EVIL
SEASON

D0956176

EVIL
SEASON

MICHAEL BENSON

PINNACLE BOOKS
Kensington Publishing Corp.
http://www.kensingtonbooks.com

Some names have been changed to protect the privacy of individuals connected to this story.

PINNACLE BOOKS are published by

Kensington Publishing Corp.
119 West 40th Street
New York, NY 10018

All Kensington Titles, Imprints, and Distributed Lines are available at special quantity discounts for bulk purchases for sales promotions, premiums, fund-raising, and educational or institutional use. Special book excerpts or customized printings can also be created to fit specific needs. For details, write or phone the office of the Kensington special sales manager: Kensington Publishing Corp., 119 West 40th Street, New York, NY 10018, attn: Special Sales Department, Phone: 1-800-221-2647.

Pinnacle and the P logo Reg. U.S. Pat. & TM Off.

ISBN-13: 978-0-7860-2761-3
ISBN-10: 0-7860-2761-4

First Pinnacle Mass Market Printing: August 2013

eISBN-13: 978-0-7860-3283-9
eISBN-10: 0-7860-3283-9

First Pinnacle Electronic Edition: August 2013

10 9 8 7 6 5 4 3 2 1

Printed in the United States of America

Acknowledgments

The author wishes to thank the following persons and organizations for their assistance during the writing of this book: Michelle Andersen; Assistant State Attorneys Lon Arend, Karen Fraivillig, and Suzanne O'Donnell; production editor Robin Cook; Marcia Corbino; Gary Crowell, former employee of the Starlight Park Barber Shop; the Honorable Deno G. Economou; my agent, Jake Elwell, Stephanie Finnegan, Harold Ober Associates; Deputy Thomas M. Gilliland, Harris County (Texas) Sheriff's Office; super editor Gary Goldstein; Kay Kipling; Jeffrey C. Monk, Administrative Manager, Houston Police Department; Reedy Photoprocess, especially president Stan Reedy and longtime employees Paula Burfield and Lynn Bushner; JoAnn Smolen, at the Lynn N. Silvertooth Judicial Center; Sally A. Trout; Margaret Wood; Stanley Beishline, Sergeant Curt Holmes, Cynthia Maszak, Cheri Potts, and Sharon Wood, at the Sarasota Police Department.

And Elton Brutus Murphy.

Author's Note

Although this is a true story, some names will be changed to protect the privacy of the innocent. Pseudonyms will be noted upon their first usage.

When possible, the spoken word has been quoted verbatim. However, when that is not possible, conversations have been reconstructed as closely as possible to reality based on the recollections of those who spoke and heard the words.

In places there has been a slight editing of spoken words, but only to improve readability. The denotations and connotations of the words remain unaltered. In some cases witnesses are credited with verbal quotes that, in reality, only occurred in written form.

Prologue

Now that the "clay" for his sculpture was more cooperative, he went to work on it. He shaped it so that it was to his liking—a nude. Nudes were his favorite. His artistic forte was the grotesque aesthetic, forcing people to see beauty even in the ghastly. It was hard to pull off. Some of the surrealists had been good at it. Salvador Dalí! Man Ray! How about the Black Dahlia Avenger, now there was a surrealist artist!

They said that a sculptor could see the statue inside the block of marble, and he liked to believe he had that ability. He would make his feminine sculpture on its back, legs open, arms positioned as gestures. The sculpture's hand pointed to an article in a nearby magazine on the floor. A clue, perhaps. The head, to one side, would be almost severed from the body, but not quite. Cloth would be draped, as beautiful as he could drape it, over her limbs, careful not to obscure the part where viewers would first want to look. The artist knew where they were going to look.

With his sharp tool he cut and dug, cut and dug, and removed from the piece a large chunk, a key chunk, which he put in a plastic bag. When people first gazed upon his masterwork, their eyes would go first to that void he'd created.

Setting was important. He would place his piece among other pieces of art, more conventional artwork, so that the difference in impact between his and others' work was more dramatic.

All of this thinking was just more evidence of how special he was. Of course, he was a great artist. How could he not be? He was the Homo superior, a cross between man and God—not just a spiritual man, but a man with a spiritual following. So it didn't shock him that when he was done and his artwork was ready for public viewing, he hardly had any blood on him at all, and washing up was a snap.

Time to make the stew.

PART I

THE GROTESQUE AESTHETIC

Chapter 1

Discovery

Sarasota County, Florida: a beautiful little section of Florida, but one with pretensions. Nothing sinister, of course, just a community that enjoyed casting itself as *artsy*. There was opera. Ballet. And a strip of art galleries on one of downtown Sarasota's main drags, North Palm Avenue.

More accurately, Sarasota considered itself *still* artsy. There was no argument that this had once been the case. Back in the day—historically— Sarasota had an artsy vibe oozing from its pores.

But that was before suburban sprawl turned much of Sarasota County into a world of McDonald's franchises and Kmart stores, largely indistinguishable from anywhere else in the United States.

Just how artsy Sarasota really was these days could be argued, but the important thing was that art and culture were important facets of Sarasota's self-image.

Members of Sarasota society distinguished their world from that of the riffraff, which was why it hit the town where it lived when the horribly carved body of Joyce A. Wishart was found on Wednesday, January 21, 2004, on the floor of her Palm Avenue art shop, the toney Provenance Gallery, a storefront at the base of the Bay Plaza Apartments.

James Jay McClelland had been a maintenance man at the Bay Plaza Apartments for four years. When there was a mess, he was the guy who had to clean it up.

At about eleven o'clock that Wednesday morning, McClelland received a phone call from Peter Delisser, one of the co-owners of Sage Capital Investments, a storefront space at the base of the Palm Avenue building.

"There's a foul smell coming from somewhere," Delisser complained.

He'd first noticed it on Tuesday. He didn't know if the smell was around before that. There had been a long weekend because of Martin Luther King Day and the stores downstairs had been closed on Monday.

Delisser explained, "I have smelled this sort of

smell before. It usually has to do with the sewer system. Wherever it's coming from, they should run the water in all of their faucets for ten minutes. That worked for me."

McClelland said he would investigate, and he did. The odor was strongest when standing outside the front door of the Provenance Gallery, the space immediately south of Sage Capital. It didn't smell like garbage or the sewer to him. It was the pure horrible smell of putrefaction.

He informed Nancy Hall, the Bay Plaza condominium manager, of the situation. Deborah Anderson, the Bay Plaza concierge, tried to contact the Provenance's owner, Joyce Wishart. She didn't get an answer and left a voice message: If Joyce didn't call back soon, someone was going to enter her gallery to check on the odor.

Hall told McClelland to get a key to the Provenance at the Bay Plaza's front desk. He would also need the alarm code. At one o'clock, after almost two hours of dread, he asked Anderson for the key and security code. The keys for all of the spaces in the building were kept in a file cabinet, which itself required a key.

McClelland told himself that there was nothing to be afraid of. Once, when he first started working at the Bay Plaza, there'd been a similar odor. It turned out to be a rat that died in the ductwork. That was probably what it was this time, too.

At 1:18 P.M., he used a key to open the Provenance's

front door; the odor was now overpowering. He immediately entered the four-digit code to turn off the alarm.

He expected silence, but instead heard classical music from the store's sound system—the soothing Muzak of a generic string quartet.

"Mrs. Wishart? Mrs. Wishart! Anybody home?"

McClelland took small tentative steps toward the back of the gallery. He glanced to his left into an alcove, briefly looked at the bloated gray-green body on the floor, and—without touching anything, his heart pounding from his chest and nausea churning in his stomach—he ran back outside, and didn't stop running until he got to Hall's office.

"Dead . . . dead body," McClelland panted.

Hall called 911 at 1:20 P.M.

Chapter 2

Death and Violins

The first responders, police officers and fire-fighters, were practically blasted backward by the smell. Veterans will tell you, you never get used to it.

They noted the classical music. Death and violins. That was different.

Detective Anthony DeFrancisco, of the Sarasota Police Department (SPD), observed possible blood on the front door's interior dead bolt handle and on paper, which was taped to the interior side of the front glass window, next to the door. He also noticed possible blood on the cover to the alarm panel, to the right of the front door.

It wasn't a large space, with more depth than

width. There was the gallery itself, where approximately two hundred works of art, both paintings and *objets* on consignment, were displayed.

In the back, where there was privacy from those who might look in through the front window, paintings were stacked up, or rested on the floor leaning against the wall. All the way back, there was an office and a storage room.

There was no back door.

It was a crime scene no one would forget—no matter how hard they tried. The body—an older woman, with red hair—was posed supine and obscenely spread-eagled. The body was stretched out on a carpet in an alcove, out of view from the street, on the north side of the building.

Her head was lying in the direction of the northwest corner. The alcove contained artwork both hanging on the walls and lying on the floor. The body, discolored and bloated from decomposition, had one arm stretched outward, and the left leg was partially covered with her clothing, which had been cut asunder.

Immediately visible were multiple stab wounds to the chest, and a slash wound at the throat all the way down to the bone. It looked as if the killer might have tried to behead his victim.

The most disturbing part wasn't what was there, but rather what was not. The victim's vagina and lower abdomen had been surgically removed.

There was just a large raw hole between her legs, a grisly negative space almost impossible for even the toughest professionals to gaze upon.

But Detective DeFrancisco had to look. It was his job to see it all. The victim was an older white woman, approximately five-eight in height. Weight was more difficult to estimate because of the decomposition bloating.

The legs had been spread far apart, pointing eastward, toward the front of the store, demanding attention be given to her gaping crotch wound. In addition to the large throat wound and the many stab wounds in the woman's exposed breast area, he also noticed defensive wounds to both of her hands. Her forehead, shoulders, and back were also deeply cut.

The detective thought it was going to be impossible to tell if she'd been sexually assaulted. Of course, he meant in a conventional sense—rape. There was one small blessing, however. The crotch surgery appeared to have been postmortem.

A person who had been opened up like this, neck slit, would have bled out. Blood would have been in a large pool on the body. Instead, he noted, "The body had very little blood on the skin and around the injuries." It appeared the killer wiped the body clean.

DeFrancisco did however see blood and body fluids around and underneath the body. Plus, he could see, the victim's clothing was soaked with blood.

There was no blood spatter on the upper walls or ceiling of the alcove.

The victim had been wearing a green pantsuit. There was a green-and-brown scarf around her neck, a white shirt, white bra, white panties, tan panty hose, and bronze-colored shoes with gold trim. The shoes rested symmetrically, toes facing the victim's opened crotch. To stand in those empty shoes would be to hover over that horrible void. The scarf had been damaged in the attack. It had slits in it.

The victim's hands and bare feet were purple. Her suit top and shirt were pulled up above her chest. Her bra, panties, and panty hose had been cut away, and were partially lying beneath the body. On her left wrist the victim was wearing a watch mounted on a brown leather strap. Her other jewelry was a pair of earrings. Her clothing had been cut by a bladed instrument. The clothing wrapped around her lower left leg turned out to be her pants.

There were indications that the killer had played in his victim's blood. In some cases the artwork was stained by what appeared to be a combination of blood and bits of flesh. In some cases there was wiping across the spatter as if a halfhearted attempt to clean up had been made. Or, perhaps, the killer just wanted to "finger paint." The killer had lingered at the scene after the murder. Not only had surgery been performed, but there was blood in many places, indicating the killer had wandered around after the murder.

In the rear of the business were two bathrooms, a shower stall filled with boxes, a refrigerator, and a microwave.

On the floor in front of the refrigerator, DeFrancisco found a brown leather purse and a black nylon bag containing miscellaneous items. Someone had gone through their contents. The key to the gallery's front door was in the purse. Items were dumped out.

In the southwest bathroom there was an area of watered-down blood on the floor, near the door, in and around the sink, and on a plastic OPEN sign that was lying on the floor in the corner near the toilet.

The watery blood on the tiled bathroom floor had been smeared with an artistic, if not infantile, playfulness. Again, it appeared as if the killer had been painting—perhaps using his toe as his brush—in blood on the bathroom floor.

Otherwise, items in the room looked neat and orderly. There were no bloody items in the garbage can. The northwest bathroom, it seemed, was used mostly for storage, and contained a ladder and cleaning supplies. There were also some personal-care items in the sink.

The scene was so obviously organized that details, which might have been considered irrelevant at the scene of another murder, were carefully scrutinized here.

One of the pieces of art most spattered was a serigraph, hot stamp, embossed on black Arches paper, called *New York, New York.* The work was signed in all caps *ERTE,* the *nom d'art* of Romain de Tirtoff.

The work was part of the artist's 1987 "New York/Monaco Suite." It was 28½ inches by 23½ inches inside a 45-by-38 frame. The price was $7,500.

That piece of art rested on the floor and leaned against the wall, right behind the victim's head. Her red hair was touching the glass near the bottom of the frame.

The glass front was pushed in—perhaps by the killer, perhaps during a struggle—and was speckled with blood and hair. The killer had intended for this work to be viewed as the scene's backdrop.

The pushed-in glass had blood smudging. Above it, below the spot where it had been hanging on the wall, there was blood running down to the floor. Perhaps, the detective thought, the victim initially fell into this picture, striking her head against the glass.

A second picture, called *Eighteen Degrees,* had also been knocked off the wall hanger and was lying on the floor in the same corner. There was blood running down the front of the picture frame and glass.

Nearby, on the floor, were a variety of items: a pair of blood-spattered eyeglasses and a Provenance Gallery news release from November of the previous year, announcing an exhibition of animal dolls by artist Linda Salomon.

The wall had scrape marks on it, some of which may have come from the falling picture. In that same area there were gouges and slice marks on the wall, which also looked as if they'd been made by a bladed instrument.

A key part of the scene was a bloodstained copy of the November 2003 issue of *Sarasota Magazine*. The body was posed, face turned to the left, left arm placed outward, hand resting atop the magazine, seemingly gesturing toward the magazine, which was opened to an article called "A Fine Madness, True Tales from the Days When Sarasota Was an Artists' Colony." The article described Sarasota in the 1950s and 1960s, a time when it grew from being a Gulf Coast fishing village into a small city with an affluent-yet-beatnik eccentric ambiance.

Noteworthy residents of the past included Julio de Diego (the onetime husband of Gypsy Rose Lee), who walked around town in a bizarre hat and cape; Boris Margo, whose artistic style twisted reality and was called decalcomania; Lois Bartlett Tracy, who brightened the world with her spontaneous abstract watercolors; Jon Corbino, whose heroic paintings depicted conflict and violence; Ben Stahl, the prolific magazine illustrator, who never threw stones, or hung paintings, because he literally lived in a glass house; and John Chamberlain, who had made art films showing himself and female Andy Warhol protégées making love in unusual places, such as in a tree. Sarasota residents lived their art through unconventional lifestyles.

Sarasota first leaned toward the artistic during the early 1900s when circus baron John Ringling spent much of his life scouring Europe for Baroque masterpieces to place in a Sarasota museum.

For generations circus folk speckled the population. It was not unusual to see "circus midgets" and their families, with chins held high, strolling down the city's most toney streets, while Rolls-Royces drove past them, with their occupants smoking cigarettes through long holders.

Chicago socialite Bertha Palmer moved to a ranch outside Sarasota and metamorphosed into a rootin'-tootin', ropin' and ridin' cowgirl as she bred prize-winning cattle. John D. MacDonald wrote his murder mysteries; MacKinlay Kantor wrote about the Civil War and won a Pulitzer Prize for Fiction. The author known alternatively as Ed McBain and Evan Hunter placed his Matthew Hope series of murder mysteries in a thinly veiled version of Sarasota.

Back then, Sarasota was a true artists' colony, and everyone knew each other. It wasn't all business and creativity, of course. With all of those characters around, there was a lot of strange fun as well. That was the image Sarasota wanted to maintain, but it was hard with the annexation of sprawling suburbia that had grown there. Still, there were about sixty art galleries in Sarasota, the majority of those downtown.

The victim's hand was clearly gesturing toward the "Fine Madness" article. Plus, there was evidence that this article had been a deliberate choice.

Though the magazine was open to page 86, crime scene investigators (CSIs) would later discover blood on page 88, indicating the killer flipped pages to find the one he liked best. On page 88 was the portion of the article about Ben Stahl, the guy with the glass house.

Along with *Sarasota Magazine,* an old April 1971 issue of *New Magazine* was also placed near the body. (The victim had apparently been studying Sarasota's artistic history, so she could chat up the locals.) The second magazine had a photo of Ben Stahl on its cover, and appeared bloodstained. The victim's hand gestured most specifically to a black-and-white photo of a man in a sporty cap, with an impressive moustache. His photo rested beside the article's title and its caption, in a scripted-handwriting font, read, *Fletcher Martin.* Police subsequently learned that Martin was an American artist who had lived from 1904 to 1979, much of that time in Sarasota, where he had painted beautiful expressionistic paintings. Some of his better-known pieces were *The Smoker, The Picador,* and *Young Girl at the Beach.*

The victim's right hand was lying near a gallery art identification card. Also near the right hand was a white piece of paper, which had been used to wipe a bladed weapon clean.

The piece of paper had the name *Werner Pfeiffer*

written on it. Police found Pfeiffer's "profile card" and learned he was an artist whose work was also for sale in the gallery.

All the people who saw the crime scene tried desperately to erase it from their minds, but it was seared into their memories. They knew they would never again get to sleep at night without first thinking of this moment, of this traumatizing attack on civilized sensibilities.

To see the victim in that condition, a person couldn't help but imagine the surgery that must have taken place, the feverish cutting by a killer who played in his victim's blood. To have viewed the scene was to have one's imagination run amok, visiting places the mind didn't usually like to go.

It wasn't like any crime scene the respondents had seen before. It was a set piece, a photo out of *Fangoria* magazine, a carefully constructed piece of horror-film art direction.

Detective DeFrancisco tried to make sense of it. Was this poor woman killed and posed this way as some sort of sick social commentary?

There was something sophisticated about it, yet so sick, so primal as to be unthinkable.

Was this a cannibal's work?

Was it the work of a dark artist—maybe a Black Mass–type guy who painted men with the heads of goats in the blood from his altar?

Was it both?

The killer had apparently taken the victim's female parts with him. Was it to dabble in cannibalism and/or necrophilia? Or was this most horrendous of mutilations merely a matter of cold-blooded practicality? If the victim had been raped, the mutilation might have removed some or all of the potentially damning DNA.

DeFrancisco took a closer look at the pieces of art in the alcove with the victim and saw something that made him shiver. Leaning against a tripod was another picture, signed *J. Gaddie,* and it showed a woman with one arm outstretched, just as was the victim's.

Was the real-life victim posed to resemble that particular picture—and if so, why?

There was further evidence that this particular piece of art was important to the killer. The art identification card that the victim's right hand appeared to be gesturing to was for an untitled work of art by an artist named Jennifer Gaddie.

DeFrancisco stepped away from the body for a moment to get the big picture. He observed the open office area behind the alcove, as well as the hallway with two bathrooms behind the office. Three tables had been set up. A computer and other office-type items sat on the tables. There were two white bookshelves in a small alcove near those tables with various items displayed, including a credit card machine and a fax machine, with its receiver off the hook, dangling from a wire to the floor.

It was later discovered that the phone line to the fax machine had been cut, and there was what appeared to be blood on the wire. A digital clock was stuck on January 20, 10:44 P.M.

The entry to the hallway was on the back left side of the gallery. A louver door separated the hallway from the office. There was blood in the area of the louver door handle, and also on the light switch to the right of it.

DeFrancisco again visited both bathrooms, this time looking more carefully. He didn't observe any blood on the right bathroom, but there was much blood on the other side.

The door trim, wall switch, sink, floor, and towel dispenser were bloody in the left bathroom. Just left of the pathway between the alcove and the back hallway was a table, and resting on that table was a bloody frameless picture.

A roll of white plastic garbage bags lay on the left, and a single bag was lying on top of the desk.

There was a computer on the desk, a phone, a daily planner, and other odds and ends. The office was not in disarray.

The victim was presumed to be the Provenance's proprietor, Joyce Wishart, who lived on Wagon Wheel Circle in Manatee County. A positive identification wouldn't be made until the next day.

Of the victim's multiple stab wounds, at least three could have been fatal, in particular the throat slash.

Police learned that no one had seen Joyce Wishart since before the previous weekend. And that was odd. She was usually around. Saturday was a big shopping day.

An errand boy from Jessica's Picture Framing Studio, who had a package for the Provenance, pounded on the gallery's door on Monday, January 19, but no one was home. It started to rain, so he dropped the package off next door, at the Allyn Gallup Contemporary Art Gallery.

A brief initial investigation revealed that Wishart had incorporated the Provenance Gallery two and a half years earlier, on June 25, 2001, and had appointed herself its registered agent. Over that time she'd displayed a wide range of art, some abstract yet commercial, which she chose herself. A typical framed piece—painting, drawing, whatever—cost thousands of dollars. Notices of the gallery as a "Thing to Do" in Sarasota appeared on websites dedicated to Florida's winter-rental business and tourism.

The presumed victim drove a 1994 four-door green Honda, which was found in the nearby parking garage in her reserved spot. Locked up and untouched. Nothing suspicious there.

Criminalist Valerie Howard, who responded along with Officer Lawrence Europa, officially pronounced the victim dead at 2:15 P.M.

Officers secured the crime scene. Officer Europa

taped off the front of the business to prevent pedestrians from inadvertently contaminating the crime scene. Rope was added to the tape to make the barrier appear more formidable.

Sergeant Howard Hickok ordered Officer Ford Snodgrass to take front-door duty. Snodgrass stood just outside the gallery's front door (where, thankfully, there was at least some fresh air) and recorded the names and time of everyone who entered and left the crime scene. Hickok notified the Criminal Investigation Division (CID) and Criminalistics that this one was special—a bizarre, beyond-belief crime scene. As soon as Hickok was relieved at 3:30 P.M., he got the hell away from that art gallery and its gruesome final exhibit.

Detective David Grant entered the gallery at 3:45 P.M. Twenty minutes later, Dr. Russell Scott Vega and Kevin Brown arrived from the medical examiner's office.

The technicians on the scene were James Tutsock, Jackie Scogin, Walter Megura, and Valerie Howard. Scogin thoroughly photographed the crime scene with a Nikon D100 digital camera. Tutsock covered the same territory with a video camera. Megura looked for fingerprints; when he found some, the location of the print was photographed by Howard, also with a Nikon digital.

As the others continued working inside the gallery, Scogin went across the street, to parking garage level 4B, space #153, the first parking space in from the center staircase, and photographed the victim's car.

Dr. Vega, the medical examiner (ME), was an expert in anatomic and clinical pathology. He earned his degree at the University of South Florida College of Medicine in Tampa, and trained at the Hillsborough County Medical Examiner's Office.

Now, inside the gallery, Dr. Vega became the first person to move Joyce Wishart's body, lifting the head, and thus discovering that there were additional wounds to the victim's head and the back of her neck. He noticed that when the bra was cut, it was not with one clean cut, but with several jagged cuts. The same sawing motion had been used to cut the pants and panties. The cut was just to the left of the bra's hook mechanism, and the bra cups were pulled to one side so that the breasts were exposed.

The medical examiner observed that there were early-to-moderate changes in the body due to decomposition. The skin was slipping in places and there was some green-brown discoloration, along with some subtle marbling on the torso and extremities. There was some bloating but no evidence of insect activity.

The decomposing changes were less noteworthy on the victim's hands than they were elsewhere on the body. The fingertips were hardened and dry, a manifestation of mummification-type changes.

The most noteworthy feature of the corpse was

the essentially complete excision of the perineum, vulva, and vagina. He couldn't tell with external examination alone if the anus was still intact.

Dr. Vega noticed that the multiple stab wounds in the victim's chest were "paralleled" by matching holes in the bra and sweater.

The major throat slash extended over the entire lateral and anterior aspects. Dr. Vega saw no obvious trace evidence over the surfaces of the body and clothing.

Before the body could be removed from the scene, the medical examiner wanted criminalists to take a look at it and the surrounding area, using an "alternate light source," an ultraviolet light that cops called the "crimescope."

Scogin and Howard returned briefly to the Criminalistics Unit Laboratory, picked up the crimescope, and returned. Tutsock and Megura used the crimescope with the body in the alcove area to search for trace evidence.

Other criminalists processed the front door and window exterior glass for fingerprints. When photography and crimescope observation of the body was complete, Tutsock bagged the victim's hands and feet, so whatever they picked up during the attack could not be polluted during transport.

It is normal procedure for the Criminalistics Unit and the medical examiner's office to take many photographs of a murder scene from all possible angles—but they were particularly thorough in that art gallery. The crime scene was so bizarre, so straight out of hard-boiled fiction, that literally everything could be a clue.

Detective DeFrancisco contacted James McClelland, the building employee who reported the odor. McClelland emphasized that he didn't touch anything when he briefly entered the gallery and discovered the body. He wanted DeFrancisco to know that he didn't take the decision to enter the gallery on his own lightly. He'd tried to contact the gallery's owner, Joyce Wishart. He called the gallery and Wishart's home. No answer. He left messages, waited two hours, accessed the key and alarm code for the gallery, saw the body, and skedaddled to tell Nancy Hall what he had seen.

DeFrancisco talked to Hall next. She verified that it was she who had told McClelland about the odor. Yes, she'd given Joyce Wishart's contact info to McClelland.

"I also have a message to relay to you from the building's valet supervisor, Bart Winer," Hall said.

"What's the message?"

"He said her car has been parked in her spot in the Bay Plaza Garage for at least two days."

"When was the last time *you* saw her?"

"About a week ago. Joyce said sewer water was coming up through her sink. I told her that wasn't the building's responsibility, that she'd have to call a plumber herself."

More bad odors.

* * *

Top brass arrived. Chief Peter Abbott, Deputy Chief Lieutenant Ed Whitehead, and Captains Tom Laracey and Stan Duncan were at the scene.

After summarizing for the chief what he'd learned so far, DeFrancisco called Allyn Gallup, the business owner of the building next door, and asked him what he knew.

Gallup said he'd smelled the bad smell as early as Monday morning. He also knew that an employee from Jessica's Picture Framing came to the Provenance on Monday, but no one answered the door. Gallup took the delivery and promised to give it to Joyce as soon as she was around. Gallup said he'd knocked on the business door Monday through Wednesday, because of his concern. But, obviously, there was no response.

"When was the last time you saw Joyce Wishart?"

"Thursday. Last. That was, what? The fifteenth. I have no idea what time of day it was."

"She married? Have a boyfriend?"

"I don't know about that. I know she has a son."

DeFrancisco next spoke to Bay Plaza employee David Sekelsky, who worked at the front desk and usually parked right next to Wishart on the parking garage's third level. He worked until 11:00 P.M., so Joyce's car was always gone when he left—except it wasn't gone last Friday. He remembered thinking it was odd that she was working so late. Sekelsky didn't recall the last time he had seen Wishart, and had no clue regarding her love life.

As the major case supervisor, it was Sergeant Norman Reilly's job to keep a checklist to make sure no aspect of a complete investigation was omitted. First task: coordinate the immediate area and begin canvass searches. Then make sure the various roles had been appointed: The CID commander was Captain Tom Laracey. Reilly listed the detectives working the case. The investigators quickly knew their roles: Detective Jim Glover was appointed the case's lead investigator, assisted by Detective Carmen Woods, the department's sex crime specialist, and Mark Opitz. Detective DeFrancisco would be the investigator in charge of the crime scene. Sergeant Hickok was placed in charge of crime scene security. Communication channels had to be kept open between the detectives and canvassing officers. Communication with other law enforcement agencies and non–criminal-investigation personnel was also key. All physical evidence needed to be documented and collected. Search warrant requirements needed to be determined; those search warrants needed to be acquired and carried out. The body needed to be positively identified by the medical examiner, and next of kin had to be notified. (That was on Sergeant Reilly's personal list of things to do.) The division commander needed to be briefed; a flow of communications was required to be maintained through the Criminalistics Unit; all leads needed to be followed up. Investigative reports had to be written; daily case reports written; eventually a summary of the investigation—when the killer was caught—would be supplied to the prosecutor.

During the early evening of the discovery, Sergeant Reilly called James "Jamie" Wishart, the presumed victim's son, to inform him of the body in the gallery.

Jamie was so upset by the news that his girlfriend, Karrie Good, had to take the phone from him and complete the conversation.

Reilly emphasized to Good that a "positive identification had yet to be made."

Good told Reilly that only recently she had assisted in hiring a private detective to locate Wishart's ex in an attempt to improve her Social Security payments. Good didn't know if Joyce had had any contact with her ex. She never mentioned if she had.

Reilly next called Patricia "Patty" Wishart, Joyce's daughter, who told them that she already knew about the body in the gallery because she and other members of her family were getting an onslaught of phone calls from the local media. Patty said she was busy getting in touch with the rest of her family and making arrangements to get herself to Sarasota as soon as possible.

* * *

Night fell. Criminalist Valerie Howard was processing evidence within the gallery. It would be Howard's job to keep each piece of evidence separate and correctly labeled. She did this by photographing each piece of evidence in its place, then filling out a form that described the evidence, giving the location of where it was found and the ID number of who found it.

For example, *Description: Swab from toilet tank. Where Found: Northwest bathroom. Recovered by: #1432. Photo: #1622.*

Detective DeFrancisco arrived at 6:30 P.M. Tutsock retrieved the victim's keys, which were still in or near her purse. The key ring had keys to both Wishart's business and her car. Tutsock gave the business key to DeFrancisco. The car keys he gave to Scogin.

Scogin and Howard again crossed the street to the parking garage. They'd previously photographed the car. Now, armed with the keys, they performed a preliminary search of the victim's vehicle for fingerprints, without luck.

At 6:45 P.M., Scogin drove the car to the SPD, where it was secured in the sally port.

A half hour later, two body-retrieval personnel from the ME's office arrived, Jeff Parris and Brian Lang. They would transport the body from the crime scene to the medical examiner's suite, where it was scheduled to be autopsied. At 7:44 P.M., the body was placed in a bag and removed on a stretcher. At 10:10 P.M., the investigators called it a day. The gallery remained under guard, but most of the peace officers and technicians left, locking the front door behind them.

The officer guarding the front door remained until 2:49 A.M., when he was relieved by a fresh officer, who'd remain till the morning.

Chapter 3

Autopsy

Dr. Russell Scott Vega began Joyce Wishart's autopsy at the Sarasota Memorial Hospital morgue at 8:30 A.M. on January 22. Representing the SPD at the procedure were criminalist Walter Megura and Detective Tom Laughlin.

Megura took digital photographs throughout the postmortem. He tried to take the victim's fingerprints, but this was impossible because of decomposition. He injected Sirchie Tissue Builder Solvent into the fingertip areas. The resulting inked fingerprints were of little value due to the advanced decay of the skin itself.

Dr. Vega verified his earlier conclusion that the victim's clothes had been opened to expose her after she was dead. The stab wounds on the body had perfectly corresponding holes in the clothes she'd been wearing. The body weighed 160 pounds and was five-eight in height. She was wearing a medical-emergency bracelet on her left wrist that read: *Lymphedema Alert No Blood Pressure No Needles in This Arm.* That meant she had a blockage of the lymph vessels that hindered the drainage of fluids from tissues in that arm, perhaps as a consequence of cancer or cancer treatments. (The victim's medical history would indicate that she had been a cancer survivor.) The hair on Wishart's head was red and varied in length from four to six inches. The scalp hair was slipping easily from the scalp because of decomposition. Her teeth were all real and in a good state of repair. The bloating from decompositional gas was most notable in the abdomen, which was distended due to suffusion. *The back and anus are unremarkable,* Vega wrote. There were numerous stabbing, slashing, and incised wounds. There were twenty-three distinct stab wounds, including three over the right side of the forehead, two on the scalp, four on the right side of the neck, one on the back of the neck, five on the back, four on the chest, three on top of the right shoulder, and one on the left shoulder. Those wounds resulted in several perforations of the lungs and one of the heart. The neck wound started at the angle of the jaw and went all the way to the other side, an "ear-to-ear throat slashing." Five separate confluent strokes with a sharp instrument had resulted in the single throat slashing, which was, when finished, thirteen inches in length.

As the corpse lay on Dr. Vega's table, the throat wound hung open, four inches at its widest. All of the large vessels in the neck had been severed. The larynx was opened up, and the sharp instrument had cut into the cervical spine.

Dr. Vega itemized the defensive wounds on the victim's hands, some of which were extremely superficial, before turning his attention to the gaping hole between the victim's legs. There was excision of the skin and subcutaneous fat of the lower abdominal wall, vulva, vagina, and part of the anal skin. The margins of the excision were smooth; and the wound was accomplished, he could tell, by at least four smooth skin strokes and multiple, additional deep soft-tissue strokes. All of the excised tissue, he noted, remained missing. The overall defect, Dr. Vega measured, was ten and a half inches in length and seven inches wide. There was a skin tag where the wound came closest to the anus. (He originally wrote that "some" anal skin was missing, but later changed this to "most.") There was a dip in the wound at the point where the victim's buttock met her thigh. In between these areas the skin margins of the wound appeared smooth. The outer edges of the wound took at least four strokes to create, and there were probably many more strokes to remove the entire crotch from the body. The excision had gone deep. Partially removed was the fat under the skin along the victim's abdominal wall. On the left side the wound was so deep that muscle was exposed. No bones were disturbed. Only the outer half of the vagina was gone. The back of the vagina was still in the body, as were a portion of the urethra, bladder, and rectum. The reproductive system had been removed, as if the killer had attempted to perform a crude hysterectomy with his sharp instrument. The uterus, fallopian tubes, and ovaries were missing.

Dr. Vega left the wound between the body's legs and returned to the head. Peeling back the scalp, Dr. Vega examined the skull. There were no fractures, despite the stab wounds in her scalp. The top of the body's skull was then sawed off to expose the brain, which was green-brown in color and of normal weight. A thin layer of mucus coated her upper respiratory system, but there were no obstructions. Her tongue was uninjured. Her body cavities contained nothing unexpected, and her cardiovascular system appeared to have been healthy. Except for the fact that a sharp object had perforated them, her lungs were normal as well. Liver, gallbladder, pancreas—all normal. The stomach was empty and the digestive system looked normal. Kidneys, pituitary gland—normal.

She'd been a remarkably healthy woman. She had beaten cancer. There was no indication that the disease had returned.

Dr. Vega then organized the pieces of evidence

that would require further testing, such as the bags that had covered the victim's hands and feet as the body was transported from the crime scene to the morgue. The medical examiner took fingernail clippings. If the victim had managed to scratch her assailant during the attack, she might have taken some of her killer with her: DNA evidence that could not be removed by amateur surgery. Dr. Vega also confiscated pulled hair with the root still attached, and the victim's watch, scarf, medical-alert bracelet, and a pair of white pearl earrings. Also bagged as evidence were the victim's jacket, pants, sweater, panties, bra, panty hose, the sheets the body had been wrapped in before being placed in a body bag, as well as oral, vaginal, and anal swabs. Yes, vaginal swabs were taken from the remaining vaginal tissue. A sample of the victim's brain and liver was also taken.

As the victim's identity was assumed rather than confirmed during the autopsy, the name of the deceased on all documents was listed as *Doe, Jane*. The entire autopsy, from beginning to end, took just shy of seven hours; it was completed midafternoon. All of the evidence seized during the autopsy was turned over to Valerie Howard.

The following day Dr. Vega would be provided X-rays via Joyce Wishart's dentist, and a comparison proved that the victim was, as assumed, Wishart. *Doe, Jane* was removed from the case's file, replaced with *Wishart, Joyce*.

* * *

The autopsy helped determine that the murder probably took place on Friday, January 16, 2004. The victim's work computer revealed that she had logged off at 4:52 P.M. The gallery was to close at five o'clock. Best guess was that the killer entered the building during those eight minutes. In addition to the locking of the doors, the victim would have turned on the gallery's alarm system at five o'clock, but a check of the alarm company's opening and closing records revealed that the alarm was never turned on during the evening of the sixteenth. According to the preprogrammed schedule, the alarm system was to be on from 5:00 to 11:00 P.M., so the system must have been turned off before five on Friday.

On the street and at police headquarters, the initial thinking was that there might be a connection between the murder and the Sarasota Film Festival, which had attracted upward of thirty thousand strangers into town. Investigators thought it doubtful that robbery was the motive. There wasn't any money in the galleries. Transactions were made with checks or credit cards.

The other best theory was that Wishart's allegedly abusive ex-husband, whom she hadn't seen in years, was responsible for her death. Many locals, in fact, were *hoping* that the ex-husband had done it. Though tawdry, it was a solution that would have ended the fear. The alternative was that there was a psycho on the loose, perhaps still walking among them.

Anyone who'd seen the crime scene knew that there was a madman on the loose, a pseudo-artsy psycho who had confused destruction for creation. Those officials knew that the posing of Joyce Wishart's remains had been a sad and sick swipe at art.

Chapter 4

Sarasota Nerves

Sarasota women, used to going out at all hours without fear of danger, were now nervously looking over their shoulders and asking men to escort them to their cars.

Neighbors of the Provenance Gallery were in shock. During the days following the discovery of Wishart's body, Jamie Jones, of the *St. Petersburg Times,* interviewed some of them, including Vicki Krone, who worked at Admiral Travel on North Palm, "just across the driveway" from the murder. She explained that police had asked her if she'd seen anything unusual during the past week. Her first reaction was, she'd never seen anything unusual *ever.* This was the very last place on Earth she would expect something like this to occur.

Now that it had occurred, Krone was looking at

every stranger in a new light. "Now I find myself looking out the window, wondering about people. It's changed our everyday pattern," she said.

Police and reporters canvassing Palm Avenue crossed paths; and when they could, they exchanged information. Officer Europa spoke to sixty-three-year-old neighbor Allyn Gallup, who recalled last seeing Joyce Wishart on the afternoon of January 15, the previous Thursday. The deceased had been in her gallery.

Europa spoke to sixty-year-old Phyllis Becker, two doors down, who didn't remember when she last saw Joyce. "I'm certain that I didn't see her yesterday, because her shop was closed yesterday," Becker said.

Two witnesses who knew Wishart—one walking his dog, the other driving by—noted that on Friday night that the lights in the rear of the Provenance were on, and it wasn't like Wishart to work late.

Europa interviewed thirty-nine-year-old Bart Winer, the building's valet supervisor, the one who had informed Nancy Hall of Joyce Wishart's un-moved automobile. He didn't remember the last time he had seen Joyce Wishart. Winer explained that among his jobs was washing the residents' cars, so he had a reason to pay attention to Wishart's car during the days before and after the murder. He'd noticed that there was a nail on one of Wishart's tires. It wasn't between treads however, as it would probably be if someone had purposefully attempted to flatten her tire.

* * *

At eight-thirty, Thursday morning, the day after the discovery of the body, Detective Jack Carter was given the task of gaining access to the victim's financial statements. If she owed money, that might help provide motive.

Turned out Joyce Wishart owed just shy of $2,000 on her Visa card. The most recent activity had her purchasing gas at a Hess station in Sarasota on January 14.

Carter didn't always get the info he wanted. At one bank he was told they couldn't release any info without a warrant. However, they would flag her account and contact police if there was any fresh activity on her credit or debit card. The bank was able to divulge that the card's last usage was at Publix on Ringling Boulevard at 7:00 P.M., on January 15.

Carter tried to gain access to the surveillance video to verify that it was the victim who used the card, but he was frustrated to learn that the Ringling Publix couldn't find the tape that covered the period of January 13 through 19. Further investigation revealed that it had never been made in the first place. A Publix spokesperson blamed "human error."

The surveillance video from Wishart's bank was available, proving that it *was* the victim, by herself, who had last used their drive-thru ATM. State-of-the-art photo-enhancing techniques were used and it was determined that there was no one in the car with her when she used the ATM.

Financial records could be used to determine the victim's customers as well. Using those records, Carter located Donald F. Goldsmith, who had recently purchased a large painting from the Provenance for $4,300.

Carter contacted Goldsmith, who said Joyce Wishart and Jamie delivered the painting and subsequently took it back and redid the frame for him. He described the son Jamie as five-ten, slim, maybe 150 pounds, with brown hair. In Goldsmith's presence, mother and son discussed Jamie living in Italy and visiting Morocco. Goldsmith said the victim seemed like a very nice lady and all of his contact with her had been related to business.

A police check of the Bay Plaza security shift–activity reports revealed that there were no logged-in security checks between three-thirty on Friday afternoon and eleven o'clock on Saturday morning. At five after eleven, on Saturday morning, the storefronts were visually checked by a security guard, who reported seeing nothing extraordinary. The first indication to Bay Plaza security that something was wrong came with the foul-odor reports of the following Wednesday.

That same morning, an SPD investigator contacted the coordinator for the Violent Criminal Apprehension Program (ViCAP), Lesa Marcolini. After hearing the details of the Wishart murder, Marcolini went to work and came back with the disconcerting news that there were twelve similar, unsolved cases in the United States. It was a sick sex thing; mutilators usually started with the sex organs.

The matriarch of Sarasota's art scene was Marcia Corbino, widow of Jon Corbino, one of Sarasota's most famous artists, and a longtime historian of Sarasota's "fine madness." She was also the author of the magazine article, "A Fine Madness," that became part of the crime scene.

Why her article had been chosen, she had no clue. Perhaps it had something to do with her husband. Jon Corbino had been one of the most acclaimed American artists of the twentieth century. According to his widow, he was a "young rebel." Back in the 1930s, his work was in sharp contrast to the quiet of American Scene painting. His paintings used, she explained, "smoldering color, monumental figures, and violent action."

Born in Vittoria, Sicily, on April 3, 1905, Corbino came to America at age eight. On the way he saw the devastation of an earthquake that destroyed the city of Messina. His ship was caught in a hurricane at sea. He recalled these images when he began painting a series of disasters, which also included floods in Montana and the horror of the Spanish Civil War.

"In the late 1940s, Jon changed his aesthetic vision," Mrs. Corbino said. He moved "from the heroic themes of social and political crisis to the fantasy of the ballet and circus. Although these paintings featured action and color, there was an aura of illusion as opposed to a physical reality."

In the early 1950s, Corbino began a series of "Crucifixions," a theme painted by all the great artists of the past.

During his career his paintings appeared on the covers of art magazines, and feature articles about Corbino appeared in *Esquire, Time,* and *Life,* as well as in art magazines and newspapers. He was listed in *Who's Who in America.*

Corbino died in Sarasota of lung cancer in 1964. Today, almost a half-century later, his paintings remain in museums and galleries throughout the country.

Marcia Corbino had been his widow for forty years when Joyce Wishart was murdered. Now, in the days after the murder, Mrs. Corbino felt the fear.

"The women in the neighborhood, and there were almost all women, were terrified for a good six months," Corbino later said. "Every one of them tried to get their fathers, their husbands, or some other male to come to work with them for protection."

Not surprisingly, Mrs. Corbino knew the victim.

"I met her at the gallery," Mrs. Corbino said. "She was having a show of a friend of mine. Then a mutual friend of ours suggested that she invite me for lunch, to get some ideas about running a gallery.

She was such a nice person, and so eager to make her gallery the best it could be. It had been a life-long dream of hers, and now that dream was coming true. She knew nothing about running a gallery, but she was eager to learn, and a mutual friend recommended we get together."

Corbino had operated a gallery with her son for eighteen years and knew the ropes. Wishart had no experience and was hungry for all of the advice she could get. Wishart was a quick study, as it turned out. She usually featured the work of artists who had been recommended to her, and those whom she had thoroughly researched.

Mrs. Corbino—who had no idea her writing was considered an integral part of the crime scene—still assumed that she would be among the first to be interviewed by police. As it turned out, they didn't get to her until several weeks later.

A woman named Kay Yount contacted SPD sergeant Philip DeNiro and told him she'd seen a possibly abandoned satchel in an alley near the Provenance on Sunday, January 18. It was gone by the time police looked for it.

Officer DeNiro interviewed Linda Joffe, who said she was a friend of Wishart's, although she was not familiar with the details of her life. They knew each other because she was marketing director for the West Coast Symphony at the same time Wishart held the same position for the Asolo Repertory

Theatre. It was her impression that Wishart had four children, but two were estranged from her. One was believed to live in Italy. Two had not forgiven her for changing her lifestyle.

Joffe said that when Wishart left the Asolo, it was on a harsh note. She'd had major conflicts with the theater's executive director. Joffe thought there might still be a lawsuit pending. Joffe thought Wishart had a lover, but she didn't know his name. Joffe was pretty sure it was a long-distance relationship, that the guy was from out of state. They only saw each other a couple of times a year.

DeNiro quickly found the theater's managing director with whom Wishart had had difficulties. Her name was Linda DiGabriele, and she said she hadn't seen Wishart in more than a year, the last time at an arts event at the opera house. She said there was nothing remarkable about Wishart's leaving the theater, that her contract had come up for renewal and it was not renewed. She recalled no harsh note. There was no lawsuit. She only knew Wishart as a coworker and knew nothing of her personal life.

"She was a very pleasant woman," Marsha Fottler told DeNiro. Fottler served with the victim on the city's arts council, and wrote the "Shop Talk" column for *Sarasota Magazine*, where she once plugged Wishart's gallery.

Fottler got to know Wishart through working on committees with her, such as Smart Talk, the

Sarasota Arts Council, and the Sarasota/Manatee Breast Cancer Committee.

"The gallery was the joy of her life," Fottler added. The thing that bothered Fottler the most was that the gallery became the place of Wishart's worst and final agony. She died horribly in the place she loved the most.

DeNiro interviewed a Sarasota artist named Linda Salomon whose work was exhibited at the Provenance. She said she had a fifty-fifty deal with the gallery. Anything that sold, she got half, and Wishart got half. Sadly, she said, her opening was supposed to be that night (January 22).

A preview of Salomon's show was in the December 2003 issue of *Sarasota Magazine*. There was a photo of Salomon and her animal dolls and a pull quote saying how Salomon's friends teased her because she became attached to her dolls and didn't want to part with them.

Salomon told DeNiro that she last saw Wishart on January 8, and last received an e-mail from her on January 14. She'd always gotten along with Wishart, but she had heard verbal arguments between the victim and employees of the nearby A Step Above Gallery.

A Step Above Gallery was DeNiro's next stop. No one there remembered an argument, but Lois Ross, the owner's wife, said she last saw Wishart on Friday afternoon, talking with a man outside the Provenance, a man dressed nicely but not in a suit. The sighting was either at one o'clock in the afternoon, when Ross was on her way to an appointment, or at four o'clock, when she was returning.

A woman named Margaret Pennington had gone into the Provenance around noon on the day of the murder to admire Linda Salomon's animal dolls. Wishart was very pleasant and introduced herself. No sign of trouble. She couldn't remember what Wishart was wearing. "I was looking at her red hair most of the time," Pennington said.

DeNiro made a list of all of the callers on Joyce Wishart's caller ID, both home and at the gallery. One by one, he tracked them down, looking for suspects. He found the chapters of Joyce Wishart's life—old friends, neighbors, her dentist—but not a clue regarding her death.

On the victim's caller ID was Elaine Fox, who knew Wishart in Ohio, where they worked together at Chemlawn, and in Florida after both moved to Sarasota. Fox and her husband were the first to move south. Wishart came to visit, loved it, and she migrated as well. Fox told police that the last boyfriend of Wishart's she remembered was a guy from Denver. She didn't know his name, but she thought he worked for a government nonprofit group and had a daughter in St. Petersburg. Fox said she was under the impression that Wishart broke up with this man before she herself moved to Florida, maybe 1998. Fox said Wishart was the type of person who could make people angry, but not to the point of creating enemies. Wishart was kind of a "know-it-all," Fox said, and could degrade people "without even knowing it."

Michelle Andersen, a coworker of Vicki Krone's, had worked at Admiral Travel for thirteen years, a workplace with little turnover. Many of the employees had been there for that long, and longer. In comparison, Joyce Wishart had only been in Sarasota for a couple of years and was still a relative newcomer.

Andersen admitted to not being a close friend of the victim's. Which wasn't to say that Andersen and Wishart weren't friendly. They greeted each other, "Hi, how are ya?"

Of course, Palm Avenue had beauty, glamour, and palm trees—but it wasn't all fancy-schmancy, either. There was a funkier edge to the big picture.

All of those art galleries weeded through a scattering of hungry artists—some bohemians of uncertain hygiene—all eager to find wall space for their work. Andersen figured the killer could be any one of them.

Joyce Wishart had the wall space and was not a big believer in negative space. Cluttered and busy was more like it. She had a lot of artwork displayed in her gallery and dealt with many artists, some strangers from heaven-knows-where.

There were even homeless people who were semi-regulars along the block, but they were the same ones all the time, so folks learned to pay little mind. Now it was: "Should I have been afraid of that guy all along?" Andersen sometimes saw the same—pardon the expression—"bum" three times a day, stumbling down the street. Would she ever be able to look at him the same after all this?

After the murder the cops came and didn't leave. "They were there for a long time," Andersen recalled, and by that she meant *weeks.*

One part of her felt freaked out by the persistent heavy police presence, a steady reminder of the nightmare; the other part was reassured. It was easier to get through her day when protection was only a few feet away.

The seemingly never-ending news stories on the murder, hinting at the ghastliness of the crime without being specific, made Andersen's morbid imagination go wild. She found herself wondering what it was like for the cleanup crew. What mind-numbingly horrendous things would the crew have to see and do—just so that life could *go on* in that room.

And what of the poor first responders? Joyce wasn't found for several days and her remains must've been an assault on the senses by the time her corpse was discovered. What they must have seen! Whatever the ghastly secret, they knew firsthand. It was burned into their memories. How could a person ever sleep again?

She had heard that the body was posed to resemble one of the pieces of art, but no one knew which painting or drawing it was, allowing imaginations to percolate.

Years later, Michelle Andersen's memories hadn't faded.

"It was so close! I mean really, really close!" she exclaimed.

There were popular events going on at the time, a ritzy film series and an art festival. The town was teeming. So there was an exceptional amount of pedestrian traffic along Palm Avenue. Businesses kept their doors propped open, hoping strollers would wander in.

Even when there weren't tourists to be wooed, security was never tight. Even on days when the weather might be inclement and the doors to the businesses kept shut, they still weren't locked. The proprietor would just put a little bell up on top to tinkle the news when someone entered.

Not that Joyce Wishart's end of the strip was the most traveled. Since it was at the west end of the street, not that many tourists strolled by. If they went there, chances were good that it was their planned destination.

Andersen was there late on that Friday. How scary was that? She was in and out on Saturday and Sunday. On Sunday, she noticed that it was odd that Joyce Wishart hadn't opened the gallery door. Andersen clicked on that—weird, no Joyce—and then moved on to something else. Andersen worked long hours that week. She worked her regular job, and then at night she made arrangements for the film festival, which had her working with directors. She'd probably been working alone in the office when it happened, just on the other side of the driveway. She thought out loud: "I'd been going back and forth in the parking garage alone. . . ." There must have been long hours that weekend when Andersen worked alone at night and Wishart's desecrated body lay posed only a few feet away.

After noting her absence during the weekend, Andersen didn't give Joyce another thought, until Wednesday, when all of a sudden there were cop cars everywhere, detectives prowling with a cool efficiency "across our roof and in the bushes." They came into the travel agency, where Andersen worked, asking, "The owner of the gallery next door was murdered, anyone seen anything over the weekend?" *No, no, no.* Then came a second influx of large vehicles and activity when the news media caught wind and came swarming.

No work was getting done on Palm Avenue. Folks were out in the street talking a mile a minute about what happened. Some in tears, some just stunned, their eyes a little too wide. Some felt ill. The smell, now that they knew what it was, was so damned *sinister*! Vague gossip about the crime scene spread. Someone thought Joyce might be missing a body part. Snippets of police conversation had been overheard. They were looking for something that didn't just belong to her, but was *part of her.*

No one knew the details, but it had to be bad. The Provenance Gallery's windows were covered to protect the crime scene's privacy, and they stayed covered for a long time.

Andersen had a friend, maybe more of an acquaintance, who was a cop. She asked him what it was like in Joyce's gallery. The police officer said, "Michelle, you don't even want to know." She'd known a lot of cops in her life, and she recognized his tone. Her stomach raced, spun, and dropped. She felt the little hairs at the nape of her neck prickle.

She would never be able to go to the parking garage alone again. It was too dark and creepy—a world where psycho killers lurked in shadows.

Andersen felt intense grief, of course, but news of the murder also overwhelmed her with her own raw vulnerability. That feeling was common with her neighbors. She thought about how the storefronts on Palm, built as they were with no back doors, could turn into a trap. She remembered the shock—and the indignity—felt by the Palm Avenue crowd. Sarasota was special and this sort of thing didn't happen here. This—and it shouldn't even need to be mentioned—was *not* Middle America!

Some wondered if keeping the details of the murder from the public was such a good idea. "It leaves your imagination going crazy," said a Palm Avenue neighbor, interior designer Sherry Simons. "We will all feel better when they disclose how it happened."

The shops along Palm Avenue were thinking in terms of security for the first time. Sherry Simons's boss, Sally A. Trout, said that she grew up in Sarasota and it had always been one of those charmed cities, relatively untouched by modern dangers.

"No one locked their doors," she recalled. "Mom would take us all to the beach and just drop us off. It was an easy time. We were all so innocent."

She thought back to all of the times she'd been in her office alone. It had never occurred to her in a million years that she was in danger.

She did recall—well, it wasn't really a problem, but rather an annoyance from homeless people. They would move up and down the street looking for handouts. A lot of them were familiar; but every once in a while, there would be one who was creepier than the others.

Now everything was different. She planned to install a buzzer on the front door and keep the back door locked at all times—precautions that had not previously occurred to her.

Trout's interior design space was only a couple of doors down from Wishart's gallery. Sally herself had done business with Joyce. She bought a painting, only two days before her murder.

Trout remembered vividly the shock that Wednesday when all hell broke loose on Palm Avenue. She had been working with a client, when all of a sudden it seemed as if an ambulance and police cars were coming from all directions. She went outside to see what was going on; eventually word got around that Joyce Wishart had been murdered. Curiosity seekers couldn't get close to the gallery. The front of the business was monitored, to keep pedestrians from accidentally contaminating the crime scene.

Trout had heard the rumors that there was a psycho killer at work, but she didn't give them any credibility. "I can't believe that this was a random crime," she said.

But if it wasn't random, that would mean that Wishart had an enemy, which was every bit as difficult to believe.

In the days following the murder, a dark cloud hovered over the street. It was a sadder and quieter world. No one spoke loudly. Neighbors, who had shouted greetings across the street only days before, now settled for a silent wave. In the nearby grocery store, where people once conversed at a distance, neighbors now stood closer and exchanged pleasantries in hushed tones.

The gallery and travel agency were not on the busiest sections of Palm, because there were no restaurants on that side of the street. The Provenance's end of the strip was quieter and darker to begin with. After the murder the block was deserted, and there was a tainted feeling to the air.

Like Michelle Andersen, Joyce Wishart's friend Lois Schulman felt positively *traumatized* by the murder.

"I've been a nervous wreck," Schulman said. "I have been talking to God, asking that he hold her in his arms. Think of how horrible the end must have been, looking at her killer in the eyes." Schulman had a personal friend who was a psychic, a gifted man. She was sure he would do whatever he could to help the investigation.

Also playing amateur detective was Nancy Hall, the Bay Plaza condominium manager. According to one coworker, Hall thought she was going to solve the mystery for the police. Compared to Wishart's other neighbors at work, Hall was very chatty on the subject of the murder.

Chapter 5

Joyce

Police quickly filled in the victim's biography. Joyce was nineteen years old in 1961, when she married twenty-two-year-old truck driver Robert Wishart in Cincinnati.

The couple had four children, two boys and two girls. The youngest was seven when she filed for divorce in 1981, accusing her husband of adultery and abuse.

The victim's longtime Columbus, Ohio, neighbors, Don and Bonnie McPeek, were very helpful, telling police how Wishart metamorphosed from a housewife and single mom into a career woman.

It was a transformation to be reckoned with—inspirational, even—and the McPeeks helped as often as possible. Don fixed Joyce's car for free and

Bonnie offered babysitting services after school let out.

Wishart was not going to allow material matters, such as the fact that she didn't have a lot of money or possessions, deter her from her goal.

"She didn't have a whole lot. She was scrounging the bottom of the barrel, trying to keep her head above water. It would have been easy for her to give up—but she never did," Don said.

"She went through a lot of trials and tribulations," Bonnie added. "But I tell you, that girl pulled herself up by her bootstraps and got through it."

Her financial problems were only compounded when her ex-husband failed to keep up with his child-support payments of $240 per month. She had to take him to court to avoid losing her house to creditors.

She took night and weekend college classes at Dublin College, a small private college near her home in Columbus, and earned her first college degree, an associate's, at age fifty.

She attended Dublin during the years 1990 through 1993. In 1991, she began to date a fellow student named Jim Beauchamp, who was her boyfriend until 1996. But even after they broke up, they remained good friends.

Her bachelor's degree was in business administration and came from Ohio Dominican University. She subsequently earned a master's in executive management from Ashland University. She clearly had her future mapped out. Her master's thesis was in the economics of running an art gallery.

She and her children had competed to see who could get the best grades. While Joyce was excelling in college, her kids made the honor roll on their own, both in high school and college.

As is true with any brood, some of the kids flew farther from the coop than others. Friends said that Wishart's two oldest children, Scott Wishart, who was forty-one years old and lived in South Carolina at the time of his mother's murder, and daughter Kirsten Whitehouse, thirty-nine, who was still in Ohio, were not close with their mother. Joyce's younger children, Patty Wishart, thirty-two, and James "Jamie" Wishart, thirty, had remained close and visited their mother regularly in Florida. Patty, in fact, had been planning to move in with her mother sometime during the spring of 2004.

Joyce had started her own marketing consultancy called Portfolio Place in 1990. Soon thereafter she was elected president of the Columbus Chapter of the American Marketing Association. In July 1998, she was the subject of a profile in the business section of the *Columbus Dispatch* newspaper. She told the reporter that Portfolio Place—for which she was general manager—provided strategic planning, finance, marketing, operations and sales plans, advertising design and placement, pre-press and print production, training, public relations, and communications programs for both profit business clients and nonprofit organizations.

Asked for a quick review of her résumé, Wishart said that she started with Chemlawn Corp. in marketing, and moved over to its subsidiary, Chemlawn Services, where she worked her way up to national marketing director by the time she left in 1989. She moved to CheckFree Corporation and worked in a similar capacity until September of 1990, when she left to start Portfolio Place.

Asked what her first job was, she said, "Running errands for neighbors." What did that job teach her? Well, first of all, she learned that her neighbors had more money than she did. She was a kid at the time and it was a revelation that when she did the same types of jobs for neighbors that she did at home, she received a lot more money than an allowance. "It was probably my earliest introduction to a free-market economy," she commented.

What was her management philosophy? "Tell me what you can do, not what you can't do," she replied. The biggest mistake she made during the early stages of her business career was being trustful. She'd been an innocent and believed that because she was honest, everyone was honest—and nothing could have been further from the truth. Also, she assumed that everyone had the same perseverance that she had, and this also proved to be false. "There are so many people who have the best of intentions," she said, "but never follow through." It didn't make them bad people, just ineffective people—these were folks who had poor time-management skills, who either overbooked their days or grossly underestimated the amount of time it would take to complete a task.

How did she compensate for her overestimate of peoples' honesty and stick-to-itiveness? "I learned to put everything in writing," she explained. "It saves so much confusion. Being able to concisely state terms, dates, activities, exceptions, et cetera, in writing with required dates to be met usually resolves the issue. Sometimes people just need a frame of reference or a date to work toward." She understood that marketing was a business that never allowed one to rest on her laurels. She constantly had to educate herself to the latest trends and techniques or risk being passed by the competition.

What was her biggest complaint about Columbus? "Clouds and orange barrels—and not necessarily in that order," she said.

She was asked where her favorite place to business lunch was. Being diplomatic, she said there were far too many to choose just one. She did, however, list the ingredients that make a restaurant a suitable place to conduct business: "The important thing for a business lunch, though, is that the place is not exceedingly noisy, the wait staff is not interrupting your conversation every few minutes to ask if everything is okay, and the table is larger than the size of the plate."

She said that she enjoyed travel and golf as relaxation. Her most recent vacation, she told the reporter, was to Sarasota, Florida, where "the Gulf and the golf" were both great.

As a closing note she said that her neighbors still had more money than she did, but at least she was closing the gap.

She was asked what her "dream job" would be, and she answered, "I'd like to be the owner of an art gallery in a warm, sunny climate."

Joyce vacationed in the Sarasota area before she moved to Florida permanently in the late 1990s. She sold her house in Ohio and moved to Manatee County in suburbia. After a stint doing contract work with NovaCare Employee Services in Bradenton, she landed a $45,000 per year job as the marketing director for the Asolo Repertory Theatre, a job she held from August 1999 until 2001. In addition to good money, the job served as a letter of introduction to a "who's who" of the area's arts community. It was a tough club to get into. You didn't need a lot of money, but you did need to pay your dues—and that meant community involvement.

Joyce Wishart's friend Lois Schulman described it this way: "You have to do things for charities that need your help. You have to give away your talents to make Sarasota a better place."

Joyce had no problem with that. She volunteered with Artists Helping Artists and served on the county's Arts Council. She further ingratiated herself with the ladies by being quick with numbers. She became the go-to gal for anyone with an accounting problem. She could take an idea, whether it was hers or someone else's, and project the economic feasibility.

Anyone who might have thought Joyce, being a divorcée from the Midwest, might have trouble fitting in with the artsy crowd in Sarasota had it backward. Her friend Denise Roberts, who was the executive director of the Sarasota nonprofit Family Law Connection, remembered meeting Joyce in 2001 and thinking how elegant she was, maybe too elegant and too cultured for the group. "She was *Vogue* and I was Target," Roberts remembered thinking when they met.

But Joyce made everyone feel comfortable. It was as if she had always been one of the ladies of Sarasota culture. She seldom talked about life in Ohio. It was as if her first fifty years hadn't happened. When she started over, she started over. The ladies frequently complained about their husbands or their ex-husbands, but Joyce did not join in on those conversations.

It was after leaving the Asolo that she opened up her own art gallery. That was September 2001. The opening earned a blurb in *Sarasota Magazine.* Marsha Fottler, in her "Shop Talk" column, said Provenance, opening in October, was perfect for those seeking fine art at discount prices: "*Now collectors who are downsizing, redecorating, or editing their inventory have a place to send their fine art for resale,*"

Fottler wrote. *"And buyers will be able to acquire original paintings, sculpture and photography at big savings."*

A consignment gallery accepted works from artists or collectors. Wishart determined prices by doing Internet research. If there was a sale, she kept half the money.

The pieces on display at the Provenance revealed a curator of eclectic taste. Wishart chose works she liked, seemingly regardless of category. There were lithographs, etchings, watercolors, European paintings, modern sculpture, and American folk art.

Although she was relatively new to the community, she fit right in with the half-dozen ladies of the town who were at the heart of the city's cultural scene.

She even hosted monthly get-togethers, serving drinks and dinner for the ladies right there in her gallery, where the gals would gossip, talk about their lives, and exchange recipes. There was always candlelight, and Wishart prepared the meal right there in her kitchenette.

According to Kathryn Shea, one of the women, Wishart seldom led the conversation, but she did act as moderator. She took particular delight in the group's lampooning of then–commander in chief, President Bush.

Fottler told the *Herald-Tribune,* "I never heard her be critical of anyone. Some of us are not like that. She would always try to find a way to resolve an issue, or to see it from a different perspective."

Less than a month after opening her own art

gallery, Wishart learned that she was battling breast cancer. She told the ladies over dinner.

"I'm going to beat it," she said at the time, and she did.

During her chemotherapy treatments her friends pitched in, giving her rides to and from the doctors, and keeping the gallery open when she was too weak to work.

Her hair, naturally brown, fell out. She bought a red wig, and then purchased clothes to go with it. When people told her how good she looked, she would reply, "You should see me in the morning. I look in the mirror and say, 'My God, where did the alien come from?'"

There were times when she was so weak that her friends feared that she wasn't going to make it, and she endured a full year of treatments before she was declared cancer free. Friends recalled that one of the pleasant aspects of her ordeal was that her dark brown hair grew back a beautiful red color after chemotherapy—seemingly in imitation of the wig she'd been wearing.

Of course, a beautician may have been responsible, but the notion that nature had given her red hair to compensate for her ordeal became a part of her story—and she conveniently continued wearing all of the clothes she'd bought to go with her wig.

During one of her monthly dinners, Wishart admitted that the gallery was not turning a profit, nor did Wishart anticipate that it would for its first five years. During the past year she had been trying to expand her business, which she hoped one day to franchise. At the time of the murder, Wishart was preparing for Arts Day. She had spoken on the phone to some of her old friends in Ohio and had expressed her excitement.

Chapter 6

"Bike Man" and Other Suspicious Characters

On Friday, January 23, Detectives Jack Carter and Jeffrey Steiner interviewed a man named Greg Parry, forty-three years old, who said he might have been one of the last people to see the victim alive.

The interview took place at the Sarasota Opera House, not far from the crime scene. Parry was the opera's director of marketing and communications. Greg knew Joyce from when she was a marketing rep for the Asolo Rep Theatre, before she left to start her own business.

He saw her on Friday at about four in the afternoon. The detectives were impressed, as law enforcement felt that was less than an hour before the murderer had entered the Provenance Gallery.

If one put the pieces together, Parry could have been the well-dressed man, seen by Lois Ross, talking to the victim on the afternoon of her murder.

Parry said he also talked to Wishart several times on the phone on the previous Tuesday. Wishart wanted to put a couple of posters from the opera house on display for an upcoming show, and Parry had them. The posters were for Puccini's *Madama Butterfly* from 1980 and *Orpheus in the Underworld* from 1983.

"I walked in, door was open, and there was no one in the front. I walked to the back and found Joyce seated at her computer, talking to another woman," Parry said.

"Was it unusual for her to have her door open like that?" Detective Carter asked.

"Not at all. If it was a nice day, she wanted the front door to look welcoming."

He described the woman as white, gray curly hair, maybe five-five, stocky not fat. Joyce might have introduced her as "Ingrid" or "Inga," but he couldn't be sure. The woman left before he did.

He gave the posters to Joyce; she thanked him, placed the posters on a shelf near her desk, and escorted him out the front door and onto the sidewalk. They conversed briefly about a vase on display on the right-hand side of Wishart's window. After saying their good-byes to one another, she reentered the gallery and he returned to the opera house, seeing nothing suspicious on his way.

Detectives wanted to know Parry's relationship

with Wishart. He said they'd had drinks together a couple of times on a group basis, and sometimes he "stopped by her gallery, due to its proximity."

Parry told the detectives that Wishart had been preparing a show that was to open February 6, featuring local octogenarian graphic designer Alex Steinweiss, who was best known as the innovative designer of record album covers, such as Oscar Levant's recording of Gershwin's *Rhapsody in Blue* and the Philadelphia Orchestra's performance of the *Peer Gynt Suite*. Before Steinweiss, record albums—78 rpm's in those days—had plain covers of dull brown or green paper. "They were unattractive and lacked sales appeal," Steinweiss said in a 1990 interview. It was a simple idea—a graphic image should accompany a piece of music—but Steinweiss was the first to think of it.

Parry told the detectives that he thought there might be a surveillance camera on the rear of the opera house that might point across the parking lot and Palm Avenue to show the front of the Provenance. He jotted down the name of the security guard at the opera house, who would know for sure. (It later turned out that there *was* a surveillance camera on the back of the opera house, but it was inoperable.)

"Where were you at five o'clock on the evening you last visited the gallery?" Carter asked.

"I had just left the opera. I wanted to do a spin class at the YMCA. It's on stationary bikes, lasted an hour. I was back at work at seven."

"Have you ever been to Joyce Wishart's house?"

"Once. Christmas, 2000. A little get-together for the theater marketing directors. Before the holidays."

Parry explained that he was not a U.S. citizen. He was Canadian and had been a resident of the United States, and Sarasota, for three and a half years. "My frequent residency status is up for grabs," Parry concluded.

After speaking with Parry, detectives checked the crime scene and found the two posters on the shelf near Wishart's desk, right where he said they would be. Police were routinely asking male witnesses to provide a DNA sample, so they could be crossed off the suspect list. Parry talked to his lawyer before complying, but eventually he gave investigators a DNA sample.

A check of the victim's security contract by Detective Mark Opitz revealed that Wishart's friend Mary Jane Goldthwaite was the person to contact in case of emergency. She was also the keeper of the Provenance's spare key, which she kept unidentified on a magnet on the refrigerator. That key had gone nowhere in years, Goldthwaite maintained, and had nothing to do with how the killer got into the gallery. Goldthwaite said she was Wishart's golf buddy and knew Wishart had an ex-husband, who was long gone. Wishart didn't talk about her love life much. Five years before, Wishart said, she had dated "a rich man in Ohio."

A check of Wishart's records showed where she had her hair cut. Her stylist, Robert Bombardier, was interviewed and said he'd cut her hair only once or twice. He "barely remembered her."

On the afternoon of January 23, Detective Steiner called Sarasota Memorial, Doctors Hospital of Sarasota, and Manatee Memorial to see if anyone had gone there with cuts to the hands. This turned out to be difficult to determine. The computer at Sarasota Memorial and at Manatee didn't sort patients by injury type. At Doctors Hospital, the emergency-room (ER) records were hand searched; no knife injuries had come in.

That Friday night, one of the victim's friends, Kathy Killion, hosted a get-together for all of Joyce's friends, some of whom were meeting each other for the first time. The ladies drank wine and shared stories of the woman they loved.

On Saturday, January 24, 2004, three days after the body was discovered, a bit of excitement erupted on the street outside the Provenance Gallery. At about 4:30 P.M., an officer guarding the shop, Cliff Cespedes, was looking at the parking garage across the street when he saw something that grabbed his attention. On the garage's third floor at the southeast corner, Cespedes saw a man's silhouette move slowly into view, then slowly back out of view, as if fearful of being seen. Cespedes called "Zone 3" and notified them that he had a suspicious person at the scene of the Wishart murder. He also called dispatch and asked for units to be dispatched to the scene.

With Cespedes was Officer Ronald Dixon, who got in his car and drove up to the garage's third floor to investigate. Cespedes, in the meantime, visually secured the southeast perimeter of the garage. About two minutes later the suspicious man exited the garage through the stairwell at the southeast corner. Cespedes was on him immediately. The man, who was wearing a Bay Plaza jacket and had a radio, identified himself as forty-five-year-old Stephen Garfield (pseudonym), the head security guard at Bay Plaza. Cespedes called dispatch back and canceled the request for backup.

Later, when writing about what he had seen, Officer Cespedes still thought that it was "peculiar" the way the man had slowly appeared in the shadow and then slowly backed away.

It was as if he were attempting to conceal his presence, Cespedes wrote. He made a mental note to keep tabs on Garfield.

As Stephen Garfield was observed moving in mysterious ways, Detectives Jack Carter and Jeffrey Steiner checked nearby buildings to see if any surveillance cameras might have picked up the front of the Provenance during the crucial period of time. They talked to Captain Powell Holloway, the security supervisor at the nearby Zenith Building, which had such a camera. Holloway said he would have a CD with the pertinent footage—3:00 P.M. on January 16 to 6:00 P.M. on January 17—to police in a matter of hours. The images provided were not as helpful as had been hoped.

As Detective Carter later noted, "The image quality of individuals approaching the storefront are polluted to a large extent by the reflections of the interior lights against the front windows during evening hours and by the back lighting against individuals during daylight hours."

A few hours after the Garfield incident, the area outside the gallery was used by Chief Peter Abbott and Captain Tom Laracey for a brief press conference. For reporters looking for fresh headlines, there were slim pickings. "Homicide . . . multiple stab wounds . . ." Not much else. Nothing they didn't already know.

There was some noise as reporters raised their voices while questioning, but the press was respectful of the crime scene and everyone remained obediently outside the police tape.

Later that night, at eleven-thirty, Officer Tom Shanafelt was guarding the gallery, when he was contacted by a twenty-four-year-old pedestrian who identified himself as Mark Saunders. The guy said he might know something helpful. Saunders lived down the street a ways, but he was frequently down on this end of Palm.

"I saw a suspicious man out here, along this stretch of street. I don't remember exactly when, but it was about three days before the body was found," Saunders said.

"Why was he suspicious?" Shanafelt asked.

"I saw the guy out here asking someone for money." Saunders didn't know who was being asked, another unknown white male.

Saunders said, "I didn't know the guy and came right out and asked him what he was doing. He told me he was waiting for a friend."

"Okay, he was panhandling and loitering. Anything else suspicious about him?" Shanafelt asked.

Saunders admitted that seeing a man panhandle on Palm Avenue was not unheard of, but this guy was new.

"The last I saw of him he was walking toward the art gallery," Saunders said.

"Can you describe him?" Shanafelt asked.

Saunders said the man was about forty years old, five-eleven, 190 pounds. His hair was black; he wore nice clothes.

"What do you remember about the clothes?"

"I just remember he was wearing a designer black leather jacket."

A panhandler in a designer leather jacket? That was odd.

Investigators went through the recent case files to see if their guy had done anything else to attract attention to himself. One interesting case was a report that had come in at two in the afternoon of January 15, the day before the murder.

Jolie McInnis had been in a building on North Palm Avenue, only a few blocks away from the murder scene. McInnis told responding officers that she'd been at the rear of the building, looking out the window. Behind the building was a private parking lot, and back there was a man going through the Dumpster.

McInnis called out, "This is private property. You can't go through there."

Hearing that, the man slammed down the lid of the Dumpster and said, "I know what's good for you. I'll slit your fucking throat."

McInnis got away from the window and called the cops. She described the man as five-ten, thirty-five years old, wearing olive green pants and a blue nylon jacket. He had brown hair and she said she could identify him if she saw him again. The man was last seen walking east on First Street. Police searched but found no one matching the description.

Detectives Carter and Steiner continued canvassing Palm Avenue for potential witnesses. Cheryl Gilbert, who worked at Chasen Reed, on the corner of Main Street and South Palm, said she last saw the victim at around noon on Friday. Gilbert was on her way to the bank and waved at Wishart through her shop window. Robert Wilson, of Wilson Galleries on South Palm, said he knew who the victim was, but he had never had any dealings with her. He had a manager, he said, who knew Wishart, but that guy quit two weeks earlier, saying he found the job too stressful. Doug Carpenter and Morris Apple, proprietors of Apple-Carpenter Gallery on South Palm, said they knew the victim well. Carpenter and Wishart had worked together recently on a Palm Avenue brochure. They agreed she was a nice lady, but they knew nothing of her friends or associates. Werner Meier, of Design Impressions, said he didn't know the victim, but his wife might have.

Mary Bates, of the Palm Avenue Gallery, knew Wishart to be thoughtful and helpful. Bates kept her promise to call the police when she saw anything suspicious; from then on, every transient who looked in her store window was reported. One of those drifting window-shoppers was a fellow named Mark, who, when contacted by cops, reported a couple more transients whom he thought suspicious. Cynthia Retz, of Gallery 53, said she knew nothing, but she asked if it was true what people were saying about what was done to the victim. And on and on, it went.

A witness named Nikki Meyer spoke to Detective Mark Opitz on January 24, saying that she was a friend of Wishart's and had had dinner with her on several occasions. Wishart had confided in Meyer that there was one particularly valuable work of art in the Provenance, which she did not keep displayed.

"It was a Renoir etching of a ballet dancer," Meyer said. "She kept it in a zippered folder." Wishart said the etching was worth up to $12,000. Meyer didn't know if Wishart had a customer interested in the Renoir.

Meyer told Opitz she was optimistic that police would be able to find out if there were customers interested in the etching because "Joyce was compulsive about logging everything in on her computer."

"Did Ms. Wishart ever express anxiety about being in her gallery alone?"

"Not at all. On the contrary, Joyce felt very secure in her gallery."

Meyer knew nothing of Wishart's romantic life. She'd seen her with men, but some of them were gay.

The following day, Sunday, January 25, Officer Stanley Beishline was patrolling Sarasota's Gillespie Park section—which included a portion of Palm Avenue—when he was approached by a homeless couple in their thirties. They identified themselves as Dennis and Ann Collins and explained they had information regarding possible suspects in a recent homicide. Dennis told the officer that there were four white males who hung out near U.S. 41 and Main Street, two blocks south of the crime scene.

"They are very violent when they've been drinking, and I haven't seen any of them since Thursday," Dennis Collins explained, speaking about January 22, not January 15.

"If you got a victim over there who has been stomped on with boots, then these are the guys you are looking for," he added. When those guys drank, they beat up people and robbed other homeless people. The leader was a white male by the name of Chris. He was very violent, the most violent of the bunch, and he carried a large folding knife, about six inches long, with serration on the back. Chris had a fat wife and two kids, but the kids were taken away from them before Christmas. Cops caught the whole family sleeping together in the cemetery, and that was why they took the kids away. It made Chris mean. He'd been kicked out of most of the places where homeless people could go for help— Resurrection House and the Salvation Army, to name two—and was desperate. Dennis said he bet there were people at the Resurrection House and Salvation Army who knew Chris's last name.

"What about the other guys in this group?" Officer Beishline inquired.

"The second guy is named Mike, but they call him 'Salamander,'" Dennis said. Mike was responsible for robbing a homeless man named Robin and smashing in his face.

There were two other guys, but Dennis didn't

know their names. One was blond, had a moustache; the other had freckles all over his body.

"If I need to get in contact with you two, how do I do it?" Officer Beishline asked.

The Collinses said they could be contacted at the Resurrection House, or on the second floor of the library. That was where they spent most of their time.

Beishline followed this report up with a few phone calls, but he could come up with no further information on Chris, Mike, and the two other thugs.

That Sunday, Officer Cliff Cespedes recontacted the security guard he'd seen lurking in the shadows. He wasn't willing to let that go until he had some more information. He asked Stephen Garfield for his vital statistics, height, weight, hair and eye color.

Garfield said that during his shift he jiggled the doorknob to the Provenance Gallery each time he passed. That was part of his job. He'd done that every day from January 16 to January 21; he had noticed nothing out of the ordinary. He wouldn't have been able to tell if there was an odor coming from the Provenance because he had a head cold and couldn't smell anything.

The only thing unusual about that stretch of time was that Garfield was training a new security guard, taking the rookie on his rounds with him, showing him what to do.

He remembered that maybe eight months before there had been a false alarm at the Provenance, the alarm went off for no apparent reason, and he had talked to the responding officers. He had no recollection of ever being inside the gallery. (The false alarm actually happened two years earlier. Officer Cespedes subsequently found a report dating back to 2002 regarding the Provenance's security system's false alarm. The system had been inspected, and Wishart's motion detector was replaced. Wishart was fined by the Sarasota Police Department for having a faulty motion detector. She was told she'd been in noncompliance with a city ordinance. This ticked Wishart off, and she officially requested that the fine be excused. Red tape was sticky and it wasn't until the summer of 2003 that the SPD Support Services Division decided to excuse the malfunction for this incident only. However, the incident would still count toward possible future "multiple malfunctions" penalties.)

Cespedes asked Garfield, "What's your address?"

Garfield gave the address of the Bay Plaza, where he worked.

Cespedes said, "No, home address."

Garfield, at that point, became vague. Only after repeated probing and follow-up questions did the officer ascertain that Garfield lived with a friend on Garden Road in Venice. Garfield said he didn't remember the street number.

"You don't know your own address?"

"I'm only going to be staying there for two

more days and then I'm moving into a Howard Johnson's."

Although it was like pulling teeth, the officer finally induced Garfield to spit out the whole story. Until recently he did have a permanent address in Venice, but he had been asked to leave because of marital woes. His wife of five years, in fact, had taken out a temporary restraining order against him.

"Why did she do that?"

"She's afraid of me."

The restraining order, he admitted, dated back to a December 29, 2003, incident in which Garfield's wife called the sheriff's department on him, claiming he had barricaded himself in the bedroom with four firearms. Deputies had to come and remove him from the home.

Garfield said that the women of the house had ganged up on him. His seventeen-year-old stepdaughter also claimed that he abused her physically. She, too, called the sheriff's department on him, but none of it was true. He was afraid of losing his job if any of these domestic troubles became public knowledge.

Cespedes looked into Garfield's claims and discovered that he had largely told the truth, although he had not been completely forthcoming regarding the ongoing nature of the conflict between the Garfields. Cespedes learned that five times in December and five times again in January sheriff's deputies had to come to the Garfield home because of family disturbances. Only recently, Mrs. Agnes Garfield (pseudonym) reported, her husband pounded nine beers before noon and then set his mind on getting his wife and her daughter arrested.

Agnes Garfield, a nurse by profession, informed police that her husband, the bum, had made a living for several months making jewelry and then selling it at art shows and flea markets. Her father-in-law was an FBI agent or a Treasury Department officer or something like that. A Fed. Agnes called Detective Opitz many times during the investigation. Every time she recalled a bit more dirt on her husband, she phoned it in without hesitation.

Garfield told Cespedes that years earlier he himself had been a cop, five years with a small-town police department in Ohio. Under persistent questioning from law enforcement, Garfield admitted he worked in the morgue and had grown comfortable around dead bodies, even decomposing bodies.

"Why'd you leave the force?"

"Got hurt. Car accident."

Detectives did some fact-checking. Opitz verified the Ohio law enforcement story. Cespedes checked Garfield's criminal history and he came back clear on all searches. Opitz verified that Garfield had served two years as a security specialist in the air force, stationed in Washington, D.C., and San Antonio, Texas, as he claimed.

Stephen Garfield remained a person of interest

until February 3, when SPD crime scene technicians determined that his fingerprints didn't match
those found in the Provenance.

Also on that Sunday, January 25, Walter Megura
went to Joyce Wishart's home on Wagon Wheel
Circle. Also there were Detective Sergeant Norman
Reilly and Detective Jim Glover. Criminalist Megura
took digital photographs of the house, inside and
out. The place was very neat and orderly. A fingerprint from a plastic cup found in the front office of
the house was processed. A computer in the den
was seized. Also found in the den was a copy of
Wishart's will, prepared by attorney Johnson
Savary, of Dunlap & Moran. In the garage was a
Honda auto registered to Wishart's son Jamie, who,
just back from Europe, had visited over Christmas.
A search of the master bedroom uncovered no
items of interest. Ditto for the small bedroom,
which contained items belonging to Jamie Wishart.

While there, Glover was approached by a neighbor and friend of Wishart's named Sue Sweeney.
Before Wishart became ill with cancer, they had
been tennis buddies. Sweeney said she thought
Wishart had two boyfriends, both from somewhere
in the Midwest. She last saw Wishart on Tuesday,
January 13, when she stopped into the Provenance
to visit.

"Nothing seemed to be bothering her," Sweeney
said. Joyce was very upbeat and positive. Her

daughter Patty was there, but she did not partake in the conversation. "Who would want to hurt Joyce?" Sweeney wondered.

Later that day Detectives Jim Glover and Carmen Woods interviewed Thomas Kearney, who'd been a coworker of Wishart's at the Asolo Repertory Theatre. After she left the Asolo, he helped her build the website for her art gallery. They'd had a falling-out when she became "very demanding" regarding his time. He had not spoken to her in over a year.

Captain Laracey and Sergeant Reilly separately interviewed Patty and Jamie Wishart, who had flown in from the home the siblings shared in San Jose, California. Patty was thirty-two years old, distraught, and said she'd just recently visited her mother, from January 8 to January 13. She flew out of Tampa International Airport on Delta Airlines. Nothing was wrong. Nothing was bothering her mom.

Her mother and father were divorced in 1982 and hadn't had any contact since the early 1990s. Recently her mother had hired a private investigator to find her ex-husband. Patty thought her dad had been found in Dayton, Ohio, but she wasn't sure and had no address for him.

"I haven't spoken to my father since I was in tenth grade," Patty said. Basically what she remembered about him was that he was drunk and abusive.

"He used to tell me about abusing cats when he was a kid."

Patty said her father was the only person she could think of capable of killing her mother. There hadn't been one incident in particular that led her to that conclusion, just a pattern of abuse. "My dad had a hunting rifle above the fireplace. Mom would freak out when a domestic argument occurred."

The two Wishart kids who didn't talk to their mother (or their father) were Kirsten and Scott. Joyce and Kirsten had a falling-out because the mother didn't like Kirsten's husband. Similarly, Joyce had a falling-out with Scott after he married Becky.

Patty said her mom had a couple of boyfriends back in Columbus, but she didn't think she'd had any contact with them since she moved to Florida.

She explained that the Wishart children had been born in two sets of two. Kirsten and Scott were older, born close together; then she and Jamie came later, also practically back-to-back. Glover asked why the older siblings were estranged from their mother, and Patty, not eager to discuss familial woes, said she wasn't certain.

Police interviewed Jamie Wishart next. He was born November 3, 1973, and gave his address as the same as his sister Patty's. He had also been to visit his mother recently, staying in her spare bedroom from December 17, 2003, until January 7, 2004. He visited his mom immediately after returning from Italy.

Jamie said his mom and dad were divorced when he was only eight or nine and he hadn't spoken to his dad in fifteen years. According to Jamie, his mom didn't talk to his oldest two siblings because they had insisted on maintaining contact with their dad, which his mom took as a personal betrayal. He remembered how violent his mom and dad's marriage had been, that mom had once been hospitalized because of the abuse she suffered. Jamie was of the opinion that on that occasion his father would have killed his mother if his older brother, Scott, had not intervened.

Where was Dad? Ohio. Mom had Jamie hire a private detective to find him. Jamie said that was for Social Security purposes. She wanted to claim wages that Robert earned during the time they were married to bolster her Social Security income and retirement.

When the interviews of the victim's children were complete, Patty and Jamie accompanied Detective Glover to their mother's home. Glover asked them to walk through the house with him and see if anything looked out of the ordinary.

Patty said "someone must have entered" the home since she was there last. A framed photograph of her mother had been placed in the den. That was new. The photo showed Joyce Wishart standing with a guy in a chicken costume. Numerous documents, not there before, were now resting on the couch in the den. Nothing else was touched. The matter was investigated briefly. The items were probably moved during a previous police search. Glover came to the quick conclusion that whatever had happened, it had nothing to do with the murder.

Patty told Glover that her mom was having business trouble. According to the daughter, the Provenance's financial health was even worse than Joyce had admitted to her friends. The gallery wasn't making money. The lease was up in June. She planned to sell or just close up. She'd already submitted three job applications at local businesses.

"Did your mother carry large sums of cash on her person?" Glover asked.

"No," Patty replied. "Fifty, sixty dollars. Rare she would have more."

"Did she wear jewelry?"

"Nothing fancy."

When music played at the Provenance, it was usually classical. Her mom liked that vibe for the gallery.

"Your mother carry any life insurance?" Glover asked.

"I don't know," Patty replied.

Jamie Wishart supplied the name of the investigator who'd found his dad. The guy was a friend of his from back in Ohio, named David Hayes. Sergeant Philip DeNiro gave Hayes a call.

The private eye told DeNiro he and Jamie Wishart were old friends. Back in the day they'd even dated the same girl. Hayes said that during the summer of 2003, Jamie had wanted him to find his deadbeat dad, who owed child support.

Joyce's kids had made it clear that the investigation had nothing to do with child support; it merely had to do with Social Security, but DeNiro let it slide.

Hayes did find Robert Wishart, and he gave the son an address and phone number in Dayton. Hayes never made physical contact with the dad, but he did call him. Hayes told DeNiro that the man who answered the phone became nervous and stammered that he'd never heard of Robert Wishart.

DeNiro called Dayton police and learned that Robert Wishart did not have a criminal record. He was clean—with the exception of a parking ticket in 1993. Ohio DMV supplied DeNiro with Robert's photo, but it was faxed and the quality was not very good.

DeNiro called the landlady at the address he'd been given for Robert Wishart. She didn't have anyone living there under that name. Not legally, anyway.

"There is a squatter named Bob," she said, and he turned out to be Wishart. Bob lived with a woman named Rose. He worked at the Salvation Army in Dayton.

The landlady said she didn't peg Bob as a violent guy, just a ne'er-do-well. He drove a truck, gambled his money, and spent his winnings on alcohol.

A sergeant with the Dayton police agreed to interview Bob Wishart at the Salvation Army and get back to DeNiro. That was done. Bob turned out to be old and frail—and he had an alibi. He was in Dayton at the time of the murder, many miles from Sarasota and his ex-wife.

On January 26, a sixty-three-year-old freelance photographer asked permission to photograph the gallery. He was granted permission to take pictures of the gallery's exterior only.

That same morning, criminalists were back inside applying luminol to the alcove walls and ceiling area, without success. Luminol was then applied to the carpet; this search bore fruit. Blood droplets were discovered in a line from the alcove to the bathroom. When the blood-revealing chemical was applied to the hallway louver, and bathroom doors, blood was revealed at both locations—blood spots that had been wiped clean, no longer visible to the naked eye. This was more evidence that the killer took his time after the murder, operated on the corpse, attempted a cleanup, staged the scene to give it style and maximize the shock value. The CSIs went to work at nine in the morning and were out by ten-thirty.

Meanwhile, criminalists Jackie Scogin and Valerie Howard were in the sally port, where they were giving the victim's car a more thorough exam. Howard lifted one fingerprint from the passenger-side visor mirror. Only two prints were found in total on and in the car; neither was of comparative value.

Officer Harry Ross was guarding the crime scene on January 27 when he was contacted by a white female who would identify herself only as Rusty. She said that back on January 23, she saw a suspicious person near Main Street and Palm Avenue. It was a black male—and not the usual vagrant who frequented that area. This was someone she hadn't seen before. Rusty asked to be contacted by an investigator and left her phone number.

Luminol and photography had been the criminalists' last tasks. Following a last once-over by Detectives Anthony DeFrancisco and Frank Puder, the crime scene was released. At eight-twenty at night, Tom Shanafelt cleared the scene and the SPD's twenty-four-hour presence at the gallery was discontinued.

Just in case the killer returned to the scene of the crime, a police surveillance camera and recording device were set up inside the gallery, looking out the front window.

After five days the surveillance experiment was discontinued. The camera and recording device were removed from the front of the gallery.

The resulting footage picked up a few curiosity seekers, and a regular visit from the Bay Plaza security guard on duty, but nothing helpful.

* * *

In the meantime Detective Jack Carter examined the victim's daily planner, but he found little of value. The January 30, 2004, entry on her daily planner had *Angels and Demons* written above the word "Library." This was no doubt a reference to returning the Dan Brown book by that title, and not a reference to any real-life cult-type activities.

More promising was Detective Opitz's interview with Mary Jane DeGenero, the president of the Bay Plaza Association. She said that she and her husband were having coffee at the coffee shop at the corner of Palm and Main, when they encountered a fifty-nine-year-old artist named Thomas Monaghan, who said he was a good friend of Wishart's. Monaghan was quickly located and explained that Wishart had sold three of his paintings, and she owed him money. (That got the investigators' attention. Did debt equal motive?) He said that he still had a few pieces for sale at Wishart's gallery. There was a vase to the left when a patron first walked in, a wooden block with a fishing village on it. He'd last seen Wishart on either Thursday or Friday, meaning the day before or the day of the murder.

Opitz asked if Monaghan had any history of mental illness. Monaghan said it wasn't his favorite thing to talk about, but at one time he'd had depression and drinking issues. He hadn't had a drink in twenty-two years, he quickly added.

After talking to the victim's closest friends, they

learned that Wishart kept a Sony camera at her gallery to take digital photos of the artwork. No such camera was found. The camera needed to be charged by a Sony power cord. To download photos from the camera into a computer, a USB cord would be necessary. Detective Opitz contacted five local camera shops to see if anyone had purchased, ordered, or inquired about any of these items. One camera store worker said there was a guy who came in asking about a digital camera. He was shown a photo of Thomas Monaghan. The guy said he looked familiar, but he couldn't be 100 percent certain.

Police tailed Monaghan for a time and learned that he had recently been evicted from his apartment, where he still kept some of his belongings in storage. Without a home he had been sleeping on the front porch of his old apartment house. His car was at Upman's Towing. Monaghan signed a waiver allowing cops to search his stuff. A polygraph exam was administered on January 29 by Jim O'Connor, of O'Connor Polygraph. During the pretest interview, Monaghan was asked what he thought had happened to Wishart. He replied that he thought "someone walked in off the street who is a psychopath." Monaghan passed the polygraph and the shadow was discontinued.

The January 6 entry in the victim's daily planner mentioned Greg Parry and the posters Wishart wanted for her upcoming show. Of potential interest were written mentions of someone who Wishart hired to set up her website, but whom she'd eventually had to fire. No name was mentioned, however, but police recognized this as a reference to Thomas Kearney. Among Wishart's computer records was an e-mail from her son Jamie that informed her of the whereabouts of her ex-husband in Dayton, Ohio.

Detective Carter received a tip from Doug Carpenter, of Apple-Carpenter Gallery. He'd talked to a woman named Joyce Whidden, who said she, in turn, knew a man named George Danford (pseudonym), who "was infatuated with Joyce" and "Joyce thought he was scary."

Detective Opitz spoke to Misty Whitley, who said that about a year before, a homeless man had come into her art gallery. When Whitley told him the place was closed, he became belligerent and at one point grabbed her. She threw him out of the gallery and hit him with a broom. The guy was about forty-five years old, white, with sandy blond hair. The last she saw he was departing the scene on a bicycle.

This "Bike Man" may have reappeared in the vicinity of Amy Shepherd, who said that she knew of a man—blond, forty years old, thin—who approached women on the street. This was on Main Street, only a few blocks from the murder scene. The guy would flatter a woman and try to hold her hand. He was persistent, but she'd never seen him angry.

"He rides a bike and honks his horn at people," Shepherd explained.

On January 30, SPD criminalists submitted a variety of crime scene items to the Florida Department of Law Enforcement (FDLE) Crime Lab. The idea was to find fingerprints that had been left on surfaces upon which fingerprints are difficult to find: paper, the victim's left shoe, eyeglasses, cut pieces of the telephone cord, and envelopes taped to the back of framed art. The criminalists submitted with the package the partial set of prints that had been taken of the victim at the autopsy. The FDLE had some positive results. Two fingerprints with comparison value were found on the taped envelope. A palm print was found on Werner Pfeiffer's artist profile card.

No other usable prints were found. The fingerprints on the envelope matched those of the victim, but the others didn't—which might have been because they were made by someone else, or just that the victim's comparison prints made at autopsy were of poor value due to skin decomposition.

The SPD also submitted a piece of carpet from the crime scene and two rolls of thirty-five-millimeter film containing images of the carpet. The FDLE found images of shoe prints in the photographs that were suitable for comparison purposes. Now they just needed shoes to compare them with. The

FDLE kept copies of the photos and returned the negatives to the SPD.

Detective DeFrancisco delivered a subpoena to the Selby Public Library for the library records for a list of sixteen individuals, including George Danford and Greg Parry. The library search was unsuccessful. None of the persons of interest had withdrawn any books considered significant by investigators.

The nervousness lingered. The public remained jumpy. Imaginations took off, untethered. The mundane became sinister. Hookers reported johns with unusual tastes. Transients looking for a place to sleep, irate artists who felt their work hadn't been properly displayed, anyone who left town around the time of the murder, became homicidal maniacs. Investigators continued to hear a wide variety of theories.

One woman reported seeing a young man on Palm Avenue. Asked what was suspicious about him, she said he was exiting one of the Provenance's neighbor galleries while carrying a skateboard.

A woman named Linda Bailey reported that twice, once a couple of months before, and once on January 28, a thin black man, whom she believed to be homeless, barged into the rear office of Louise's Paperie on Main Street, where she worked, and asked to be hired to wash the front windows. The first time she didn't think anything of it, but the second time she thought, *Well, that's just the sort of thing that might have happened to Joyce.* Because of that, she reported it. Bailey was unable to give a more precise description.

Folks around the vicinity of the United Methodist Church, which was on Pineapple Avenue, complained about a tall, thin white male who was aggressively panhandling, doing his best to intimidate those who wouldn't give him money. No one knew if he arrived at the church on a bicycle.

The owners of Jack's Restaurant, located on Main Street, complained that on January 21, a week earlier, someone had broken in at night through the ceiling, but they didn't take anything.

On January 29, Detective DeFrancisco interviewed a woman who thought she was being stalked. Her name was Rita Cullanane (pseudonym). The guy was a white male, thirty-five to forty years old, with "blond short, shaggy hair."

"How do you know he's stalking you?" DeFrancisco inquired.

"He parks his car across the street and sits there staring at my house," Cullanane replied.

The guy drove a gray Reliant K. He always left before she could confront him. Now someone was calling her phone and not saying anything. Just heavy breathing. She saw the same guy park in front of her house another time—only, he was in a different car, a green Lincoln, which might have been a taxi.

Forty-five-year-old Elizabeth Whittington, of

Omega Lane, came to the SPD's front desk to tell them that on a Thursday, during the first week of December 2003, about five weeks before the murder, she'd been invited by her friend Jo Ellen Silberstein to attend the opening of her show at the Provenance. "I met her at the dog park I go to. She told me that it was going to be a very big VIP event, with over seven hundred invitations going out." In reality, however, there were only about ten people attending Silberstein's "retrospective" of some thirty years of work. The small attendance made Whittington feel most uncomfortable. She left quickly and, after spending a brief time in a nearby gallery, went home. After that, Silberstein became "persistent and insisted" that they "get together for meals." As they dined together, Silberstein told Whittington that she was from a prominent Sarasota family, that her mother was very big in the city's ballet and circus. The family also owned homes in New York State. Whittington was clearly frightened by the murder, and there was a chance her imagination had gotten the better of her. Situations that might have been mildly irritating before the murder were now terrifying. She complained that since the murder she'd had "very odd people coming into" her life—a fact that had her so freaked out that she was not staying in her own home.

Silberstein herself was interviewed and also remembered the occasion. Instead of focusing on the poor turnout, Silberstein focused on a helper

Wishart had around. It was a man named Jim, who carried paintings from one place to another and things like that. Jim gave Silberstein the creeps. She didn't know why, but she thought it was something the police should know.

Silberstein knew something was wrong over the weekend. Wishart's gallery was either open or the CLOSED sign was up. But that weekend she wasn't there, and yet the sign was not up. She said of Wishart's four kids, Joyce only spoke to two; the others hadn't even called her when she was sick. Her ex-husband had been abusive and once injured her foot so severely that she required several surgeries.

Sergeant DeNiro talked to Gloria Owens, who was also familiar with Jim. "I felt uncomfortable around him, too," Owens said. "He was very strange. I can't put my finger on it. I just had the feeling that he wasn't right."

Jim turned out to be Jim Arthur (pseudonym), a retired airlines employee originally from Illinois, who had been the weekend box office manager at the Asolo Theatre when Wishart worked there. Arthur had had a key to the Provenance for a time when Wishart was ill, but he returned it a long time ago.

A woman named Andrea Briggs told police that she'd found a homemade doll just down the street from the Provenance, and she didn't know if there was voodoo going on or what, but she thought it might be important. The doll, police noted, had no face and wore an acorn for a hat. It was spooky.

A private detective called SPD to report a hunch that had him troubled. He knew of a ne'er-do-well with the first name of Cloud, who had a history of taking things that didn't belong to him and forging checks. Cloud claimed to be a Native American. The interesting thing, though, was that he was a regular at art shows, where he tried to sell knives he had made, with blades ranging from one to ten inches in length. "Some of them were very odd-looking," the private eye reported. "They looked more like scalpels to me."

Some 911 callers didn't even have a concrete occurrence or sighting to report. "I just have a funny feeling I'm being followed," one woman complained to the emergency dispatcher. "Especially when I'm downtown," she added.

Sometimes the caller interested cops more than the complaint. A man called to say he "knew something" about the murder. A background check on the caller revealed that he had an arrest record for false imprisonment and selling porn to kids. He just wanted to get "inside" the investigation because he'd heard there was kinkiness involved.

Chapter 7

Carlie

The community's fear and shock were compounded when, only two weeks after Wishart's murder, an eleven-year-old local girl, Carlie Brucia, was abducted and murdered in Sarasota.

Carlie was walking home from a friend's house in broad daylight on February 1, 2004, and was abducted by a man in a car. She was raped and strangled to death. Her body was dumped in the woods on the grounds of the Central Church of Christ, hidden with tree branches, two and a half miles from the site of her abduction.

The body was not discovered for four days; by the time of its discovery, it was partially decomposed and eaten by insects and animals. Dr. Vega, who performed Joyce Wishart's autopsy, was also the medical examiner for the Carlie Brucia case.

The case broke when it was discovered that Carlie's abduction was caught on video by a camera mounted on the rear of Evie's Car Wash, on Bee Ridge Road, in southwest Sarasota, exactly five miles southeast of the Provenance Gallery.

The abductor's family members identified him, and police arrested Joseph P. Smith, a thirty-nine-year-old auto mechanic. Wishing and praying, police looked at Smith as the possible killer of Joyce Wishart. There was disappointment when they found he wasn't the guy. They also investigated Smith as a possible perp for the abduction of twelve-year-old Jennifer Renee Odom, who disappeared in Pasco County in 1993. Again, no connection.

Smith was subsequently tried, convicted, and sentenced to death. No prior connection between abductor and victim was found. Carlie was apparently a random victim.

At the time of Carlie's murder, reporters sought to create sensational headlines, and so used details from Dr. Vega's autopsy report to draw parallels between this crime and the murder of JonBenét Ramsey.

Those similarities included the fact that both victims were strangled with thin string ligatures. Circumferential abrasions on the necks of both victims were horizontal, with just a slight upward deviation on the back.

Both victims had had their hands bound together. Both had bruises and abrasions in addition to ligature marks. No semen was found on the body in either case. In both instances a tiny spot containing male DNA was found on their clothing.

Dr. Vega noted that the ligature had been applied from the back, due to the slight upward slant in the back. Great strength would not have been necessary to complete the murder, as only about eleven pounds of pulling pressure on the ligature would have been necessary. Dr. Vega said the victim was killed by the ligature's compression of the carotid arteries on each side of the neck.

The prosecution got its conviction when the spot of DNA material on Carlie's shirt turned out to be Smith's semen, and fibers found on Carlie's shirt matched those found in the station wagon Smith had borrowed on the night following Carlie's abduction. Strands of Carlie's hair were also found in the car.

Although the ligature used to strangle Carlie was never found, Dr. Vega felt strongly that a shoelace had been used.

Testifying at the trial, Smith's brother said that Smith had confessed to him to having "rough sex" with the victim.

According to the coroner of Pittsburgh, Pennsylvania, Dr. Cyril Wecht, pedophiles have been known to use "erotic strangulation" during the abuse of little girls, as it causes mild convulsions and seizures that, to the pedophile, resemble sexual climax.

The dark clouds over Sarasota hovered for months.

It wasn't until the summer approached and the weather got very hot that some of the sadness left.

"Hotter'n hell," folks kvetched—this small talk seemed so normal compared to the thoughts they'd been forced to think for the past few months.

By the time of Carlie Brucia's murder, DNA experiments were already being conducted on blood foreign to the victim found at the Joyce Wishart crime scene—and though no match for the DNA had yet been found, there were a few conclusions that could be drawn.

After a profile of the foreign blood was created by the FDLE DNA scientists, that profile was sent by SPD detective Glover to DNAPrint Genomics on Cocoanut Avenue in Sarasota for a bio-geographical ancestry analysis. The corporation doing the analysis had developed proprietary technologies for efficiently targeting "single nucleotide polymorphisms," which predict a subject's gene pool. This analysis concluded that there was a 96 percent chance that the killer was of European descent. He was a white guy.

One of the white men police talked to was Peter Hooten, who said he'd known Joyce Wishart for about a year. He went into her gallery once a month. He characterized her as a woman constantly on the Internet, trying to learn as much as she could about art. He was an art collector and had purchased one painting from Wishart. He'd been out of town, in Claremont, on the night of the murder. When Detective DeFrancisco asked Hooten if they could collect a DNA sample, he said he'd prefer discussing the matter with his lawyer first. DeFrancisco subsequently received a letter from Thomas D. Shults, of the Kirk-Pinkerton law firm, saying that Hooten would not be supplying a DNA sample for "privacy reasons."

Another white guy whom police interviewed was Robert Lyman Ardren, who made it onto the suspect list because he was a contributing writer for *Sarasota Magazine,* the periodical that had been found near Joyce Wishart's body. Robert "Bob" Ardren worked as the director of public affairs for the Ringling Museum of Art, and he was curator for a time for the Ringling Circus Museum. He told Detective DeFrancisco that he worked full-time for the Pelican Press, and part-time for *Sarasota Magazine* and the *Herald-Tribune.* He hadn't seen anything odd. He believed if there had been something odd, he would have seen it, since he was constantly hanging out in downtown Sarasota, in particular at that "new coffee shop where Charlie's News used to be."

How well did he know Wishart?

As far as he could recall, he'd never had much conversation with the dead woman. Just hello and good-bye.

"I haven't spoken to her in a while, maybe a couple of months," Ardren said. "Is it true what they are saying?"

"Is what true?" DeFrancisco asked.

"Is it true that she was . . . sexually mutilated?"

"I can't talk about the crime scene," the detective replied.

Ardren took that as yes. In his humble opinion, he told DeFrancisco, that this was no crime of passion. Maybe it was supposed to look like a crime of passion, but no.

"I believe this was the work of the Colombian Mafia," Ardren said.

DeFrancisco asked Ardren for a DNA sample. Ardren said no problem.

Mark Ormond, a local art consultant who wrote a column for the magazine, was also asked for a DNA sample.

Jimmy Dean, the executive publisher of *Sarasota Magazine,* was interviewed twice by investigators.

Bottom line: If you were a white guy and knew the victim—even slightly—chances were good the Sarasota police asked for a DNA sample. Even non-acquaintances were asked for samples if they had been known to "hang out downtown." Investigators had high hopes for one guy who was known to loiter downtown and "say inappropriate things to women." But his DNA, like all of the rest, didn't match that found in the gallery.

During the afternoon of February 2, Detective Glover interviewed Kevin Elias (pseudonym), who had worked for two and a half years at the parking garage across the street from the murder. He said he saw nothing out of the ordinary on January 16, but there were elements of his bio that intrigued the investigator. Elias told Glover he'd grown up in a military family that frequently moved from place to place, and once had been arrested for burglary. He didn't know the victim. Didn't even know what she looked like. Glover asked Elias what he thought had happened. Elias said he only knew what he'd heard: how the victim had been stuffed into the exhaust vent, how she'd been mutilated, cut to pieces, and then reassembled. Glover asked what type of individual might do such a thing, and Elias said some strange things: "I feel a little guilt for what I did," he said at one point. "I hope I'm not involved," he said. The killer, he believed, might have been "a veteran."

Detective Carmen Woods interviewed a man in a wheelchair named Henry Gibeau, who was among the last to see Wishart alive. He had visited the Provenance at two-thirty in the afternoon on the fatal day. During his visit he engaged the victim in conversation. They were soon joined by a man, who had gray hair, who tried to dominate the conversation. Gibeau did not feel that Wishart was afraid of the man, but she did ignore him.

A human resources director at a local museum asked cops to check out a peculiar ex-employee.

The SPD heard from the friend of a psychic detective. The psychic, the friend said, had touched the door of the Provenance and had "seen many images."

Detective DeFrancisco interviewed more friends of the victim, Sara Dechart and Barbara Derfel, in Dechart's home. Dechart had been one of Joyce's best friends at one time. When Joyce was getting the shop ready to open, she'd been the one who helped out painting. And she had helped keep the gallery running when Joyce was sick and had gone off to the H. Lee Moffitt Cancer Center in Tampa for treatment. For a long time Dechart had a key to the gallery, along with the electronic gate opener for the parking garage. However, she had given those items back in May 2003 when she and Wishart had a "falling-out." In fact, she hadn't spoken to Wishart since then.

Derfel said that at one time she had a key to Wishart's house, in case of emergency, but she had never had a key to the business. Like Dechart, Derfel hadn't spoken to Wishart since the spring of the previous year.

On February 9, Detective Woods spoke with a post office worker named Cindy Lizarralde, who complained that she'd had a coworker back in 2002 who was creepy. She'd gone out with him twice and was never sure she knew his real name.

He said he was "Charlie Brown."

He threatened suicide and would sometimes utter horrible things: "Go fuck yourself, whore. I'm going to slash your face and stab your heart." She'd been to his apartment and he hardly had any furniture. He liked clowns and deviant art. He *was* a clown and visited kids' hospitals in makeup, which she remembered thinking was not a good idea.

When a lady at the post office died of a drug overdose, Lizarralde asked Brown if he killed her. He didn't deny it, but instead referenced another clown, saying, "You mean like John Wayne Gacy?"

The witness remembered where the guy lived, and this was how Detective Woods learned his real name (which wasn't Charlie Brown). Woods determined that, though the man was bipolar and had anger issues, he was miles from Sarasota at the time of Wishart's murder.

On February 18, a little more than a month after the murder, Detective DeFrancisco returned the key to the Provenance to the victim's son Jamie. Leads were still pursued, but with each new crime the murder of Joyce Wishart pushed closer to cold-case status.

On February 24, police learned of two more Bike Man sightings. Two Sarasota women, Martha Fuller and Barbara Sperling, reported to police that on the day of the murder, a thin, middle-aged white man on a bicycle had creeped Fuller out, riding past her slowly in the street and staring at her. A man named Douglas Berdeaux reported seeing a man on a bike on the night of the murder, standing at the corner of Pineapple Avenue and Ringling Boulevard. The man was staring back toward the crime scene for such a long time that Berdeaux became concerned about his behavior.

During another night in February, a man was discovered wandering alone through downtown Sarasota. The guy turned out to be an insomniac who loved antiques. "It's safer to walk here than where I live," he explained. Police swabbed him, anyway.

The owner of a furniture store reported that a strange man came in and said her shop's carpets smelled like "gunnysacks used to hold dead bodies." The odd customer added that he was a stump remover by trade, and owned a wood grinder that could grind up "anything, including a dead body."

Another man aroused suspicion when he told his bartender he'd heard that the killer cut out Joyce Wishart's ovaries. Police found the guy, who said he'd heard the rumor from his boss, who, in turn, said he'd overheard it from another customer while having coffee at Sarasota News and Books, a place where you could browse while simultaneously sipping award-winning coffee.

More than a month after the murder, weirdos were still coming out of the woodwork. One man reported that a man he knew was a murderer who made snuff films.

Detective Grant had a chat with the new tenants of the Provenance's space and advised them what to do if anyone appearing suspicious entered the premises. What a way to start a new business! When the space reopened, it was under police surveillance, and one man was investigated because he stood for an extended period of time at the approximate spot where Wishart's body had been posed.

Posing bodies in order to make an "artistic statement" was not a new concept. The most famous instance of this was the still-unsolved "Black Dahlia" murder in 1947 Los Angeles. It was the most famous American murder case not involving a celebrity. The victim was Elizabeth "Beth" Short, a twenty-two-year-old wannabe starlet, who was drifting around Southern California, depending on the kindnesses of strangers. Her body was found naked, severed into two pieces at the hips, the pieces arranged at the edge of a vacant lot, only inches from a sidewalk. Faceup, her arms were over her head; like Joyce Wishart's body, the legs were spread. Short's upper body was parallel, but off line with her lower half. A Sardonicus smile was carved into her face. Portions of her breast and thigh were cut out. A rose tattoo, or perhaps a rose-colored birthmark, on her leg had been removed and the skin containing it shoved up her rectum. The crime scene was exquisite, emulating as it did artwork of the grotesque aesthetic school. The murderer wanted everyone to see the beauty in this unthinkable ugliness.

It is typically more common just to pose bodies
in order to shock. One of the most vivid examples
of this occurred in Florida with the gruesome murders of the "Gainesville Ripper," who turned out to
be Danny Rolling. During the late summer of 1990,
five students from that college town were found
murdered and mutilated in their apartments. Most
famously, one coed's head was severed and placed
on a bookshelf facing the door.

Mrs. Marcia Corbino, Jon Corbino's widow and
author of the crime scene magazine article, had
thought that she would be among the first to be interviewed by police, but it wasn't until February 11
that Detective David Grant knocked on her door.

Years later she remembered some of the police
officer's questions as "mystifying." She explained
that the article in *Sarasota Magazine* had been an
excerpt from her book *A History of Visual Art in
Sarasota*. She talked about Ben Stahl, explaining
who he was. Corbino told Grant that many of
Stahl's paintings had been stolen in the late 1960s
from the Museum of the Cross. Stahl died in 1987.
She gave the investigator contact information for
Stahl's children. His son, she said, still sold his
father's paintings every once in a while.

She was also asked by police about another magazine found at the scene, probably *New Magazine*,
but not about the one that contained her article.

Mrs. Corbino still didn't know that her magazine article had been referenced by the killer when creating the crime scene. At no time did she get the impression that the policeman who questioned her had any idea who she was.

After she learned of her unique role in the murder case, she wondered if the killer read the magazine that he'd used. Had he made a conscious decision to leave the magazine open to a particular page? If the killer spent some time in the gallery after Wishart was dead, perhaps he had time to do some reading. She felt guilt. She knew it wasn't rational, but she couldn't help it. It was because of that guilt that she decided to write about the murder, a story called "A Mecca for Murder," which was eventually published in a literary magazine.

"I tried to answer the unanswerable question of why? Why did it happen to her, and why did it happen here? It all seemed out of synch with the universe," Corbino said.

For the rest of February and into March, Detectives Grant and Glover received copies from crime analyst Bruce Steinberg of all loitering, prowling, and burglary reports in Sarasota dating back three months before Wishart's murder. They then checked out each one: Where was the guy now? Where was he when Wishart was killed? Since this was a transient crowd, many of these individuals didn't have solid alibis. Police asked them for voluntary DNA samples.

During spring 2004, Detective Sensei DelValle worked on possible leads found in Wishart's address book, handwritten, and on her home and work computers. Nothing.

Jack Carter's investigation carried on throughout the summer of 2004. He used the victim's financial records and personal effects as the basis of his investigation.

It had been months and the investigation into Joyce Wishart's past had yielded little. It was a frightening prospect for an investigator, but it was appearing more and more as if the answer did not lie with the victim. It seemed that this was a randomly selected victim killed by what may be a serial killer at the very start of his career.

If the rough surgery performed on the victim by the killer was an attempt to remove DNA, the effort was in vain—and the DNA end of the investigation continued full-speed ahead. One suspect who wouldn't give a voluntary DNA samples had to be tricked. DNA material was confiscated from a cigarette butt and the top of a soda can.

Meanwhile, the FDLE's psychological experts carefully considered every known factor of the murder and came up with a general description of the man whom police were looking for. He was white, had a maturity level in the early thirties, was well groomed, was likely to have moved from job to job, lacked sincere relationships in his life, and—though he might be able to mask it in public—held a contempt for society.

Police were six months into the investigation, and had checked out more than four hundred leads without success, when it happened.

The case broke.

On July 26, 3:30 P.M., Detective Glover received a phone call from a very excited analyst at the FDLE Lab. She was Suzanna R. Ulery, and she had great news.

"We've got a match," she said.

"What's the name?"

"Elton Brutus Murphy."

PART II

ELTON BRUTUS MURPHY

Chapter 8

The Orange Groves

This is the story of Elton Brutus Murphy's life. For the most part it's Murphy who's telling it; and from what we can tell, most of it is true. Murphy admits that he wasn't entirely candid at times, but it was nothing personal. He knew that prison officials would be reading this book one day and he didn't want to be "locked up even worse than I am now." He was very appreciative of the interest in his story and hoped that what he had to say would help contribute to a "dynamic and compelling work of literature." He wanted you to imagine it was a movie called Invitation to Murder, *with special effects, maybe animation, and a soundtrack of mind-blowing Pink Floyd records and the anthems of Bon Jovi. Perhaps the director could squeeze into the soundtrack his favorite song of all time, "Beds Are Burning" by Midnight Oil.*

* * *

Elton Brutus Murphy was born in Wauchula, Florida, on February 3, 1957. He was the son of Elton Murphy Jr. and Betty Jo Murphy. His childhood home was a pastoral scene: a lovely two-large-bedroom cement block single-story house painted a pastel color, nestled under two huge oak trees.

How rustic was it? "Chickens and roosters roamed our yard," Murphy explained. "We had two monkeys during my youth, and a female goat that my dad milked daily. Dad would drink the goat's milk, but the rest of the family preferred cow's milk. There was a donkey and two horses, one regular and one miniature."

His dad drank and his parents fought constantly: mostly verbal, some physical. There was some scuffling with the old man before the first-born son eventually left the house, no injuries or anything like that.

"I only remember one whipping in my life from my father." It occurred when he was ten or eleven. "Just on the bottom," Murphy said. "It wasn't like my dad beat me up."

His dad taught him practical stuff, paid him for the work he did, and made him start a savings account at the bank.

The fights between his parents were what he remembered most. His parents had endurance and could fight all night. Murphy couldn't remember a good night's sleep until he was maybe ten years old.

Predictably, his favorite childhood book was a forget-your-troubles fantasy entitled *The Wonderful Flight to the Mushroom Planet,* written by Eleanor Cameron. It was about the adventures of two boys named Chuck and David who visited the planet Basidium in their homemade spacecraft.

The family didn't use "Big Elton" and "Little Elton." They called the boy "Brutus," after his middle name. Murphy was known as Brutus to most people for most of his life.

When his parents fought, it wasn't just yelling. Stuff was thrown, smashed. One time his mom and dad were arguing and fighting over a .22-caliber pistol and the thing went off.

"I just knew one of them had been shot, but thank God neither of them were," Murphy said.

According to Murphy, his father was a drunk *and* a coward. Another brouhaha when Brutus was ten resulted in Betty Jo calling the sheriff's department. When the deputies arrived, his dad was hiding beneath the marital bed. As deputies coaxed the father out from under the bed, and then held him at bay, Brutus and his mom packed their stuff and got the hell out.

The separation didn't work out. Brutus and his mom were gone for only a few months when they returned with a promise from Elton that he would go on the wagon. Elton went to Alcoholics Anonymous for a while, and stayed dry for a decade, not hitting the bottle until after he and Betty Jo divorced. Once he started drinking again, his health abruptly went south. He was dead within a year. That was 1980. Elton died when he was forty-three.

"I have no hard feelings toward my parents," Murphy said years later.

Elton Brutus Murphy was a bundle of creativity as a kid. He was musical, too. When he was about ten, his parents decided he should take steel guitar lessons. For three full years, he did.

"Mr. Yagle was my teacher," Murphy remembered. "I got where I was pretty good at it." His favorite tune to play on guitar was the theme from the TV show *Bonanza.*

After three years, however, the steel guitar lessons ended, and so did Murphy's interest. But only temporarily. When he was fifteen, he got back into it, taking Spanish guitar lessons for a year. His teacher was Terry Yagle, Mr. Yagle's son.

When Brutus was a teenager, and it was normal to argue with parents, he could remember getting into only one verbal altercation with his dad, and he could no longer remember what it was about. He never fought with his mother, ever!

"My parents' problems were with each other, not with me," he said.

That said, the domestic turmoil was enough to make any boy sulky. Young Brutus sought solace from his troubles by wandering the sixty acres out back that his family owned, fifty acres of orange grove, ten of dense woods. He wasn't into sports, being on a team or anything like that, and preferred roaming the woods alone, both on his family's property and that of others.

That didn't mean he wasn't athletic. He loved to swim, and spent hours gliding across the large pond behind his parents' house. On days when he didn't feel like a swim, he'd grab his fishing pole and fish in that same pond.

"Brim [regional name for bluegill, sometimes spelled bream], catfish, and bass," Murphy recalled.

For a time, when he was a kid, they had a boat. That was when his dad was still around. And if he wasn't roaming or swimming or fishing, Brutus could even hunt on his own land: deer, squirrel, and rabbit.

As he matured, his walks in the grove changed. He went from fantasizing about war, Indians, and treasure maps, to thinking almost exclusively about, as he put it, "easy girls and women."

In the movie about his life—the imaginary one playing in Murphy's head—the soundtrack for this part was by the Beatles, the Monkees, the Beach Boys, and Johnny Cash.

"I now consider where I grew up a small paradise," Murphy has stated.

But paradise didn't last. In 1970, a hard freeze came and destroyed the orange grove. It was never replaced. Most of what had been the grove, forty-five acres of it, was fenced in and the Murphys raised cattle.

The remainder of the cleared land and part of the woods were converted into a nursery in which they grew a wide variety of shrubberies. Murphy had to find someplace else to wander alone— someplace that could never be as magical.

Those acres became a setting for labor rather than relaxation, for he worked in the nursery every day after school until he was sixteen. After that he worked for another nursery and stayed there until he finished school.

At first, Brutus liked playing Spanish guitar. Better than steel guitar. He enjoyed his lessons. But interest dwindled when he was sixteen and bought an electric guitar.

Before long, Brutus was playing in a small group, all teenaged musicians. He played rhythm, along with Randy. Billy was on drums; Charlie on lead; Karen and Judy sang. Randy, Billy, Karen, and Judy were siblings.

They practiced in a barn about a mile from the Murphy house. "We were so loud that my parents could still hear us!" he said. "We played a couple of dances in Arcadia, at the National Guard Armory." They played the rock hits of the day: Creedence Clearwater Revival, Deep Purple—"Smoke on the

Water" was a crowd favorite—some ZZ Top. They played slow dances, too: "Help Me Make It Through the Night" and "Green, Green Grass of Home." The band never had a name. They'd talked about giving themselves a name, but they never got around to it.

Throughout the rest of his life, Murphy usually had a guitar. He figured he owned fifteen different guitars over his life. As an older man, long after the high-school dance days, Murphy liked to play the songs of Gordon Lightfoot, whom he saw in concert in 1982. He would perform "Sundown" and "The Wreck of the Edmund Fitzgerald."

Throughout his youth, and really throughout his life, there was one constant for Murphy. He was always in tip-top physical condition. Even when he was having deep problems, he was still buff.

"I always exerted myself in daily exercise," he said. "I started out as a teen working out with the weights several times a week." As an adult he always belonged to a gym. He'd lift, run, swim, and relax in the sauna. He also kept exercise equipment at home.

He got himself in such good shape at one point that he was running eight miles a day, six days a week. When that got rough on his joints, he'd ride his bike, sixteen miles a day, and would swim two miles daily.

In jail, of course, there wasn't much to do other than exercise, and it was while behind bars that Elton Brutus Murphy ended up setting his personal records.

He boasted: "I was in the Leon County Jail, and in one day I did eighteen hundred push-ups. Not at one time—in sets of twenty throughout the day!"

Chapter 9

Eco-Adventures

Murphy lost his virginity when he was fifteen. At the time he was camping with his family in South Central Florida at the Fisheating Creek Campground. The titular creek was supposed to be the most "pristine" in Florida, west of Lake Okeechobee and north of the Everglades.

It was a standard camping place: paddleboats on a cypress swamp, hiking through the hardwood forests, activities that were known in camping advertising as "eco-adventures."

Murphy had an eco-adventure, all right, and it was a doozy. The girl was also fifteen. She was from Miami and very good-looking.

"Dark brown hair and a medium build," Murphy said. "I do not remember her name."

They took a walk around the campground in the

dark and did it on a picnic table. He did remember an awkward moment as they tried to achieve penetration with her panties just pulled down. It was he who realized that they'd be a lot more comfortable, and successful, if she took off her underwear altogether.

"It was great!" Murphy exclaimed. "And it did wonders for my fifteen-year-old self-esteem."

At age sixteen, he discovered scuba diving. He fell in love with it and decided to make diving his career, either as a scuba-diving instructor or as a deep-sea diver.

He went to Hardee High School in poor, rural Hardee County during the 1970s. Although he claimed not to remember her, Murphy's classmate Debbie Gulliver remembered Brutus well—and she had nothing but nice things to say about him. He wasn't the type to get in trouble. In fact, he was considered one of the "smart kids."

Brutus's favorite high-school subject was drafting and auto mechanics, which he took during the first semester of his senior year.

Brutus was athletic, but he wasn't a jock. He didn't play sports and was not a spectator at sporting events. Every once in a while, he'd watch a football game. His favorite sport on TV was the Olympics, especially the Winter Olympics.

* * *

Hardee County, population fifteen thousand, was not exactly the land of opportunity, and the people there were most likely to work in the citrus, cattle, or phosphate-mining industries. Anyone with another ambition split.

During high school, Brutus wrote to all of the diving schools, read the brochures, and picked the one he wanted to attend. He saved most of his money for two years so that he'd be able to attend a "diving instructor college."

As a teen he didn't require as much solitude as today, and on weekends he could be found raising a little hell.

"I used to go out drinking with my friends," Murphy remembered.

His best friend during those years was Ralph Lovelady (pseudonym). Brutus was with Ralph the first time he ever got arrested: 1973, possession of alcohol by a minor.

"We had to spend the night in jail," Murphy recalled. "Kind of funny now. Lovelady went on to be a sheriff's deputy out of school."

The rest of Lovelady's story wasn't quite so funny.

"Lovelady was still in his early twenties when he himself became a suspect for a series of crimes in Hardee County. When his colleagues at the sheriff's department came to arrest him, Lovelady shot himself."

Others in Murphy's carousing crowd were Danny Yeomans, of Zolfo Springs, a crossroads a couple miles south of Wauchula, and Randy Wiggins and David Smith, who lived in Wauchula proper.

Murphy's other close high-school friend was Randy Newsome, but he wasn't a drinking buddy. He, too, went into law enforcement for a time, working for the Wauchula Police Department (WPD). For some reason he didn't stick with it, and Randy ended up driving a truck.

"I haven't seen any of them since high school," Murphy said sadly.

Brutus Murphy went out on the occasional date during high school, but he had no long-term girlfriends. A couple of the girls he went out with were Deborah Clanton and Lorraine Baucum.

Then there was Rose. Ah, Rose. He remembered many things about Rose, but her last name wasn't one of them. She was from Arcadia, which was about twenty miles south of Wauchula, along Route 17.

But his most memorable experience with a girl during his teen years occurred on his eighteenth birthday, and her name was Sheryl Hayes.

"I'd been socializing with her at Hardee High. She'd agreed to give me some on my birthday," Murphy recalled. Trouble was, she was only fifteen.

Brutus and Sheryl, his brother Dean and his girlfriend, and a couple of other couples went camping near Sheryl's house. Dean was Brutus's only sibling, fourteen months younger than Brutus.

If only everyone had kept their yap shut, then everything would have been great: "Sheryl made the mistake of telling her younger sister where she was going. So here we were, all camped down by a creek in a pasture, and I had a condom on about to do the deed, when out of nowhere here comes a truck tearing out across the pasture with its lights on coming toward us. Sheryl says, 'That's my father, Brutus! You better run and hide!'"

Brutus took the advice and scurried—no shirt, pulling up his jeans—behind some brush and trees along the creek bank. He peeked out and he could see three men, all with guns, who looked like Sheryl's father and two brothers. He heard Sheryl's dad barking orders. The whole party was ordered into the back of his truck. Then Brutus heard the man calling out to him.

"I have everyone in the back of my truck at gunpoint. Unless you want something to happen to them, you will come out of your hiding!" the man shouted.

So Brutus came out and got into the truck with the others. The two brothers held guns on them.

Sheryl's father said, "Brutus, how old are you?"

"Seventeen," Murphy lied.

"It's a good thing you're not eighteen," Sheryl's father said, "or I'd break your scrawny-looking neck, you being with my daughter the way you were!" He was a big man, outweighed the teenager by a hundred pounds. "Brutus, I called your folks and they are going to meet us at my house," he said.

When Brutus's parents arrived, his dad defused the situation. The teen had to promise never to have anything to do with Sheryl ever again, and it was a promise he had no trouble keeping.

He went to his senior prom with the new girl in school, named Vanessa Coons. "We had a good time there, but that was it. Afterward, we went our separate ways," Murphy recalled.

Looking back on his life, Murphy feels like high school was kind of a blank, a waiting period. "It wasn't until after high school that things began happening to me," he said.

Brutus moved to Jacksonville, Florida, and attended PADI, which meant Professional Association of Diving Instructors. It was the best school out there. Their registered motto was: "The Way the World Learns to Dive." PADI was, and is, the world's leading scuba-diving training organization, although Brutus got the impression that tourism was their bread and butter.

The school offered courses right there, locally, of course; but it also offered courses at a variety of global vacation spots. These were courses designed, it appeared, for folks with serious coin.

It was cool that they didn't just teach scuba diving. They did things to help the world as well, through their conservation efforts. The school was less than a decade old, to boot, founded in 1966 after a couple of friends—one teacher and swimming instructor, and one a salesman for U.S. Divers—came up with the idea over shots of Jack Daniel's. Both had come to the conclusion that scuba-diving schools were poorly run and made entry into the world of underwater breathing much more difficult than it needed to be.

Murphy took the ten-week resident training course designed to graduate open-water scuba instructors. He completed the course in December 1975 and received a variety of certifications. He became an instructor, equipment repair specialist, senior lifesaver, and American Red Cross instructor of cardiopulmonary resuscitation (CPR).

Certificates in hand, Brutus Murphy moved to Key Largo, Florida, where he was self-employed as a scuba instructor at the Bryn Mawr Marina & Campground. He concentrated on speed, and became convinced he could train and certify scuba divers faster than anyone else around. He got so fast that he could do it in three days.

"I definitely taught the shortest course in the United States," Murphy boasted.

Chapter 10

Bermuda

While teaching scuba diving, Brutus did his best to stay up on all of the latest developments by reading *Skin Diver Magazine,* which featured ads for—and feature articles about—new equipment. There was lots of gorgeous photography, and the magazine was part travelogue, with articles about the latest hot spots to dive, always suitable for a luxurious vacation, and other things to do while there. He always learned something with every issue. They had Q&A columnists in different categories, like technology, medicine, teaching, and "turning pro."

In one issue of *Skin Diver,* Murphy read an article about U.S. Navy underwater photographers. It sounded like the perfect job, he thought—and so he enlisted in the navy in 1976. He endured boot camp in San Diego, California; then he moved to the Naval Air Station Pensacola, where he attended the navy's School of Photography.

From there he spent the remainder of his five-year hitch at the Naval Air Station Bermuda. When it came to military service, this was about as good as it got. Murphy loved it there. He worked in the base's photo lab, which was part of the Atlantic Fleet Audio/Visual Facility.

"It was a great job in a paradise of a location," Murphy reminisced.

The base he lived on had been an air force base until 1970. He lived in Bermuda for four years. During that stint he took thousands of photographs, both as part of his job and on his own. He was a photographer for the base weekly newspaper, the *Bermuda Skyliner.* For years on end, Murphy had photos in every issue. He eventually got to the point where he was Bermuda's number one naval photographer, photographing naval events at both bases on the island, as well as all sorts of related activities.

Murphy offered a quick aside: The United States left Bermuda in 1995, but the island remained, for obvious reasons, a great place for reunions, not that Murphy ever attended any of those.

"Not that all of the events I photographed were that exciting," he admitted.

If the military loved one thing, it was ceremonies. There was a ceremony every day, awards, promotions, whatever. Lots of marching, bands playing . . . Brutus Murphy took pictures of them all.

And, then again, some photography jobs were very, very exciting. He was in charge of the aerial photography as well, and he got to ride in a Huey H1N helicopter once a month.

In sharp contrast he also worked as the base portrait photographer and—his camera mounted on a tripod—took thousands of studio portraits of base personnel.

But home base for Murphy during those years was the darkroom, where he spent many enjoyable hours, becoming a master of developing film and printing photographs.

Some of his tasks were downright spooky, in a secret agent James Bond kind of way. Murphy served a role in the then-ongoing Cold War with the Soviet Union.

"I had clearance to handle classified material and developed aerial photo surveillance photos taken from a P-3 Orion reconnaissance plane," Murphy said.

The P-3 was a land-based, long-range, anti-submarine patrol aircraft, flew at 28,300 feet, had a mission radius of 2,380 nautical miles. And, if things got nasty, the P-3 could bite back, as it was capable of holding ten tons of ordnance. Judging by the photos taken from the P-3, Murphy figured there wasn't a Soviet ship or submarine in the Atlantic Ocean that the U.S. Navy didn't know about.

Murphy says that his photographic work became of such a high quality in Bermuda that he was offered a job teaching photography at Los Angeles Community College-Overseas. Brutus explained that he didn't have a college education, but the lady from the college said none was needed. And besides, Brutus came highly recommended by Chief Clinton. And that was how he ended up teaching Photography 101 for three semesters. The course covered photographic and darkroom techniques. After his second semester as a teacher, the college presented him with a "provisional teaching credential."

Yeah, yeah, yeah, but Bermuda was mostly just fun. Murphy and a friend of his, fellow Photographer's Mate John Pappas, bought an inflatable boat and motor together. They decided to get the best, so they bought an Avon, the number one manufacturer of inflatable boats since the 1950s. Their boats were built by hand from tough materials and came with a ten-year warranty.

He joined the base dive club, the Reef Roamers, and dove in the ocean at least once a week for the entire time he was there. One of the best things about the club was access to underwater cameras.

"I shot hundreds of underwater photos, including shots of the various shipwrecks along the ocean floor off Bermuda," Murphy said.

* * *

In 1977, his life took an unexpected turn. That year, he was sent back to Pensacola for some advanced photographic training.

"I wasn't there long, just long enough to meet Elaine Crabtree and fall in love with her," Murphy remembered.

His friend Mark Klothacus introduced them.

"Back then, I was a deeply devout Christian, and so was she. We met at United Pentecostal Church."

The church taught the Bible standard of full salvation, which was the absolute essentiality of repentance; baptism was immersion for the remission of sins; the speaking of tongues as the "Spirit gives utterance."

Brutus and the woman saw stars immediately, and their initial romance was brief. He had to return to Bermuda after a week. Once returned to the base, he couldn't get his mind off her. He recorded a marriage proposal and mailed the cassette tape to Elaine; she agreed. Several months later he returned to Pensacola to be married.

The groom was twenty; the bride was twenty-two. He recalled a beautiful ceremony, at the same church where they'd met. A beautiful sun-drenched white church on Sun Valley Drive, right across the street from an equally sunny gas station.

Both sets of parents were there, as well as a contingency from the church's congregation. Best man was fellow navy photographer's mate second class (PH2) Mark Klothacus, the same man who'd introduced them.

The honeymoon was brief, in more ways than one. The vacation was short and the romantic glow quickly faded. The new couple moved to Bermuda and lived in base housing. They were together for three years.

"For the first two of those years, we were Seventh-Day Adventists," Murphy said.

That group believed that God's greatest desire was for worshippers to see him clearly—not so much to see his face, as some thought, but to see the quality of God's character. As worshippers experienced God's love, they came to see their own lives more clearly as well.

"For the third and last year together, we mutually agreed to become vegetarians," Murphy added. "The preacher's wife, also a vegetarian, taught Elaine how to cook a variety of nonmeat dishes."

Murphy was the one who ended the marriage.

"I allowed the devil to get to me," he later said. He flew to the Norfolk, Virginia, Naval Base for about a week. There he made contact with a woman in the navy he'd worked with in Bermuda. She'd been reassigned to Norfolk and they got together a couple of times in her dormitory room on the base.

Brutus confessed to Elaine that he had sinned and had brought pain upon their marriage through the act of lusting after other women.

Contrary to his wants and needs, Elaine initially

forgave him for his lust and stayed with him. She was definitely not getting the hint. For three weeks Brutus had to save up all of his meanness and say every nasty thing he could think of before Elaine agreed to leave Bermuda.

"She moved out on our third anniversary, in 1980. She returned to Pensacola, and I have not seen her since—not even for the divorce," Murphy said.

She did try to make a collect call a couple of years later, but Murphy didn't accept the charges. But, even in 2011, he knew her current address, including her remarried name and an alias she used sometimes. With his vegetarian-cooking wife gone for good, Murphy spent the rest of his time in Bermuda living the footloose and fancy-free life of a single man.

Rid of Elaine, and swinging, Brutus rented an off-base apartment and dedicated his leisure time to entertaining a string of tourist women—oh, my—and one naval wife. Oh, the naval wife!

While teaching his photography class, Murphy had a student who was a "delightful-looking twenty-eight-year-old wife of another naval photographer."

Her husband, apparently, lacked the patience to teach his own wife how to take photos. She needed college credit, so she took Murphy's class, and they hit it off right away.

"I could tell that she liked me a lot, right from the start. She kept looking at me as if I were an ice-cream treat she wanted to eat," Murphy boasted.

At one point during the course, Murphy informed his students that he did a lot of underwater photography as a hobby—and that he was a scuba-diving teacher before he was a photography teacher. After that class his favorite student asked him if he would teach her underwater photography. She said that she already knew how to scuba dive because she and her husband enjoyed diving on the many wrecks off Bermuda.

"We own an underwater camera, but I don't know how to use it," she said.

Brutus happily agreed to go diving with her, and to teach her how to use her own and other underwater cameras. He met her at the front gate of the Bermuda Naval Base, and got her a visitor's pass. She brought her own scuba equipment and camera with her. He was familiar with her camera, a Nikonos, because he'd once owned one just like it. He had his own equipment ready, so together they drove out to the NASA tracking station, which was connected to the base.

"Before we went into the water, I gave her about an hour class in underwater photography, including specific instruction in using her camera," Murphy said.

They changed into their scuba equipment and entered the water. They only had to go out about sixty feet from shore, and they were in forty feet of water surrounded by a beautiful coral reef and many tropical fish—lots of stuff to take photos of.

The other man's wife began taking photos, and

Murphy got close to her in the water so he could assist her in setting the controls. Murphy had his own camera with him, and he took some pictures of her taking pictures.

"I could tell by her facial expression that she was having a blast," Murphy said.

They were in the water for about an hour. They surfaced and climbed out of the water. They sat together on the lava rock, their feet dangling into a tidal pool. He made her review what she had learned, and he explained in greater detail the usage of different types of underwater cameras.

"All of a sudden, out of the blue, she told me she had an ulterior motive for getting me alone," Murphy said. "She asked me if I had a wife or a girl-friend."

He said he was separated from his wife; she was back in the States. She said she was happily married to a good man, who was twenty years older than she was—not that age made a difference, of course. And she'd been faithful to her husband for the entire six years of their marriage.

"It's just that I'm beside myself from thinking about you," she said. It happened right away. Her eyes had started to twinkle the first time she laid eyes on him, on the first day of photography class, and they had been twinkling ever since. "I don't know how you feel about me, but I would really like to be with you. I would like you to make love to me. Oh, God, I can't believe I just said that out

loud! Please tell me that I didn't just make a fool
out of myself."

"No, you didn't," Brutus said, with a comforting
tone. "And I am very flattered that you find me
interesting. Well, I guess our photography lesson
is over."

He smiled at her and made his move. He em-
braced her and made love to her right there in the
tidal pool.

"It was great, and so was she," Murphy said.

After that, Murphy and the other guy's wife
met a few more times, always in Murphy's small
apartment. They had wine and piña coladas and
fantastic lovemaking. After that, the woman said
she needed to call it quits, needed to get back to
concentrating on being a good wife.

"It was fun while it lasted," Murphy said. "Great
memories."

He played hard, and he worked hard. His service
to his country was lauded. He received several letters of appreciation for a job well done.

"I was awarded the Good Conduct medal and the
Navy Achievement medal," Murphy said. The latter
was for doing an excellent job as the petty officer in
charge of the Atlantic Fleet Audio/Visual Facility.
His rank at that time was actually E5, petty officer
second class.

After all of those millions of photos Murphy took

of naval ceremonies, now he got to be the subject of just such a photo, proudly receiving his medal. The photo ran in the *Bermuda Skyliner*.

Brutus Murphy was discharged honorably in 1981, and, largely because of the skills he'd learned while in the navy, made a seamless reentry into the civilian world. He quickly got a job in Clearwater, Florida, processing film in a darkroom.

Chapter 11

Mary

His love life didn't suffer, either, now that he was out of uniform. On Clearwater Beach he met a beautiful woman named Mary Border. They were both in the water swimming, riding the waves.

He asked her what she did for a living and she had to answer him several times because he had water in his ears. She got right in his face and said, "I cut hair." It was love at first sight for him. He wasn't sure how she felt about him. When they did meet, there were times when he thought she liked him, and then there were times when his insecurities took over and he thought he was just fooling himself. But she *did* like him.

She was model gorgeous, statuesque, five-ten, so tanned, naturally blond hair as golden as the Florida sunshine, very slender, and muscular.

As was true of all of his relationships, once it started, it progressed quickly. They saw each other pretty much every day. They mostly went to the beach and strolled slowly along the wade at night, so the ebb of each wave splashed across the tops of their feet.

They'd been lovers for about a month when he popped the question. He proposed in his car, which was parked just outside Fort DeSoto Park. She said yes, and they became engaged.

A couple of weeks later he bought her a ring.

He and his new fiancée moved into an apartment together at Indian Shores. It was a large complex called the Indian Pass Apartments. There were several hundred units, with a pool in the courtyard. The apartment was right across the road from Indian Rocks Beach. It was a one-bedroom unit, with a small bath, living room, and kitchen, about five hundred square feet. There was a small porch, where they could step outside and look at the water.

Brutus went to work for Reedy Photoprocess Corporation, where he maintained the film processors and printers. Reedy was comprised of two companies. The parent company was in Minneapolis, run by president Stan Reedy.

In 1980, Reedy purchased a small processing lab at the corner of Fifth Avenue and Sixty-fourth Street South in Pasadena, Florida. The lab was comprised of many small rooms, with each step in the processing and printing procedure done separately. There was one room for correcting, another for processing. As custom printing was a Reedy specialty, each enlarger had its own separate room. At the end of the hallway were the "chemical mix" room on one side, where Murphy spent the bulk of his time, and the bathroom on the other. In the front there was a small area for customer pickup. The largest room was the office.

Many years later, Brutus Murphy's coworker at Reedy, Paula Burfield, had nothing unkind to say about him.

"To me, he was always sweet," she said. "Very pleasant."

No indications that there was anything odd, nothing a little bit off. He worked in the lab in the back and dressed casually, usually wearing a normal pair of jeans and a T-shirt. She remembered thinking at the time that he was "rather nice-looking."

Another Reedy employee who remembered Murphy was Lynn Bushner. He was "fine. Very nice. Perfectly normal."

She said that many of his duties were janitorial. In addition to keeping the machines in working order, he also swept up the place. Neither Burfield nor Bushner remembered Murphy ever processing film.

Murphy worked at Reedy for about six months. He enjoyed the job, but there was no money in it.

"Mary was making three times as much as I was, cutting hair," he said.

According to him, he spontaneously quit one morning. According to his former coworkers, he was fired after getting into a "tiff" with someone.

Murphy enrolled that same day in the barber school at Sunstate Academy in Clearwater. It was his idea to make the move, but Mary supported him 100 percent. He paid his tuition by using his GI Bill money.

While attending Sunstate, Murphy's eye for the ladies began to roam again. The lover he remembered best was an emancipated seventeen-year-old named Amber.

"The sex was without delay, and it was good," he said.

He stayed with Amber for a couple of weeks before he dumped her to go with another student. He broke off his engagement with Mary so he could pursue without guilt.

He had lived with Mary Border for a year and a half. He felt that life was filled with opportunities, and she was stifling that. She became pretty upset when he told her he needed his freedom.

Murphy sometimes still wished that he had married her.

"Absolutely gorgeous," he reminisced.

Brutus graduated from Sunstate in March 1983. On April 6, he received his Florida barber's license. His first job as a hairstylist was in downtown St. Petersburg, working at Pedro's Tonsorial Parlor.

The parlor was not far from Jannus Landing, an open-air concert venue now known as Jannus Live. He only stayed at Pedro's for a couple of months before he found a better-paying job, working freelance at Starlight Park Barber Shop in Largo.

At the Starlight, Murphy worked for the owner, a guy named Bill Mills, and his immediate supervisor was Alia Benson. Longtime Starlight employee Gary Crowell remembered how the shop looked back then, with its light blue interior, three matching chairs, and mirrors on the back wall.

The shop was part of a strip mall at the corner of Park Boulevard and Starkey Road—a very busy intersection, sitting next to a pawnshop/jewelry store. The plaza wasn't big, but sometimes it had juicy gossip. One owner went to jail for paying a cop to kill his ex-wife.

Brutus remained at the Starlight Barber Shop until early 1984, when he and his brother, Dean, invested together in a pair of hair salons in St. Pete: A Hair Emporium. The salons—Brutus ran one, Dean the other—were top-notch, but neither location was that great. They never did make much money.

And that was the way life stayed for a few years, until Brutus was twenty-eight years old and started to feel the old wanderlust again.

Chapter 12

The Madness

Sometime during 1984, while living and working in St. Pete, Brutus Murphy raped a woman. That was the start of it: "the madness"—what Murphy would come to call his "bizarre behaviorism."

It enveloped him and rendered him irresponsible.

That was the first time he felt his own personal Mr. Hyde persona ooze out of his psyche. He didn't know how to explain it, but a curtain closed on his normal self.

He was still in the plane, but he was no longer the pilot.

He thought maybe it was caused by a chemical imbalance in his brain. His conscious mind became subservient and his subconscious rose to dominance.

Murphy's neophyte madness was not the only chemical affecting his behavior.

"I was very drunk," Murphy recalled.

He was soaring. He had a strong chemical high, "a feeling of grandiosity in my psyche that I never felt at any other time."

He met the girl in a joint called the Crown Lounge, where they sometimes had B-list (maybe C-list) rock concerts: acts a full decade or more past the peak of their popularity.

"I brought her home and she fell asleep," Murphy explained. "She was wearing a skirt and panty hose. I took a scissors and cut off her panty hose and then I raped her. I told her about it in the morning, and she just laughed and said it was okay. She was a really good sport about it."

According to Murphy, she then told him that he would have to pay for his selfishness. There would be no more cutting of panty hose with scissors. He had to have sex with her again—this time so she could enjoy it. So they had a little morning delight.

It's not uncommon for American veterans to become nostalgic over their time in the service, but it was particularly bad for Murphy.

He'd had maybe the greatest-of-all-possible military experiences in Bermuda. Compared to cutting hair in strip-mall Florida, making beautiful underwater photos and dealing with top-secret film was tons more glamorous and adventurous.

He decided that the thing he needed to make his life complete was to become a Navy SEAL. Murphy sold his salon. Brother Dean kept his and continued cutting hair.

"I reenlisted in the navy for six years, and was able to reenter the service at my old rank, E5 pay grade as a photographer's mate, petty officer second class," he said.

A few weeks into his Navy Veteran Training in Orlando, Murphy took his fitness test for the SEALs and, on the second try, passed it. To pass the test he had to swim five hundred yards in under twelve and a half minutes, do a minimum of forty-two push-ups in two minutes, fifty-two sit-ups in two minutes, and eight pull-ups (no time limit). The last stage of the test was the toughest. Wearing boots and pants, a candidate had to run a mile and a half in under eleven minutes.

After completing that training, he was sent to the Naval Special Warfare Group One and Basic Underwater Demolition/SEAL (BUD/S) Training in Coronado, California. For seven months he worked as a photographer directly under the master chief of the command, a SEAL named Cliff Hollenbeck, who was a real hero, with a Silver Star and a Bronze Star to show for it. Murphy again loved the photography work because of its variety, for he took photos throughout the command, including in the SEAL Compound.

"The most interesting assignment was to go up in a CH-46 double-rotor helicopter with a bunch of SEALs and shoot photos of them rappelling out the rear of the chopper. I also photographed them fast-roping out of the bottom of the helicopter."

Passing the fitness test entitled Murphy to enroll in BUD/S Training. This program taught SEAL candidates to be men of character, to be in top physical condition, and to learn new tasks quickly. The course lasted for six months and taught physical conditioning, small-boat handling, diving physics, basic diving techniques, land warfare, weapons, demolitions, communications, and reconnaissance.

For the first seven weeks the course concentrated on conditioning, with the fourth week aptly named "Hell Week," which consisted of five and a half days of continuous training, with a maximum total of four hours sleep during that time. Hell Week was designed to prove to the candidates that it was possible for a man to do ten times the work that an average man would have thought possible.

The second phase of training concentrated on diving; the third on weapons, demolition, and small-unit tactics. The final three weeks were basic parachute training.

Murphy began his BUD/S Training during the winter. "I wouldn't recommend it," he said. BUD/S Training in winter was tough because the Pacific Ocean was downright icy!

Murphy only made it four and a half weeks into BUD/S Training. "I couldn't psychologically handle being in and out of the fifty-degree water all day long," he remembered sadly.

He preferred to think about the aspects of the training in which he did well. He handled the obstacle course with no problem. He handled the boat landing in the pounding surf. The running and the swimming—both without trouble.

"But the cold water affected me so much, I finally rang the bell, which signified that you are quitting BUD/S," Murphy admitted.

After dropping out of SEAL training, Murphy was commanded to go to his next duty assignment in Long Beach, California, aboard the USS *Peleliu.* The ship was named after the 1944 battle in which the First Marine Division, later relieved by the Army's Eighty-first Infantry Division, cleared the Pacific island of Peleliu. The battle was supposed to last a couple of days, and ended up lasting longer than two months. It had the highest casualty rate of any battle in the Pacific Theater, higher than either Iwo Jima or Okinawa.

The battle's namesake was a huge eighteen-story-tall amphibious assault ship. She was in dry dock when Murphy was assigned to her, and stayed in dry dock for many months, while he worked aboard as a photographer.

After what seemed like forever, the *Peleliu* finally went out to sea, but it didn't stay out there for long. After two weeks the captain determined that work on the ship was incomplete. It returned to dock.

"After a few weeks of being on the ship anchored to the dock, I decided to take drastic action," he said. He grabbed his backpack and his Navy SEAL combat knife, which he bought off someone during BUD/S.

"I jumped ship," he admitted. He didn't know why. "I got off work one morning and walked through the gate of the Long Beach Naval Shipyard with no intention of ever coming back. I went AWOL!"

Murphy got on a bus for downtown Los Angeles. High and euphoric, Murphy removed his military ID card from his wallet. He cut it into little pieces. He threw the pieces out the window of the moving bus. Murphy looked back at the confetti wind with a sense of profound liberation.

He was too high with adrenaline—or chemical imbalance, or whatever this new madness was—to look at reality. If he took off the delusion glasses, his reality was far more bleak.

He was beginning a four-and-a-half-month stretch during which he would live as a transient, roaming free and broke along the West Coast between Santa Monica and San Francisco. Hunger would drive him to desperation, and to crime.

He was only in San Francisco for a couple of days. For a fellow who was down on his luck, San

Francisco could be an accommodating city. There were flophouses and soup kitchens.

But Murphy was so out of it, he lacked the social skills to find those places. He slept on the coast in a foxhole he carved for himself out of the brush.

The worst crime he committed during those lost months was in a campground on Half Moon Bay. In fact, it was so severe that it temporarily ended Murphy's life as a transient.

"I tried to kill a man," Murphy explained. Again, the madness from the chemical imbalance in his brain made him do irrational and bad things—things clearly destructive to others, but self-destructive, too. Murphy said it felt like a drug, like he took too much of something and was wasted out of his mind.

"There is a dreamlike state that I am in," Murphy said. "Things slow down. Surreal. Unreal. That's a fact!"

Half Moon Bay is twenty-eight miles south of San Francisco, between forested hills along California's most scenic coastline. It was beautiful, Murphy later said, but a place where "the winds of romance blew queerly."

The guy—his name was never known—propositioned Murphy sexually. Murphy wasn't at all tempted. In fact, he was pissed off. So Murphy waited until the guy was asleep, attached a heavy lead weight to his combat knife case, and hit the guy in the head with it.

"I hit him as hard as I could, but it was obviously not hard enough."

Instead of staying unconscious from the concussion of the blow, the guy woke up very startled and frightened. Murphy hit him again with the weighted case—this time in the center of his forehead. Once more, the guy withstood the blow better than Murphy would have thought possible. Murphy had given him his best shot, right between the eyes, and the guy was only stunned.

"Then he begged me to stop, so I decided to let him live," Murphy explained.

That was as far as Murphy's compassion went. He pulled his razor-sharp combat knife from its sheath and brandished it so that the guy was good-and-properly terrified.

"I warned him if he went to the police, I would hunt him down and kill him."

Murphy hadn't planned on the guy having a skull as thick as the hull of the *Peleliu*, and had already made plans for what to do with the corpse when the guy was dead.

"I was going to dump his body over a cliff along the coast," he said.

Instead of killing the guy, Murphy stole his Chevy Blazer, his wallet, and his money. Without stopping, Murphy drove to the San Francisco Bay Area airport.

From there, he called his mother in Florida, and she wired him enough money for an airline ticket back home. After a few months in Florida, Murphy became fed up with the outlaw life, constantly looking over his shoulder, searching for military police (MPs) in the margins of his vision.

"I had my brother and his wife drive me to the recruit training command navy base in Orlando, Florida." Dean let him out at the front gate.

Murphy walked up to the sentry and said, "I am Petty Officer Murphy and I am here to turn myself in for desertion."

He stayed in Orlando for a couple of weeks, where he was free to come and go, and was allowed to socialize with other deserters. Then they put him, unaccompanied, on an airplane to Los Angeles, where he called shore patrol at the Long Beach Naval Shipyard and told them that he was at the airport. He was told to wait in front of the airport. He saw an official navy car pull up and inside was a pair of armed escorts.

"You Petty Officer Murphy?" one asked.

"I am."

Before many mildly interested witnesses in the hustling and bustling airport, Murphy was handcuffed behind his back.

He was placed in the back of the navy car and was taken to the Long Beach Shore Patrol and kept in a holding cell for a couple of hours. He was next moved back to the USS *Peleliu*, still in dry dock, and back to his former workstation in the photo lab.

"I was not confined while aboard the *Peleliu*," Murphy said. He was even allowed to leave the ship and go on the base and return. This freedom lasted for about a week. Then he was court-martialed.

As a result of that legal ceremony, Murphy was demoted from E5 to E1, given thirty days in the brig, and given a dishonorable discharge, the grounds being "bad conduct."

Murphy served his brig time in San Diego.

"That was my first prolonged incarceration, and it was rough," Murphy said.

The only good thing about the brig was the breakfasts. Those meals were huge and great, and in complete contrast to everything else about the place.

Most days he and the other prisoners were taken from their cells and sent into the harbor onto one of the ships. Half the time they would scrape old paint; the other half they would be saddled with a brush, slapping on new paint.

After his month in the brig, he was released into civilian life. Within twelve hours he was in St. Petersburg, staying with his brother until he could find a job and get a few paychecks under his belt. Actually, it was more like he was living next to Dean rather than with him. The building in Largo was not a duplex, but more of a quad-plex.

The search for a job didn't take long. Murphy had a skill, cutting hair, which was always in demand. Almost immediately he was hired by a barbershop in the Gateway Mall in northeast St. Pete. "It was a really good job," he said. "Busy location, and what made it even better was I was paid in cash daily, with a seventy-five percent commission."

He only stayed with Dean and Dean's then-wife, Brenda, for a couple of weeks. He moved out quickly. He didn't move far, however. He ended up renting the apartment right next door to them.

Chapter 13

Paula

Murphy remembered good times from that period. The brothers went out on Dean's boat, nocturnal fishing trips on Tampa Bay. About six months after Murphy's discharge, he met a lovely haircutter named Paula Cunningham (pseudonym), who would become his second wife. They met at Madeira Beach. As was Murphy's pattern, he fell in love almost immediately.

She and her family were vacationing. It was a holiday, but Murphy didn't remember which one. He ran into Paula and her sister and her girlfriend and they asked him if he wanted to play a game with them, some board game or something, so he went with them.

Brutus and Paula were married by a justice of the peace in St. Pete in 1987. The newlyweds decided to make a fresh start of it in a new town, where they would open their own hair salon and live happily ever after. They traveled around, scouting locations, visiting many towns and cities on a number of weekend trips. They visited Panama City, Tampa Bay, just looking around. Then they stopped in Tallahassee and Murphy had a real good feeling about it.

"There was something in the air in Tallahassee," he said. Smelled like home. The newlyweds found a place and moved to Tallahassee in late 1987. Just as planned they opened their own shop in early 1988—Clippercraft Haircutters. It was very romantic. Paula would cut hair in the chair right next to her husband's.

The place had seven workstations. They rented them out. They didn't have employees, and they never had more than a few independent contractors at any given time. They had a tanning bed and a massage therapist. That is, they had a massage therapist until—fingers no doubt wandering—she fell in love with one of her customers and moved out of the state.

"The environment was just short of upscale and very relaxed. We played Top Forty music on the radio all day," he said.

And that was the way it was. The Murphys were as happy as clams for just about seven years. Then the rent went up and up and up, $1,200 a month, until they were forced to change locations.

Murphy was proud of the new Clippercraft Haircutters because he did all of the work himself. "I built the walls, and all that stuff," he said.

The space had been a skin care place, but he converted it. Took about a week. He was handy with tools, good with plumbing and electricity—and completely self-taught.

The old shop was already gone, so there was no income. They needed to open the new joint quickly. Refurbishment time was at a premium.

"When I look back, the new Clippercraft Haircutters was still a little rough around the edges when we opened for business," Murphy said.

But it wasn't the interior decoration that hurt business as much as the location. Sure, the rent was cheaper, and it was another little space in another little shopping plaza.

"But cheaper didn't mean better," Murphy said. Their steady customers weren't willing to go the extra distance to the new place. Plus, starting on moving day, there was a massive road construction project right outside, making access to the shop ridiculously complicated. Customers had to drive through rutted dirt to enter the new plaza's parking lot.

"We lost a hell of a lot of business," Murphy said.

If Murphy had it to do over again, he would have stayed at the first site. Better to have high rent and a thriving business, he realized in retrospect.

* * *

It was around the time that the Murphys were struggling at their salon's second location that he began to express himself artistically. After Trevor, his son, was born, Murphy made paper airplanes. Then he graduated to cardboard and wood. He started experimenting with materials and found that he loved working with copper. He sculpted in metal, soldering and welding copper pipes into *objets*. Of course, not everyone appreciated Murphy's talent. Some only saw a weirdo collecting and mangling scrap metal.

He would find pieces of copper; he'd take copper tubing and flatten it out. He would hammer and propane it together; the next thing you knew, he had made a train! Encouraged by his early success, Murphy became more "progressive."

To maximize his ability to work in this medium, Murphy took a night class in gas welding at Lively Vo-Tech in Tallahassee. The "Vo" stood for Vocational. Whatever it was you wanted to be, they could teach you. Want to learn to fly? Step right up. Massage therapy, turn right. Beauty parlor skills, turn left. Murphy was there to learn to weld better.

And he did learn, and Murphy's pieces of art grew, both in complexity and in size. His larger sculptures were made of steel, copper, and brass. He made sculptures that were all steel, all copper, or all brass—or any combination of the three.

It got to the point where making sculptures was all he wanted to do. Night after night, sometimes all night, he would weld. Whenever he had a day off from the salon, which was great, it gave him an opportunity to weld some more.

Most of the metals he used were scrap or junk. He would go to the scrap yard every couple of weeks or so and buy scrap metal by the pound. He would bring the metal to his workshop, where he had a wide variety of bending, cutting, and welding tools.

"Eventually I made a room about five hundred square feet in our hair salon, which I used as a gallery for my works of art, my metal sculptures."

To advertise his gallery, he put a sign, BRUTUS'S BONEYARD, in the hair salon's front window, with a picture of one of his favorite metal sculptures: a skeleton made of pipes holding a spear.

Not all of his work was macabre. He made airplanes, trains, ships, automobiles, and whimsical fantasy creatures. He made an alligator and a flying machine. His all-time favorite sculpture was a six-and-a-half-foot-tall Egyptian pharaoh made of steel.

Because of the floundering business at the hair salon, and perhaps a little because of all the time he was putting into a not-for-profit pursuit, Murphy was forced to take a second job, cutting hair at the Regis Hairstylists in Governor's Square Mall in Tallahassee.

Because Regis had such a great location compared to his own place, he moved all of his customers there and developed a clientele. There was always an influx of new customers, because it was in a mall and because Regis had a nationally recognized name.

Paula tried to make it on her own cutting hair at Clippercraft Haircutters, but there just wasn't enough money. So not long after her husband began working at Regis, the Murphys closed up Clippercraft for good.

Chapter 14

C-section

For seven years the Murphys lived and worked together. Considering how much time they spent together, they hardly ever got on each other's nerves. They always remembered to take time for themselves. Paula went to the gym every day, and—when he wasn't working on sculptures—Murphy enjoyed long walks and bike rides. As the marriage progressed, Murphy spent less and less time getting fresh air, and more time on his welding "obsession."

The best things that the marriage gave him were "two wonderful children": Trevor and Darcie. One of the greatest moments in his life—maybe *the* greatest—came in 1989 when he watched Trevor being born.

"Trevor was born by Caesarean section and I watched the entire procedure," he said. The most fascinating part was when the doctor removed his wife's uterus and set it down outside the body so he could sew it up and put it back.

The moment his son was born was "one of the most emotional times" of his life. It was incredible that he could feel so much love for someone, for another human being, whom he'd seen only for a moment.

He felt the same way in 1993 when his daughter was born. Although the same doctor delivered both of his children, Darcie was born of natural childbirth, so Murphy did not get to see his wife's internal reproductive system for a second time.

According to Murphy, he always got along well with his children. He is eager to let the world know: "I never spanked or whipped my children. I don't believe in it."

He says he never "hit or slapped" Paula, either. Not that he was a perfect husband with no temper. "I admit that I was physical with her a few times. The first time was only a few months after we were married. I know that, at that time, I frightened Paula very much. What I did was throw her on the bed. Then I put my hand tightly over her mouth and told her to keep her mouth shut." There were a couple of other times during the marriage when he did the same thing to her. That was the extent of the physical abuse he dished out. He didn't really hurt her, but he was aware that he scared the "wits out of Paula" each time he did it. After each time he felt awful, but he didn't remember ever apologizing. Years later, when their marriage was over, Paula told Murphy about how scared she became when he got physical with her, how she even "feared for her life."

Murphy said, "Of all of the women I've been with—Paula, I loved the most! I really believe she is my soul mate. Even today." He still frequently dreamed about her, even though they had been apart for years.

Chapter 15

Group Sex

According to Paula, she and Murphy broke up when he became verbally abusive and threatened physical violence against the children and toward her. She said that Murphy had an inadequate-type personality. There had been an incident, she said, in which Murphy requested to watch her having sex with another man—and that, in fact, did occur.

Murphy admitted that it was true. "I had a strange obsession," he said. "I needed to see my wife with another man. So after years of coercion, I finally persuaded her to do so. Eventually we did two threesomes, with an extra guy. And we did one foursome, with another husband and wife."

Murphy found these group-sex scenes very exciting, but he came nowhere close to living out his most extreme sexual fantasies. "My swinging was on the low-key amateur level," he said. "Usually we would discuss each other's likes and dislikes and go from there."

He was always looking for new opportunities to bring fresh people into his marriage bed. He also convinced Paula that they should have an "open marriage"; that is, they were each allowed to have lovers on the side. So Murphy regularly found himself in bed with other women. Only once, however, did he tell Paula about it. "I told her before the encounter what I was going to do and who I was going to be with. Then, when I got home, I told her all about it. Paula seemed happy for me."

Open marriages are most often a precursor to separation, and that was the case here. The sex-on-the-side scenario caused the marriage to come to a "bad conclusion."

The beginning of the end came about eight months after he left Clippercraft. One day, as he was completing a haircut at Regis, he glanced up toward the reception area. He noticed a woman there, and she was holding a large manila envelope. She placed the envelope on the front desk and walked out. He completed the haircut and walked his client to the front of the shop and took her money. While there, he looked at the manila envelope and was surprised to see it labeled: *Elton Murphy: Personal and Confidential*. He opened the envelope right there in front of everyone; inside were fifty photographs of his wife and another man he didn't know. They were fully clothed, but they were kissing in one photo. The photos were taken in various locations, surveillance style. One location he recognized was outside the Legends Gym, where Paula worked out. Murphy was unnerved by the photos and found it difficult to concentrate on his work as he finished his shift. Even though he and Paula had an open relationship, she had never—as far as he knew—previously acted upon it.

That night he confronted his wife, saying, "Paula, how are things going at the gym?"

"Good!" she replied happily.

"What are you doing there?"

"I work out there. Why? What do you think I'm doing there?"

He said nothing, just handed her the manila envelope. Looking at the photos, she was flabbergasted.

"Where did you get these?" she asked.

"At Regis today," he replied. "So, who's the guy?"

"That's Bobby Bill (pseudonym), my personal trainer," she replied. "We're not up to anything. We're just friends. Who took these photos?"

Murphy admitted he didn't know. "So there's nothing going on between you two?"

"No. Nothing."

"Well, somebody thinks there is, or they would not have taken these photos. Somebody takes you two seriously."

Paula insisted that whoever thought that was wrong. Murphy was cool with that and decided to let the matter slide. About a month later, Murphy came home early from the salon and was completely overwhelmed by what he saw.

"I saw nothing! All of the furniture was gone," he recalled. "I didn't even have a bed!" He walked from room to room in disbelief; then he sat down on the living-room floor and began to cry. He couldn't remember ever being so upset, before or since.

About an hour later the phone rang. It was Paula.

"I called you at work and they said you left early. As you can see, I've left you. I'm sorry you found out the way you did, but I wanted to avoid a conflict with you."

Murphy was devastated.

Chapter 16

Psychological Haze

A few days later he returned home and there was a message on the answering machine from "some crazed girl" who claimed to be Bobby Bill's girlfriend. She was "carrying on" about finding Bobby Bill and Paula having sex in a car parked behind the gym. She called Paula "a whore." Murphy later learned that the woman on the message was named Cindy. She had been living with Bobby Bill until Paula intervened and caused them to break up.

According to Paula, after they broke up, the children showed no interest in talking to their estranged father, who appeared to be laboring in some sort of fugue state. Murphy, as we'll see, had fonder memories of fatherhood.

Murphy admitted he was hurting. "I had the wind knocked out of me" was how he put it. "I was wounded merchandise for quite a while."

He was so hurt that, about a year later, spur of the moment, he decided he could no longer live in the same town as Paula—so he packed a few things and left Tallahassee. He wanted to put some distance between himself and his ex-wife and kids. It hurt so much. He couldn't live with the fact that she didn't want him.

Murphy left Tallahassee in 1996. "I was in a psychological haze again," he said. "I think the chemical imbalance fluids were working!"

He drove to Tampa to his mother's home. She agreed to let him stay with her for a while, until he could get back on his feet again. The next day Murphy gussied himself up in his finest clothes and made the rounds of Regis Hair Salons in the area, looking for work. He got a job at the one in the Brandon Town Center, Brandon being a town right next to Tampa. They needed a hairstylist badly and he was hired immediately. He both cut hair himself and taught a class in hairstyling techniques. His manager there was a woman named Sylvie Tarlton.

The Brandon Regis gig was the best job ever. The mall was really nice and was crowded. Business was brisk. "In my first two weeks I doubled what I'd been making in Tallahassee," he said. He was excited. He felt as if he was finally being paid what he was worth. The salon was nice and the atmosphere was electric. He was a member of the Regis President's Club for several years, which was the honor the Regis chain gave to its biggest moneymakers.

"It was upscale. And while there, I had an over-abundant amount of beautiful women to build the type of clientele I had always dreamed of," he said nostalgically.

In 1997, Murphy met a woman named Jane Wingate.

Chapter 17

Jane

Murphy met Jane through her daughter, Allie. He cut the daughter's hair and she wanted him to meet her mom. Hey, no problem. He didn't even have to go anywhere.

The daughter brought her mom in, in order to get her hair cut. Jane and Murphy immediately hit it off—just as Allie had predicted. He got Jane's phone number and called her a week later and asked her out. A few weeks after that, he moved in with Jane and Allie. For a while there, at the beginning of their relationship, it was almost like a contest between the two of them: who could send whom the most flowers at work. The game made the girls at the Regis jealous.

Murphy, Jane, and Allie lived together in River-view, in a three-bedroom mobile home. He and

Jane had an open policy sexually. "We both had outside affairs, but it was me mostly," Murphy said.

During that era one of his hottest sideline girlfriends was named Deborah—she of the plentiful, super-sexy pubic hair.

"Jane, Deborah, and I almost had a threesome," Murphy recalled.

The three were all on a couch together. Jane watched as Murphy felt up Deborah. Deborah was all set to be with Jane. Jane and Murphy had discussed having a threesome with Deborah earlier, and she said she would like to. Jane chickened out when the moment arrived. According to Murphy, Jane gave him and Deborah her blessing and split.

Murphy remembered Jane as a woman with a very pleasant personality. They were about the same age. Her mother was from England. She was also exceptional with Murphy's kids when they came to visit.

They found ways to surprise one another. One time he told her to get in the car, and then he took her on a surprise trip to a bed-and-breakfast.

"One Christmas, she lavished me with expensive gifts over a few days. She gave me a Web TV unit, a Washburn guitar, a black-onyx gold ring, and a Sony video camera." She then treated him to a room at the Don CeSar, a huge, fancy resort hotel on St. Petersburg Beach, known for its rows of palm trees and the twin cupolas on its roof.

He lived with Jane and Allie for about two years. Their visions of the future were incompatible.

Jane wanted to stay flexible, mobile.

Murphy was ready to plant roots, settle down.

Murphy had gone so far as to buy a plot of land in Ruskin, a town in Hillsborough County, along the eastern coast of Tampa Bay, and purchased a mobile home to put on it.

Murphy thought the move would please Jane. Trouble was, she had just finished a job in Ruskin, had no pleasant memories of Ruskin, and the last thing she wanted was to move there. So, instead, Murphy moved into the new mobile home by himself—and he was single again.

The last that Murphy heard about Jane Wingate, she was working at the Office of Property Management in Washington, D.C.

Chapter 18

New Home, New Life

"New home, new life," he said. He loved the new place. So quiet, twenty-two miles from his job, yet close to Tampa Bay and a river. He fished frequently. He bought a kayak and negotiated the river in it. "When I was away from my job, I felt really away," he explained.

He purchased a used immersion-baptismal font, which he converted into a hot tub. He put it in his mobile home and decorated the area around it to look like an ancient ship. "I called it the pool room," he said. It was great for entertaining; his kids spent hours in it.

In 1999, not long after he moved to Ruskin, when Elton Brutus Murphy was forty-two, a neighbor found his mom unconscious on the kitchen

floor of her Town 'n' Country home in Tampa.
How she got unconscious was a matter of opinion.

Murphy remembered, "The doctor in the emergency room made the mistake of saying someone
must have pushed my mother and she banged her
head, resulting in a brain hemorrhage. The way he
diagnosed what happened, it sounded like my mom
had been thrown down or something, and that
this blow—this thing to her head—could not have
happened without some sort of force being used,
and that was what started the snowball to hell on
that incident. We had my mother pulled off life
support after three days of being brain dead. They
said there was no hope for her." Betty Jo was sixty.

Because of the emergency room (ER) doctor's
opinion, and the fact that Brutus was one of the last
people to see his mother alive, life was complicated
for a few days. He said, "I was under suspicion by
law enforcement that I might have been the one
to cause her death. Thank God, the autopsy ruled
it was an accident."

The main guy pushing the "Brutus did it" theory
was his brother, Dean. Dean already didn't trust
him. They had been apart for years.

Murphy felt that a pair of siblings not communicating much with each other was genetic. His
father had been the same way—never talked to his
brother. "He disassociated himself from everyone."

All of that suspicion squelched Murphy's ability
to mourn properly. He and his mom were close;
her death hit him hard.

* * *

During November 1999, Murphy met Elizabeth. Like Jane before her, he met her while cutting her hair. He subsequently asked her out. Elizabeth was a physical therapist—and a thirty-four-year-old virgin. They considered getting married.

Murphy might have grown sexually bored with Elizabeth if it hadn't been for some kinky games he was playing on the side. While he was dating Elizabeth, he cut the hair of a man who, as Murphy explained it, "wanted me to do his wife while he watched. The wife was twenty-six and beautiful, and they both seemed to enjoy it as much as I did." Being the third for couples that wanted to swing was nothing new for Murphy. He did it more than a few times, dating back to 1984 when, at age twenty-seven, he provided the sexual entertainment for a couple in their forties, John and Doris.

The monkey wrench in those works wasn't Elizabeth's sexual inexperience, it was her fifteen-year-old adopted son, who was a disciplinary problem. The kid had been raised in foster homes and had a terrible temper. Murphy lasted until February 2000; then he broke it off. He'd just given her a bracelet for Valentine's Day. He didn't ask for it back; he told her to keep it.

Chapter 19

Best Year Ever

At the end of 1999—maybe the start of 2000—Murphy purchased a short stack of books about the stock market and day trading. He studied extensively and opened two accounts, one with Datek Online, another with Ameritrade.

He worked at Regis during the afternoon and evening shifts, so he had all morning to play at trading stocks. He didn't try to be too eclectic. He focused on—and dealt exclusively in—Nasdaq penny stocks.

"I got to where I was getting pretty good at it," he recalled. There were several mornings when he made a quick few hundred dollars. For a time he was making more money trading stocks on his computer than he did cutting hair.

Brimming with confidence, Murphy quit Regis

so he could trade full-time. All day long he traded, five days a week. For a while there, he was having a lot of fun. Nothing got his adrenaline pumping like buy, sell, buy, sell.

He'd stayed Hollywood hot for about six months, and then his luck ran out. Broke, he was forced to return to Regis. He tried trading part-time again, but the thrill was gone. His luck never returned.

When he filed his tax return in April 2001, he reported $483,000 in trades for the previous year. In retrospect he considered that phase of his life to be a good experience. However, he recalled enjoying the renewed comfort of being on safe financial ground at Regis.

During those black-ink days, Murphy made room in his schedule for his kids, too. Despite Paula's diagnosis that he was in a "fugue state," Murphy recalled being an active dad. In 2000 through 2001, he went on several trips with his kids, camping in the northern mountains of Georgia, walking the Appalachian Trail to North Carolina, where Trevor and Darcie saw and played in snow for the first time.

The granddaddy of all the trips, though, was the ten-day camping trip to Oregon and Washington. "We camped at a different place every day," Murphy said—Mount St. Helens, Mount Rainier, Mount Hood, the Snake River, the dunes of the coast of Oregon.

Closer, but more frequent, were family outings to Ginnie Springs near Lake City, Florida. Even though Murphy and his kids lived a four-and-a-half-hour drive apart, Murphy insisted they were close and they "loved spending time together." Despite this, they never saw each other more than "several times a year." Murphy remembered quality time, trips to Florida amusement parks: Disney, Universal, SeaWorld, Busch Gardens, etc.

The year 2001 was Murphy's best ever. It was his best as a hairstylist, and the best all around. With a pair of scissors in his hand, filled with confidence, he peaked as a hairstylist. He serviced the shop's largest list of clientele. His specialty was hair color and highlighting. He loved doing the fancy updos at prom time for countless teenaged girls.

Everything was going well. He was content. He was happy with his mobile home in Ruskin, even though he spent many hours remodeling the interior again and again: new floors, new TV, the works. His tastes would change and—*bam*—he would change his home's ambiance to suit himself.

Yes, 2001 was great, and 2002 started out positively as well.

Even as his life soared, his lack of control over himself still came around to bite him in the ass. The thing that he couldn't control was his spending. He spent more than he earned—simple as that—by a lot. He was going out nightclubbing, drinking too much. He was $38,000 in debt; he was forced to file for bankruptcy.

* * *

During this time he had a hairstyling friend named Tammy Burkhart. He'd meet her at bars two or three times a week. One of their favorites was Barnacles, on Providence Road in Brandon, a place that changed dramatically depending on what hour a client was there. During the day it was a family-friendly sports bar. There were 450 TVs! At night it was a meat market—that is, a pickup joint—for truckers, bikers, and rural folk. They also enjoyed spending time in the Green Iguana in Ybor City, where patrons could get burgers and live music seven days a week.

They would drink and laugh together for hours, often till the lights flashed and the proprietor started putting up the chairs.

"I never laughed so much in my life as when I was with Tammy," Murphy remembered. "She was a real joy to be around."

Even though she was good-looking—he thought she resembled Calista Flockhart, popular at the time on the TV show *Ally McBeal*—they never did anything sexual together.

"I certainly didn't mind being seen with her in public, though," Murphy admitted.

Chapter 20

A Not-So-Beautiful Mind

"Then one morning in February, my whole life began to change before my unbelieving eyes," Murphy said. "I became immersed in a psychological nightmare. No matter how hard I tried, there was no escape." The only thing he could compare it to was *A Beautiful Mind*, the movie that was popular at the time. He would urge anyone who hadn't seen that movie to do so immediately. He also saw a lot of himself in the patients and their delusions in Ken Kesey's book *One Flew Over the Cuckoo's Nest*.

This time the madness came and it didn't leave—not until 2007, by which time his life was irreparably ruined.

It started like a scene out of a horror movie, *Invasion of the Body Snatchers*. He woke up one morning and things looked different. He noticed that every person he viewed from a distance had glowing eyes. Bright, white lights. He couldn't see their eyes at all, just the lights radiating from the sockets.

He wondered what was wrong with him, but no answers were forthcoming.

Everyone he saw from a distance had glowing eyes, while those up close sneered and snickered at him. He couldn't figure out why everyone was laughing at him. What was so *funny*? Everyone was in on the joke except him. It was unnerving.

Anytime he went anywhere, he thought someone was following him.

"I was lucky that I didn't kill one or more people that I thought were following me," he said.

He believed he'd been implanted with a tracking device, or his car had. Every time he drove from one place to another, there was someone on the other end waiting to follow him.

It got to the point where he was afraid to eat, scared that his food had been poisoned.

Then came the hallucinations. That started in a Bennigan's. He was partially drunk when faces started to change. He couldn't stop looking at everyone's lips. Lips moved very fast and turned into flying butterflies.

He thought maybe it was the alcohol that had caused it, but that theory crumbled when he hallucinated stone-cold sober: the same pattern, mouths moving very fast as if emitting comically sped-up jibber-jabber, then metamorphosing into a magnificent monarch butterfly.

He knew his phone was tapped, and he scared one poor woman who worked for the phone company. She was parked next to some phone junctions and was inside her van, peering at a computer screen. Murphy was convinced he'd found surveillance headquarters.

"Hey," he yelled, pounding on the woman's vehicle, "what do you think you are doing?"

She didn't stick around to find out the details of Murphy's beef. She started up the van and got the hell out of there. He walked away more convinced than ever that there was a massive conspiracy. He thought about the conspiracy all the time. It was on a grand scale. How could it be so big? Who could be the mastermind behind it?

He did not seek out psychological treatment. Instead, he allowed the astonishing events in his brain to erode his quality of life. The events were beyond his control, beyond his comprehension, and they became increasingly terrifying.

People stopped seeming human. He was surrounded by beings of an alien species. Everyone was an alien, except for him. He was alone in a war against everyone.

He wasn't just going to take it anymore. He was going to fight back, the lone soldier, representing the suddenly absent human race.

Since it was a war, he chose a military target: MacDill Air Force Base, which was only four miles away from where he worked. The site was intriguing because there was a contingent of Navy SEALs there.

There it was.

There was the answer he'd been searching for. It had to be the SEALs who were messing with his mind. He was the subject of some kind of psychological warfare or mind-control experiment. Project MKUltra, the CIA called it.

Murphy was guilty! He had lied, told people that he was a SEAL, even though he'd rung the bell. That was why he was the subject of the experiment, he reasoned. That was why he was being punished so cruelly.

He theorized about how it worked. He figured that the SEALs must have teamed up with a squad of cyber SEALs, a group of "Internet freaks" that haunted fake SEALs until they forced the imposters to confess. He found the cyber SEALs on his computer and discovered that there was a page on their site for confessors.

Chapter 21

An Apology and Clarification

On May 22, 2002, Murphy sat at a computer in a library and wrote a long and rambling message to a website called Apologies and Clarifications, in which he admitted to lying about his military career. He claimed that he was attempting to set the record straight. He began by admitting he was a "Liar," with a capital *L*. His lies had been about his feeble attempt at BUD/S Training in 1986. He requested out of the program "long before Hell Week." He discussed his duty on the *Peleliu,* Murphy wrote, he went UA (unauthorized absence) for four months, and during that time assaulted a man just south of San Francisco. He wanted the world to know that he was sorry about the violence and that he apologized to both the man and his family. After returning to the civilian world, he wrote, his pattern of telling lies continued. On several occasions he led people to believe that he had been a Navy SEAL. He told one fellow that he'd been on secret missions in Central America. Sometimes he tempered his lies. He admitted that he did not succeed in becoming a SEAL, but he claimed that this was because he'd suffered from hypothermia during Hell Week. Because he was almost twenty-eight years old at the time, the cutoff age for a starting SEAL, he was not allowed to roll over into another class. His lie continued to say that, even though he was not an official SEAL, he had been allowed to stay on as a SEAL photographer. He frequently claimed that he had been allowed to hang out with the SEALs and that they had taught him a thing or two about defending himself. Not true. He wanted to apologize in particular to the SEALs and thank them for all of the hard work they'd done protecting American freedom. He wanted to apologize to the SEALs who'd died in the line of duty, and apologize to their families. He was ashamed of his lies.

He wrote God bless them all. I apologize to the Hillsborough County Sheriff's Department. I was not attacked by masked men at gunpoint, another lie. Instead of working harder to achieve real achievements, I made them up. To any persons over the years I have threatened, I mean you no harm. To all persons involved with helping to show me the error of my ways, thanks, I appreciate your efforts. Forgive me if you have felt threatened. He said that these represented all of the worse deeds that I have done.

The other lies he'd told were of a personal

nature, dealing with romance and whatnot, and he didn't seem as interested in apologizing about those. He didn't feel it was necessary to go into detail regarding the lies he'd told about being a SEAL, nor did he want to get into the incidents that had led up to his public apology. He asked for an opportunity to make up for his lies, to pay back to society, and promised that he would "obtain counseling" to help in that endeavor. He concluded: I would like to serve my country in the future to help keep it free. I support our War against Terrorism! Sincerely, Elton B. Murphy.

Murphy later claimed he'd even lied in his confession, lied to humiliate himself even more than necessary. He said he'd dropped out of SEALs way earlier than he actually had. In reality he'd made it four and a half weeks before ringing the bell.

After confessing to his lies, and in a "psychological stupor," he went home to his medicine cabinet and took out a razor blade. He rolled up his sleeve and cut himself twice on the arm, then—bleeding pretty good now—called 911 and said that earlier that morning he'd been abducted by a group of men claiming to be Navy SEALs.

The deputy who came to his home thought he was nuts, and calmly told Murphy that he'd seen this sort of thing before, that Murphy's best bet was to "seek professional help." If it happened again, the deputy would have to arrest him for filing false reports.

Murphy didn't follow the advice, but he did take

action. The next morning, with the help of his brother, Dean, and Dean's wife, Murphy packed up all of his belongings into his Explorer and a U-Haul trailer.

"I abandoned my home," Murphy remembered. "I told myself that I had to get out of that crazy environment while still alive."

Chapter 22

Return of the Military Flashlights

He moved back to Tallahassee, hopeful that a change of scenery would end his troubles. He would get a new place to live, a new job, a new lease on life. He would be closer to his kids.

It didn't work. Switching cities couldn't kill the demons in his head, a sad fact he realized during his first full day in Tallahassee. He'd already procured himself an apartment on Magnolia Drive—in the same apartment complex, the Talla Villas, where he'd lived with Paula and the kids before buying a home. He'd already gotten himself a job, hired immediately at the Seminole Barber Shop, a busy three-chair shop on the edge of the Florida State University (FSU) campus.

The shop had been in business for thirty years, with FSU students making up the bulk of the exclusively male clientele. That was a big change from working at Regis, where the majority of the customers were beautiful women.

All of these accomplishments? Not bad for Day One.

Murphy was driving through town on the Apalachee Parkway, when he stopped at a red light. He glanced over to the car idling beside him and the occupants had the bright-light eyes. White, glowing, so bright—their eyes resembled intense military flashlights.

In a panic Murphy looked around to the other cars in his vicinity. All of the occupants had the spotlight eyes. When he went to work the next day, all of his customers were aliens, with glowing eyes and smirks on their lips.

Everyone in the shop—coworkers, customers, everybody—was determined to humiliate him, all part of the "cosmic collective prank" that was being pulled on him. He even felt it when he was watching TV.

The talking heads were poking fun at him.

"I felt very discouraged," Murphy recalled.

Even with his life in free fall, Murphy was not ready to fully commit to the notion that there was something wrong with his mind. He believed he was the one who was right. He didn't have hallucinations;

he had the unique ability to see the awful truth. In a world filled with villains, he was a lone victim.

No, he didn't think he was sick—but he was becoming increasingly aware that others thought so.

"There were people in my life who were certain I needed help," Murphy said. Among them was Sylvie Tarlton, his former boss at Regis (who would later testify at Murphy's trial).

His brother and sister-in-law were the most insistent. Before Murphy left Hillsborough County, he promised them that when he got to Tallahassee, he'd see a shrink.

He told himself that he was doing it to make them happy. He was okay. About a week after his arrival in Tallahassee, he visited a mental-health facility affiliated with FSU Medical Health Clinic, which occupied a truly scary, old building. The horror movie in his mind was so much scarier than anything Hollywood could make. He'd never been in a house of sick minds before, and it freaked him out. He was happy that his stay was brief. After making him wait, a woman took down his information. He told her what had been happening to him. She gave him an appointment to see a psychologist in a couple of weeks, and Murphy went home. Just before his appointment the clinic called him to verify that he'd be keeping his appointment. Murphy said he'd changed his mind. He didn't need a psychologist. A man tried to talk him into coming. Murphy said thanks, but no thanks. And it wasn't like his symptoms had eased. They'd worsened. "Escalated" was how Murphy put it, explaining: "I was driven to do some really insane things with a lot of negative incentive from all of the people I was in contact with."

One portion of Murphy's mind was aware of the self-destructive nature of his behavior, and concluded that he punished himself as penance for past sins.

He would always need to work off the blemishes on his soul, but—a revelation—he could concentrate on refocusing his punishments so that they made a positive contribution to the world.

Murphy's angels and demons waged war, and for a time the side of good was winning. Murphy dedicated his life to picking up garbage at the side of the road; he became the enemy of litterers everywhere. He walked up and down the streets and roads, sometimes from 4:00 A.M. until midnight. He carried plastic or paper bags as his receptacle. It went on for months.

There were days when working twenty hours outdoors was not punishment enough. His suffering was too mild, so he would pick up garbage for twenty hours *while barefoot*. Those were the days he would wade into snake-infested ditches in pursuit of waterlogged garbage.

The roads he patrolled were often open and desolate. When he ran out of bags, he would just make piles on the shoulder of the road, one pile every half mile or so. One time he found fourteen shopping carts in a ditch not far from a grocery store. He gathered them up and pushed them back into the parking lot, where they belonged.

Because his wanderings were never preplanned, there were many nights when he ran out of energy many miles from home. On those nights he would find the least-traveled spot—under a bridge, in the woods, in a couple of abandoned homes—where he would lay his head down and go to sleep. He slept in construction sites, in houses under construction.

The cops always hassled him. At least six times he was questioned by police. Most of the hassles were small. They looked at his driver's license and sent him on his way. On June 19, 2002, for example, deputies from the Leon County Sheriff's Office (LCSO) were called to the corner of North Meridian Road and Ginny Lane on a report of a suspicious person. Murphy showed the deputies his ID and allowed them to search his backpack, which contained clothing and a sheet inside a plastic bag. In his written report, the responding officer noted that Murphy's *apartment complex was right down the street.*

There was this phase Murphy was going through. He just couldn't stop helping people. He concentrated all of his energy on volunteering to do good deeds.

But some people were not appreciative. Some people were simply contrary and didn't want to have nice things done for them. During the day of June 19, 2002, Murphy was walking on Longview

Drive when he saw a house's slanted roof in need of cleaning. It wasn't just leaves and small branches making the mess; there were a couple of soccer balls stuck up there as well. Murphy knocked on the front door; the owner, a guy named Frank Burns, answered. Murphy offered to clean the roof and Burns told him to get lost. Murphy didn't leave. As he was compelled to clean up everything everywhere, Murphy had no choice but to find a ladder and try to climb up onto that roof.

The homeowner, as it turned out, was not cool with this. He came flying out of the house with a baseball bat in his hand. Murphy remembered the guy as in his forties and huge: maybe six-two, 275 pounds. The guy held Murphy in place, still on the ladder, until a sheriff's deputy arrived.

"Why are you doing this?" the deputy asked.

"I have to do acts of kindness in order to redeem myself," Murphy replied.

"Why do you need to be redeemed?"

"I may not be from this planet. I need to do good deeds to be accepted."

As Murphy remembered it, "They took me to Tallahassee Memorial Hospital in protective custody for a brief evaluation, and I was Baker-acted."

Florida's Baker Act, officially known as the Florida Mental Health Act of 1971, allowed a judge to commit a person involuntarily for evaluation, if he felt the subject was a danger to himself or others.

On June 26, one week after his arrest, Murphy was taken to the Apalachee Center, on Capital

Circle Northeast, in Tallahassee. At Apalachee, the slogan was "Healing Minds and Empowering Lives." It was run by a private, not-for-profit behavioral-health-care organization. Murphy stayed for a week. He shared a room with a guy in his twenties, and he was treated in a coeducational group atmosphere. Most of the people in his group had also been committed by the state. He took classes. There was recreation.

"We also ate our meals together," Murphy said. "And sang songs as a group."

He didn't remember any of the songs, although he knew one of them was a Toby Keith tune. What he did remember was that they brought in a gorgeous blonde with a pleasant personality to lead the singing, and she told Murphy she thought his voice was beautiful.

Paula and the kids came to visit. Paula's theory was that Murphy's problem was anger management. She told him that she'd fallen in and out of love with him a few times, and the "out of love" periods always followed incidents in which he had anger issues.

Paula had purchased him some clothes. She also had a five-minute meeting with one of the doctors.

"What did they say?" Murphy asked his ex-wife.

Paula replied, "They said you were bipolar and had seizures."

Murphy was stunned. That wasn't even remotely accurate. Hadn't they been paying attention?

"Doctor didn't know his ass from a hole in the ground," Murphy said.

They put him on Tegretol, an antiseizure medication and an anticonvulsant that was also used to treat bipolar conditions in patients who suffered simultaneous depression and mania.

At first, Murphy took the pills. Maybe the doctor knew something. Turned out he didn't. The meds did nothing to alter his paranoia. In fact, the pills did nothing at all, and Murphy stopped taking the pills after about a month.

The Apalachee Center was a complete waste of time. Within hours—*hours!*—of his release, he was again shirtless and shoeless, picking up garbage alongside some Tallahassee thoroughfare.

Chapter 23

The Voices

Then came the voices, which at least got him to stop picking up garbage every now and again. He'd heard voices before, but now they gained absolute influence over him.

On the rare occasions when he tried to explain the voices to someone, people tended to think that he was merely "hearing" his own thinking—but that was clearly not the case.

Most of the time the voice belonged to a woman—or women. When Murphy tried to ignore the voices, they mocked him, taunted him for hours on end. When they told him to do something, he had to do it. *Yes, ma'am!* The voices were in control.

Murphy looked back on it now and realized that he was swimming in and out of psychotic pools.

People might have thought he was on drugs, but it was his own body's chemicals doing it to him.

In his whole life he'd only done alcohol and pot, and the pot only when he was offered some by someone else. He had tried cocaine a couple of times, but it made him a reckless driver. No hallucinogens. LSD was a drug that other people took to feel like him. For Murphy, the trip seemed to go on forever.

He was still living in the apartment complex where he'd lived with Paula. One day around noon, as he was in his eighth hour of picking up trash, he found himself standing outside the McDonald's on North Monroe Street.

Suddenly there was a flash! He realized that there was a camera in his eye! That explained everything: why people always knew where he was and what he was up to. He was stunned and astonished. He knew instantly it was true.

The camera was linked to a control room somewhere, where they monitored his behavior. The powers that be had control of everything. The people he saw around him, buying french fries and Big Macs, had receivers and transmitters implanted in their brains.

But he was the only one with a camera. He was the show. Everyone was watching him all the time. His life was a reality show that aired twenty-four hours a day.

Even his dreams were transmitted to the control center. He felt various emotions fighting for attention.

He felt a sense of pride—if it was a show they wanted, it was a show he was going to give them. He felt sad, doomed even, because his final delusions of self-determination had been stripped away. He understood fully that his life was controlled by others. He was a virtual prisoner of the powers that be, the secret government, what he called "the control" and "the collective."

After years of crazy thinking, he could finally see the world clearly. He never felt more sane in his life.

One night he was staying in an abandoned building because his garbage pickup had pulled him far from home. In the morning he looked closely at himself in a mirror. He could see the camera lens, the focus whirring and spinning, the f-stop opening and closing with his pupil.

He began to think of himself as a TV cameraman, a reporter for the *Elton Brutus Murphy News*. Somewhere, probably in his ears, he'd been implanted with microphones as well, he assumed. He knew the collective could hear what he heard and hear his thoughts. He had no choice but to cooperate with the collective. He had tried to run away from them, but there was always someone at the other end of his trip, a fresh humanoid hellhound on his trail.

Once, he tried to get away from people altogether so that he might have moments of peace.

He went into the woods, to the Wacissa River, a spring-fed stream in Jefferson County that emerged from clear limestone springs, with ancient cypress trees lining its banks. He couldn't imagine a more beautiful setting. He had no food with him, only a mask and snorkel, a small backpack, tent, improvised pole spear, and a pocketknife. If his life was a reality show, he was going to give them *Survivor.*

During his adventure he came to a place in the river where it was very narrow and no longer passable. A creek led away from the river, so he abandoned the Wacissa and followed the creek until he came to a shallow area, where there must have been fifty alligators on both sides of the stream.

"It looked like a *Tarzan* movie!" Murphy recalled.

He had swum with alligators in the past with no problem; but with this many of them, it was asking for trouble. He felt invincible, however, and in he went, working his way toward the deeper part of the creek. On his left he heard a gator about ten feet long. His head was a foot wide. Murphy could tell the gator had seen him and was heading his way. Scared out of his wits, Murphy swam toward the shore, not too fast. He kept his movements smooth so as not to convey anxiety. Luckily, when he got to the bank, there was a tree root that served perfectly as a handle. He grabbed hold and pulled himself efficiently out of the water. The gator turned around in the water and disappeared.

"That's the closest I ever came to being eaten alive," Murphy said.

While he was on the river, he ate roots and raw fish. He was lucky he didn't get bitten by a snake. He kept swimming through dense patches of lily pads near the riverbank; there were water moccasins everywhere. But in his mind he was invincible, and the snakes must've sensed that.

Sometimes he entertained his viewers with adventurous, solitary games. Other times his reality show went to where the people were: like at the mall.

He spent hours and hours in department stores, out of his mind with delusions. He believed he was "shooting commercials" for the collective. He would pick up items off the shelf and, talking out loud, do a commercial for that item.

Today, Murphy thinks he is lucky that he doesn't remember all of the things he did in 2002, because the stuff he does remember is so weird.

Chapter 24

The Talla Villas
Nocturnal Playground

The Talla Villa Apartments on East Magnolia Drive became his nocturnal playground. The apartment complex was huge. The square plot of land it occupied was so big that three laps around it equaled a mile. The square plot was occupied by four square buildings, each with its own courtyard, and positioned so that there was a courtyard at the center of the complex as well, which was where the pool was.

Murphy's nighttime antics began mischievously enough, with him climbing merrily first up the stairs onto this balcony, then down and over to that balcony, stealing "everything that wasn't tied down."

He didn't want to keep the things he stole, and

he had no motives of profit. He stole bicycles and barbeque grills, only to hide them in the bushes around the apartment building, or would throw them in the big garbage Dumpster. He did keep a stolen ten-speed bike in his apartment for a while so he could look at it. He stole from at least twenty-five apartments, and each time it was completely juvenile. He was a criminal prankster, not a becoming personality trait for a man in his middle forties.

"I carried a butcher knife with me, and for a time I was cutting things," he said. The world was his enemy and this was his way of—well, not really fighting back, but of not going gentle into that good night of societal oppression.

In his own way he was disturbing the universe. He cut bicycle tires in half, severing them as he might a snake. He cut up the seats on the complex's golf cart. Many people had plants and miniature trees growing in big pots on their balconies. Murphy cut them down. He sliced through the ragtop of a Triumph convertible. He sliced the canvas top on a Jeep. According to a later police report, thirteen cars were damaged. He pulled up a small garden of tomato plants and threw them into the yard. He plucked all of the green tomatoes from those plants and left them in a straight, even-spaced trail on the lawn.

One night he threw all of the pool furniture into the pool. He remembered thinking as he did it, *Boy, Matt, the pool guy, is going to have to take a swim.*

On the patio next to the pool, Murphy wrote in

twelve-inch letters various obscenities regarding Mark and Barbara Brindley, who were the managers for the Talla Villas. The Brindleys knew Murphy from all the way back to 1990 when Murphy lived there with Paula. They were aware of the divorce, and had kept in touch with both Murphy and Paula after the breakup. So when Murphy came looking for an apartment, they were happy to rent to him— and everything was fine, at first. Then he heard voices, and gathered garbage compulsively. Why the obscene graffiti? Barbara Brindley thought it was because Murphy had written a letter, sort of a personal ad, which he'd thumbtacked up on the laundry room wall. The ad was for a lonely man looking for another lonely man. Anyone interested should meet him by the pool at a certain hour, wearing a certain item of clothing.

As one might imagine, the kicks of playing around outside apartments wore off after a while. The strong female voice in his head told him to knock off the kid stuff. Playing outside was boring; she wanted him to play around inside, too.

So he snuck through a couple of unlocked patio doors and wandered from room to room with the butcher knife in his hand, even walking into bedrooms while couples were in bed asleep.

"Thank God they did not wake up," Murphy said years later. Something very bad would have happened if they'd woken up. Of course, if they had, they could not be allowed to call out in the night.

Murphy was a veteran breaking-and-entering man by now. One time, when he couldn't find a sliding door open, he used his knife to pry an apartment door open. It was always a thrill, a real adrenaline rush. He entered the home, took food out of the refrigerator, and left. When he got back to his own apartment, he remembered that it was four in the morning.

He showered, ate the food, and got a couple of hours of sleep. At eight in the morning, there was a knock on the door. He didn't recall if it was city or county cops, but the law had come to see him. "There was quite a few of them. At least half a dozen," he said. They informed him he'd been seen throwing the chairs into the pool. As for the rest of the mischief, they just assumed it was Murphy. According to police, however, Murphy admitted to slashing the convertible tops.

"Why do you do these things?" a Tallahassee policeman asked.

"I have a chemical imbalance that I am currently taking medicine for," Murphy replied. "I have no idea why I do these things. I have no ill will toward anyone."

As it turned out, one Leon County Sheriff's Office deputy lived in the Talla Villa Apartments and had had his patrol car damaged by Murphy.

He was arrested on burglary, criminal mischief, and various misdemeanor charges. He was booked into the Leon County Jail, a white two-story building on Municipal Way in Tallahassee. It was a fairly modern facility, built in 1993, and maintained an inmate population of about six hundred.

In jail Murphy discovered that his hallucinations were vivid and the voices loud. He saw the glowing eyes, the butterfly lips, and every once in a while a fellow inmate transformed—time-lapse photography style—into a reptilian alien.

Sometimes he saw two or three of the hideous creatures at once, social reptiles, walking and talking together in small groups. He was in jail, reeling from a bad trip, for about a month. Then his brother, Dean, came and bailed him out.

While Murphy was in jail, Paula went to the Talla Villa Apartments, spoke to the Brindleys, and cleaned out his apartment—from which he'd been evicted due to his arrest. The task was more difficult than she would have hoped. Murphy had been hoarding. The space was filled with newspapers and magazines, and—for reasons she couldn't even begin to understand—many, many wire hangers.

As a postscript, the Brindleys did see Murphy one last time, in October 2002. He was wearing tattered clothing and claimed to be living in the woods, where he'd built a campsite, he said. Murphy apologized for all of the trouble he'd caused during his vandalism phase.

Chapter 25

Haven of Rest

When they let Murphy out, he called Paula. However, it was Dean who found him a place to live, at the Haven of Rest, a men's home on Tennessee Street, a faith-based rescue mission for homeless men.

As Murphy recalled, he walked all the way from the jail to his new home, picking up garbage along the way. He didn't arrive at the home until ten at night, after lights-out, so he had to find his way to his bunk in the dark.

"It was a totally new experience for me," he said. "All around me were these guys, many of them snoring."

The sleeping facilities at the rescue mission were on two floors. The lower floor, where Murphy was assigned to sleep, was a large room, maybe eight hundred square feet, with bunk beds down both sides, an aisle in the middle.

Later, when he proved he could pay by the week rather than by the day, he was moved upstairs. The space was larger up there, and there were single beds, which were more spread out.

Murphy estimated that about twenty-four men slept downstairs, maybe a dozen upstairs. Lights came on at 4:30 A.M.; and by 5:00 A.M., the men were expected to be in the chapel for "morning devotion."

After that, everyone scarfed a "more than adequate" breakfast with coffee, and then they were ushered out into the street. It was still dark outside and Murphy had hours to kill before his first order of business, which was to go to the Seminole Barber Shop and beg for his job back.

His boss turned out to be most understanding (in other words, desperate for help) and rehired him immediately. He cut hair for long hours.

When he was on break at the barbershop, he would go outside and pick up trash.

Getting back on his feet was going to be difficult. One problem: no wheels. Before he had been jailed, his Ford Explorer was repossessed.

He bought a green 1970 Plymouth, a real clunker. However, Murphy drove that car for only a couple of weeks before the voices instructed him to donate it to the first needy person he encountered—the first one with a driver's license, anyway.

That person turned out to be an aged African-

American woman who was trudging along South Monroe Street, pushing a shopping cart full of what appeared to be all of her worldly possessions.

"I stopped and asked her if she would like a free car. She said yes." Murphy made the woman show him her driver's license before giving her the keys. "I said, 'Congratulations, you are now the owner of this car, and everything I left in the trunk.'"

The contents of the trunk were a two-ton floor jack, a spare tire, and a toolbox filled with tools. "I'd never seen a black woman so happy," Murphy said. She transferred the stuff from her shopping cart into the car and drove away.

Murphy walked home—and still the voices wouldn't leave him alone. He needed to rid himself of all of his worldly possessions. He threw out clothes and kitchen utensils and food. He even threw out two computers. He made sure to smash the hard drives with a hammer before discarding the computers, because he didn't want any information to fall into the hands of the enemy, the collective. He even threw away money. He remembered being down to his last few pennies and throwing them, one at a time, across the yard.

Murphy was allowed to stay at the Haven of Rest for five weeks before he was asked to leave. The end came when he was called into the director's office for a routine meeting. The director said he just wanted to find out how Murphy was doing.

Murphy said he was doing fine. While in the

office, he stole the keys to everything at Haven of Rest. He threw the keys in the garbage can outside.

When the director accused him of stealing the keys, since he was the last one in his office before they disappeared, Murphy denied it.

The director didn't believe him. The next morning, at three-thirty, Murphy walked past the director's office, which was also the room where the director slept, and down the wooden stairs, which creaked loud enough to wake the dead. He opened the back door and crept onto the fenced-in patio, which was off-limits to residents after hours. The director heard him, caught him, told him he simply wasn't with the program, and asked him to get out right after breakfast.

Murphy was again homeless. He spent the day on the FSU campus, picking up trash, and slept that night in an abandoned sorority house less than two hundred feet from the FSU police station.

That first night Murphy triggered an alarm at the house when he entered through an upstairs window. He smashed the alarm, silencing it. He figured the FSU police were going to arrive any second, but they didn't.

His delusions were working overtime. He believed that everything in that house was trash and needed to be taken to the trash can.

"I must've made a hundred trips out the back

door, carrying every item I could find," he said. "I worked all night, and filled eleven trash cans."

At dawn he vacated the sorority house and began to clean the campus. As he passed the maintenance building, he saw several men looking at him, one pointing. Frightened, he hid inside a Dumpster.

On October 21, 2002, Murphy was arrested by FSU cops on Madison Street, where they cornered him in his hiding spot. Caught red-handed, Murphy obediently whipped out his Florida ID.

"Why are you in the Dumpster?" the cop asked.

Murphy was at a loss.

He had no idea why he was there or how he got there. He was just there. As he was arrested, he gave the Haven of Rest as his home address.

Murphy was placed in a holding cell at the FSU police station. He was then transported back to the Leon County Jail and charged with trespassing.

"I did one hundred twenty-five days in jail—the longest one hundred twenty-five days of my life," Murphy recalled.

Murphy spent most of his sentence hallucinating vividly. He believed that his twenty-four-hour TV show was now a game show, and he could win prizes if he could accomplish certain feats.

One hundred push-ups—win a Learjet.

Five hundred jumping jacks—win a luxury car.

Every time he got his hand on a book, he would

rip each page out, one by one, and flush everything down the toilet.

Following a diagnosis of bipolar disorder, Murphy was placed on mental-health probation and was released from jail. By the time he once again stepped into the fresh air, it was January 2003, and he was very disappointed that there was no Learjet or luxury car waiting for him. He was disappointed with the collective, disappointed with the control room. There wasn't even a parade!

What he did have waiting for him was a bus ticket to Punta Gorda, purchased by Dean. Murphy did some soul-searching during that bus ride. The total lack of reward from the collective was an eye-opener.

"By the time I arrived in Punta Gorda, I no longer believed in the collective," Murphy said. Other delusions lifted at that point, too. He no longer believed in the camera in the eye. That was a relief. Unfortunately, the predominantly female voices in his head didn't depart. They remained and chattered and demanded with increasing frequency. More and more, the voices were focused in a deviant and loathsome way.

"*Kill women. Rape women. Kill women. Rape women. . . .*"

At the bus station Dean met his brother and took him home with him—his home right next to Solomon's Castle.

Joyce Wishart was murdered in this art gallery—killed and horribly mutilated late on a Friday afternoon. Her remains were not discovered until five days later. *(Sarasota Police Department)*

The view of the Provenance Gallery's interior, as seen from the front door. *(Sarasota Police Department)*

The Provenance was one in a series of art galleries all in a row along Sarasota's toney North Palm Avenue. *(Sarasota Police Department)*

Police could determine the approximate time the killer entered the art gallery by the fact that the security system had not been activated. The sign in the window reads: PROV-E-NANCE 1: ORIGIN, SOURCE 2: THE HISTORY OF A VALUABLE OBJECT OR WORK OF ART.

(Sarasota Police Department)

Thinking at first that the killer might be someone Joyce Wishart knew, police went over her belongings for clues as to who he might be. Joyce's car was found in its regular parking spot in the parking garage near the gallery. Everything appeared normal. *(Sarasota Police Department)*

Police tape stopped pedestrians from walking directly by the Provenance Gallery, to prevent any inadvertent contamination of the crime scene. At the far right is Admiral Travel, the agency where Michelle Andersen worked. Police asked her if she'd seen anything unusual during the week before the murder. Her first reaction was that she'd never seen anything unusual ever. *(Sarasota Police Department)*

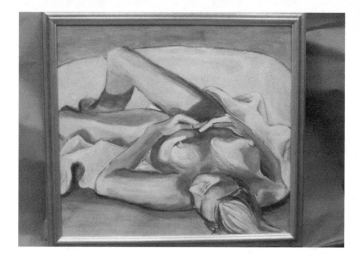

The killer used his interest in this painting of a nude as an excuse to return to the Provenance Gallery. Joyce Wishart was holding the painting when her killer attacked. *(Sarasota Police Department)*

The body was found with its head in a far corner, spread-eagled, with multiple stab wounds to the breasts. Most disturbing, her vagina had been removed. Notice the careful placement of the shoes. Though Murphy denies it, perhaps feeling it flies in the face of his insanity defense, it seems apparent that the killer was trying to create his own obscene artwork. *(Sarasota Police Department)*

Joyce Wishart's body was positioned so that her head (extreme lower right) was almost touching a geometrical abstract work, comprised of several media and various angles and shapes. *(Sarasota Police Department)*

The crime scene from another angle. The victim's legs can be seen at the bottom left. *(Sarasota Police Department)*

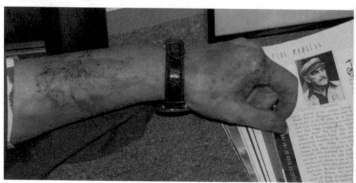

The victim's body was posed so that the left hand rested upon a copy of *Sarasota Magazine*, opened to an article by Marcia Corbino called "A Fine Madness." The feature profiled Sarasota in the good old days when it was a colony of eccentric artists, writers, and circus folk. The man with the moustache and hat is Fletcher Martin, a Sarasota artist who died in 1979. *(Sarasota Police Department)*

Joyce Wishart's right shoe, a key component in the killer's posed crime scene, had a single droplet of blood inside it (arrow).

(Sarasota Police Department)

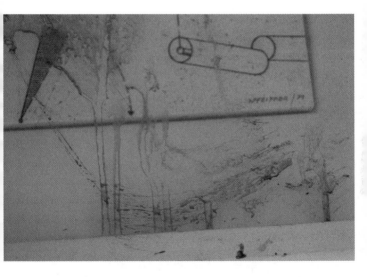

Heavy blood spatter struck the artwork in the vicinity of the murder. Sweeping marks through the blood indicated a quick and careless attempt to wipe the blood away. In several spots the killer seemed to have attempted cleanup activity, but wasn't very good at it.

(Sarasota Police Department)

A spatter expert could look at the bloodstained artwork in the vicinity of the murder and determine from which direction the blood came and how fast it was traveling when it struck. *(Sarasota Police Department)*

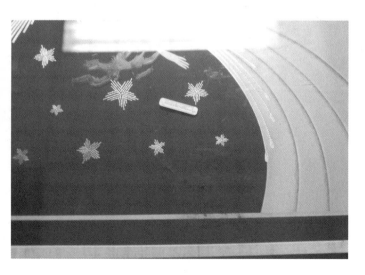

Blood and tissue encrusted the artwork. *(Sarasota Police Department)*

There was blood spatter on the tiled walls of the gallery's bathroom. Again, a halfhearted attempt to clean up had been made, accomplishing little more than to smear the blood over a larger surface. *(Sarasota Police Department)*

Police found several palm prints in the gallery, easy to see because they were in the victim's blood. *(Sarasota Police Department)*

A palm print was also discovered in this glop of blood spatter.

(Sarasota Police Department)

The key piece of evidence, "possible tissue from carpeting," was sent by the Sarasota Police Department to the FDLE's Tampa Crime Laboratory for analysis. *(Sarasota Police Department)*

The toilet in Murphy's Shade Avenue rooming house, where he said he disposed of the vagina he stole from Joyce Wishart's body. *(Sarasota Police Department)*

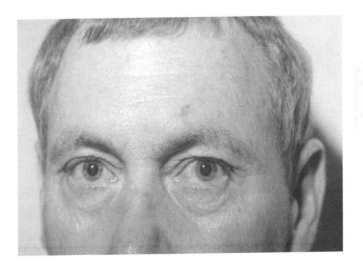

The eyes of a mutilator. *(Sarasota Police Department)*

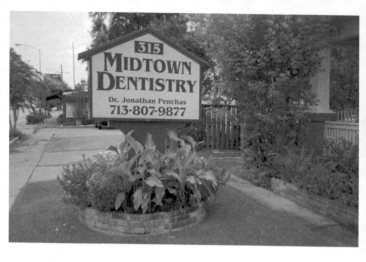

On February 25, 2004, Elton Murphy was arrested and charged with burglarizing a dentist's office. *(Sarasota Police Department)*

When arrested for burglarizing this building, Murphy was armed with a hatchet and a jackknife. He was in possession of prescription medications. *(Sarasota Police Department)*

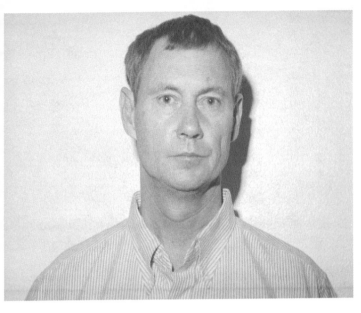

The break Sarasota Police Department had been looking for came when Elton Murphy was arrested in Texas and a sample of his DNA was confiscated. *(Harris County Sheriff's Office, courtesy Sarasota Police Department)*

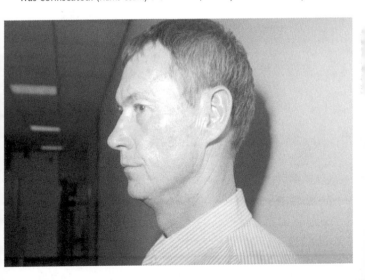

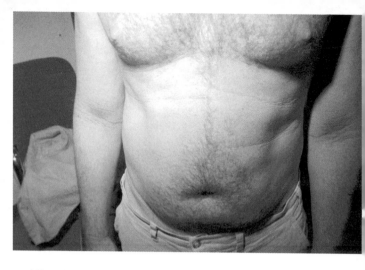

When Sarasota police officers went to Houston to arrest Murphy for the murder, they photographed him while he was dressed and undressed—here without his shirt. *(Sarasota Police Department)*

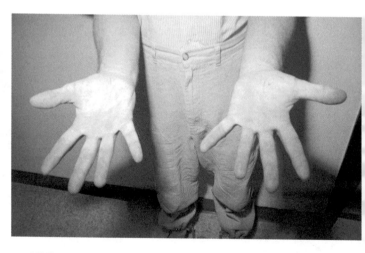

While capturing Elton Murphy's large hands, the photographer also gives us a view of the killer's ankle chain. *(Sarasota Police Department)*

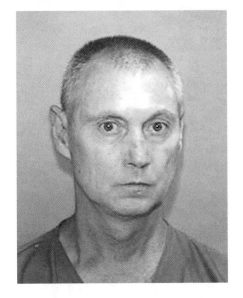

Murphy as he appears today. *(Florida Department of Corrections)*

The many faces of Elton Brutus Murphy. *(Sarasota Police Department)*

The Honorable Deno G. Economou, circuit judge, ruled in 2007 that Murphy was fit to stand trial. *(Courtesy Judge Economou)*

Prosecutor Suzanne O'Donnell handled the forensic evidence at Murphy's trial, so Lon Arend could concentrate on Murphy's sanity. *(Photo by Dawn M. Buff)*

Chapter 26

The Majik Man

Well-known sculptor Howard Solomon was Dean's father-in-law, who had created a large metallic structure in the town of Ona in Hardee County: Solomon's Castle. He built it and they came. The "castle" became perhaps the county's only tourist attraction.

Solomon's creation had eighty stained-glass windows and had been built to look like a sixteenth-century Spanish galleon. The castle had a restaurant next door.

The eatery was run by Alane, Solomon's daughter, and Murphy's brother, Dean.

Being around Solomon always made Murphy want to be an artist, always started him thinking artistically. Murphy tried to emulate Solomon with his own works of art.

Solomon would always claim that he appreciated Murphy's work, and on more than one occasion, Solomon purchased one of Murphy's sculptures.

Dean and Alane didn't believe the appreciation was real, however. Murphy's brother and sister-in-law thought Solomon felt sorry for Murphy, and this was Solomon's method of being charitable.

Alane noticed that Dean's brother never showed up in good shape. It was never a happy thing. Murphy was inevitably destitute, and looking for work at the restaurant until he could "get back on his feet."

Murphy remembered: "In 2003, for one day a week for a few months, I was working off some debt for my brother—he was selling me a car and had loaned me some money—at the restaurant. It was really a fun place to work."

Dean sold him a car on credit to help him get on his feet, a red Geo Metro convertible. His brother bought him clothes at Walmart and a pair of shoes at a shoe store.

As always, Murphy's visits to Solomon's Castle became irritating. Murphy wasn't good when it came to social prompts and cues, boundaries and taboos. There were times when he didn't know how to act.

Dean and Alane were slightly uncomfortable with some of the things Murphy was saying in front of their children, such as "God has chosen me" and "Big things are going to happen to me."

With his brother's help and guidance, Murphy

moved out of the Solomon's Castle home and into his own place, an efficiency apartment in the Port of Tampa.

Things were good. He was only three blocks from the bay. He was employed again at a Regis shop, but not the one he'd worked at before. It had been time to start over, anyway.

The women at the old place were scared of him.

It was a woman by the name of Marguerite Bradley who gave Murphy the chance. She knew he had been through psychological turmoil after a bad divorce, but she still took him on.

There was a brief period, two or three days, when Murphy felt almost optimistic. He was going to put all of his troubles behind him and make a fresh start.

"Then my agitated behavior began again in Tampa, and it got to the point where I felt like I had supernatural powers."

Elton Brutus Murphy was a "majik man," which was "magic" spelled in a magic way. He was the hero whose exploits were woven surreptitiously into the fabric of the world's greatest literature, the world's greatest music. He was inspiration itself.

Then it went sour.

It was the same delusion he'd suffered in the Tallahassee jail. It seemed everywhere he went, he was inadvertently causing accidents to happen with his mind.

When he walked down the street, cars crashed. He'd look at a waiter carrying a tray and it would drop. He'd look at a lovely set of legs in high heels and the woman would trip.

Murphy had this power now and he spent long hours contemplating how best to use it. He experimented with different methods of making chaos out of order. He drove on the interstate and stared at cars until they swerved out of control.

He believed he was a god, and it was during this stretch that Murphy first referred to himself as "The Lord God Elton Brutus Murphy."

Best title ever.

Chapter 27

Messages from Nibiru

Murphy had been living in the efficiency apartment near Tampa Bay for two or three weeks when he found himself in a Barnes & Noble bookstore in Brandon. He was in the Spiritual section, browsing, when he met a guy named Dave Gallant.

"What book are you looking for?" Gallant asked.

"I don't know," Murphy replied, open to suggestion.

Gallant recommended the books of Zecharia Sitchin, an author born in Azerbaijan, who served with the British Army during World War II. Sitchin believed that the ancient Sumerian culture was created by the Anunnaki, ancient astronauts, who came to Earth from the planet Nibiru. This planet revolved around the Sun in our solar system, past Neptune, in such an elongated orbit that Nibiru

only appeared in Earth's sky every few millennium.
Sitchin's pseudoscience hit Murphy where he lived.
Here was an explanation for bizarre phenomenon
that he, the Lord God, had been aware of for years.
And Murphy and the man who'd recommended
Sitchin became fast friends: conspiracy-theory
buddies. Gallant had read all of Sitchin's books and
was willing to teach Murphy the truth.

From the bookstore the pair relocated to a
coffee shop. They found that they had other things
in common as well. Both had recently done stints in
jail. Additionally, Gallant, like Murphy, believed
himself in possession of superpowers.

Gallant described how he could make himself
invisible. Murphy said, hey, he could do that, too.
So they went to a mall and walked up and down
without anyone being able to see them.

"I'm invisible now."

"Yeah, me too."

They laughed like children. They could see *each
other,* of course, because they shared residence on
the higher plane.

In the following days and weeks, Murphy used
his power of invisibility to commit small acts of
larceny. He'd go to the mall or a flea market and
swipe stuff right in front of people, and the vendors
wouldn't be able to see.

One day at a mall kiosk jewelry store, Murphy
deftly plucked six rings from a rotating display.

He stole a thick silver necklace off a flea market
table while the vendor was looking right at him!

Murphy returned the next day and, needing something to put on his necklace, he stole a silver skull off the same table.

During this sticky-fingers period, Murphy actually read the Sitchin books that Dave Gallant recommended, and he became a firm believer.

Murphy decided to worship some of the ancient astronauts from Nibiru: Marduk, Nergal, and Enki. Gallant worshipped Nergal exclusively, because he believed that his powers came from Nergal.

Murphy still heard the voices, but now they were spiritual in nature. Now he knew there was a logical explanation for them. The messages he received came from the ancient astronauts, from the gods—so he felt less anxiety when they boldly tempted him.

During the summer of 2003, Murphy was on administrative probation, which meant that he did not have to visit his probation officer regularly, but he did have to write him once a month and keep him informed of his whereabouts. His other court-ordered obligation was to attend monthly psychological counseling sessions with a guy named Michael White.

White wasn't a doctor. He had a master's, had undergone state testing and supervision in Florida, and had worked as a counselor for ten years. Before that, White spent a decade as a New Hampshire law enforcement officer. White treated Murphy from May till December 2003.

During that time White never found Murphy delusional or hallucinatory, and Murphy certainly had never claimed to be God or a god. Murphy showed up early for his sessions and never seemed confused. White tested Murphy for overall function, and Murphy scored well within the normal range.

"I didn't inform him of my psychological issues," Murphy later admitted.

In the meantime, on the sly, Murphy's delusions inflated his ego even further. Sometimes he thought he was a god, and sometimes he thought he was *the* God.

Murphy grew comfortable with the voices in his head. He felt less like the victim of a worldwide conspiracy and more like the controller of that conspiracy. In his mind the voices repeated their ultimate demands: kidnap, rape, kill.

If the voices wanted him to kidnap, he would— and he knew who the victim should be, a twenty-one-year-old woman at Regis named Julie. Murphy sighed just thinking about her.

"To me, Julie was the most beautiful and sexy woman in the world," Murphy remembered.

His plan was to take her at gunpoint. He knew where he could steal a gun. He would keep her for a week or so, rape her as often as possible, and then kill her.

There was a part of Murphy's freaky psyche that knew the plan was wrong and argued against it. It was a small and diminishing part, but it was there nonetheless.

"You just have a crush on her, and you can't have her because she has a boyfriend," the angel on this shoulder would say.

"Rape her and kill her," the devil on that shoulder responded.

It only aggravated matters when Julie's boyfriend turned out to be a creep and she came to work with a black eye.

Not long after getting the shiner, she announced she was engaged to the asshole. Murphy plotted to kill him as well. He built voodoo dolls out of Barbie and Ken. He had about a dozen dolls that he kept "imprisoned in a hamster cage."

He playfully poked the sweet Julie doll with needles. He cut the male fiancé doll with razor blades. He tied tiny nooses and hung them. If he got caught, he'd call it rough sex. Murphy believed the voodoo was working.

During that same time Murphy and Gallant had a brief spat. It was over something trivial. Murphy didn't even remember anymore what it was about. Murphy built a Gallant voodoo doll and threw it out the window of his moving vehicle.

Soon after that, Gallant was hit by a car and needed hospitalization. Murphy went to visit him and Gallant looked really bad, like "death warmed over"—not that he ever looked that great. Gallant was fifty-four years old at the time and had had a couple of heart attacks and open-heart surgery. When Gallant recovered, he and Murphy once again became friends.

Gallant was a good friend—and a great landlord. For rent and for food, Gallant charged Murphy only $50 per week. "What a deal!" Murphy exclaimed. The food was pretty much free. Gallant enjoyed feeding Murphy the meals he enjoyed the most. "And for me that was steaks and liverwurst-and-onion sandwiches," Murphy said.

"Dave Gallant thought he had a unique relationship with the spirit world, and I know for a fact that he does," Murphy recently explained. "He used a Ouija board in an untraditional manner to contact the beyond."

Gallant drilled a hole in the middle of the Ouija planchette. He inserted a pen through the hole and placed the planchette on a sheet of paper.

"He'd contact a particular spirit or soul, and as the planchette moved itself, the pen drew an image or signature," Murphy explained. "It was fascinating watching the planchette move by itself and draw the picture."

Murphy loved to watch, of course, but soon enough his ego troubled him: *I should be able to do this,* he thought. After all, he wasn't a mere mortal—

and this was small potatoes. He was a god, and he should be able to do whatever he wanted with a Ouija planchette!

It was best to practice alone. In solitude he set up the planchette with the pen and put it on paper. Then, brow furrowed, eyes unblinking, he stared at it and concentrated with a determined focus. Nothing. He tried again the next day. Nothing. The day after. Zip.

One time he tried it with a major storm raging outside, rolling crescendos of strong thunder, cascades of rain blasting the windows. Murphy still couldn't make the damn planchette move.

He took the frustration well, and tossed the planchette onto his bed. At that precise moment lightning hit a tree about one hundred feet from Murphy's apartment. He could look out the window and see the tree smoldering as he fixed himself a healthy snack.

Fifteen minutes later he reentered his bedroom and gazed down onto his bed, where the planchette was, "and, lo and behold, there was a huge ink blotch in the shape of a tornado" on his comforter.

The pen was completely empty of ink.

"It was a significant sign," Murphy explained.

My dry spell is over, he quickly concluded.

He placed the planchette on the paper on a table and efficiently summoned up a soul. He stared at the planchette and, "lo and behold," the pen emptied itself of ink and formed a growing blotch on the paper. The ink "steadily flowed" onto the paper. As before, the blotch formed the shape of a tornado.

This is nothing short of a miracle, Murphy thought.

He was not only transforming the pen into a bridge to the eternity, into the soul's method of communication, as Gallant had done, he was also getting the pen to drain out all of its ink and make a tornado. That was one-up on Gallant for sure.

Every day Murphy practiced his voodoo and his Ouija skills. The images created by the planchette were, under Murphy's mind power, becoming increasingly complex.

"I summoned my own soul just to see what would happen," he recalled. He used a red Magic Marker in the planchette that day. The resulting image was of a three-headed dragon complete with wings and a tail. Murphy was astonished.

The image was both exciting and disturbing, but it made him feel good because it reinforced the fact that he was unique—unique in the universe. The disturbing part was that something so hideous would be symbolic of his own soul.

What a monster I must be, deep down inside, Murphy worriedly thought.

The dragon was so well done that Murphy couldn't have drawn it as well if he'd set down to create it in the customary fashion. His artistic skills weren't that great. The dragon was beyond his scope, or what he perceived to be his scope.

Murphy was starting to believe strongly again that he had no scope. He was omniscient and his power was absolute.

Murphy knew most readers were going to think he was perpetuating a hoax, that the planchette's behavior could be explained by some trick, a sleight of hand. But, as Shakespeare wrote, *This above all: to thine own self be true,* Murphy knew he was telling the truth. That was all he cared about.

Chapter 28

Hypnotism

The other mystical power Murphy experimented with during his time with Dave Gallant was hypnotism—and Murphy eventually became proficient at it.

"It started out with Dave hypnotizing me a couple of times," Murphy said. The first time Gallant put him under, they attempted a half-successful regression. He saw ancient clothing—robes and sandals—on men and women. Another time Gallant hypnotized Murphy in a simple attempt to help him relax.

Gallant said he could hypnotize people without their knowledge. That notion appealed to Murphy immediately for selfish reasons.

"All I could see were opportunities to take advantage of people for money and frequent sexual gratification," Murphy remembered.

He couldn't wait to learn how to do it, already fantasizing about how to get what he wanted from those totally under his majik spell. (Murphy specified that when he referred to his powers "majik" was the correct spelling.)

The bad thing about learning how to hypnotize people without their knowledge was that—unlike making a Ouija drawing of a dragon—he couldn't practice alone.

It was while practicing his hypnosis techniques that he began to have problems at work with clients—inappropriately touching the ladies when he was supposed to have been cutting their hair.

His preparation for his first field hypnosis experiment had been sufficient, he thought. He had taken everything he had learned from Gallant and had added to that what he had learned from reading a book about hypnotism during several lengthy visits to Barnes & Noble.

"I was armed and ready for the unsuspecting public," Murphy said.

The hypnosis program was like throwing a bone to the *"kidnap, rape, kill"* voices in his head, like teen girls who combated suicidal feelings by seeing how often and deep they could cut their own wrist without hitting a vein.

He geared his preplanning toward haircut clients who, more than anyone else, were a captive audience. Indeed, the subjects were chosen just as rape-and-murder victims would have been chosen if he had given in to the relentlessly taunting voices in his head. When choosing subjects for hypnotism, breast size was a criterion.

He began by planting hypnotic suggestions into his usual haircutting banter. He was impressed with his own ability to blend the suggestions seamlessly into the conversation. The subject had no clue what was happening to her.

"Only once did someone catch on to my shenanigans," Murphy said. She was a pretty twenty-four-year-old, and he was shampooing her hair when she said, "Hey, you're trying to hypnotize me, aren't you? It won't work. Nice try, though!"

He only worked at the Regis in Orange Park for three months, mid-January through April Fools' Day, largely because he often had things on his mind other than cutting hair when dealing with clients.

That job ended when he had a bridge-burning quarrel with the manager, Marguerite Bradley, who didn't like Murphy's workplace demeanor. She'd warned him twice. The conversations about spiritualism, guaranteed to make anyone within earshot tense up, had to stop. The rule was, no talk about politics or religion, and spiritualism counted as religion! The first time, it was just a warning; the second time, she suspended Murphy for a week without pay. That steamed him and he quit.

(Years later, Bradley testified at Murphy's murder trial. He believed that she lied on the stand, saying he'd been fired, when he clearly remembered quitting.)

"The voices were driving me mad," he later admitted. Rape. Kill. Rape. Kill. All day and all night. "There were so many women that I nearly killed. It's unbelievable."

Murphy carried a weapon in his backpack everywhere he went. It was either his combat knife, with a seven-inch blade, or a hatchet, which he'd purchased at Home Depot for $6.

"The hatchet came in very handy during burglaries. It could be used both to smash out windows and to pry open doors," Murphy explained.

Sometime during his decline of 2003, Murphy purchased a stun gun. He used it on one occasion and was disappointed: "I found it ineffective."

The client who could tell he was trying to hypnotize her was the exception to the rule. For the most part, Murphy was an excellent hypnotist with many, many successes.

He could *thoroughly* hypnotize subjects without them realizing it. Like the planchette-and-ink experiment, Murphy knew his claims of hypnotic prowess would strike some readers as bragging. Or, worse, as evidence that he was a schizophrenic suffering from hallucinations.

"They say you can't get a person who is under hypnosis to do anything that they normally wouldn't do unhypnotized. I am telling the truth, as God is my witness, that this is not true," Murphy said. He could not only hypnotize a subject without the subject knowing it, but also without being noticed by anyone in the room. People in the waiting area and other hairstylists would watch him doing his thing, and they would have no idea what he was up to. It got to the point where practically every female who got into his chair was groped. Sometimes he would squeeze their breasts; at other times he'd get right in there between their legs and rub them sensuously on their most private areas. They would sit there in the chair like zombies, not reacting at all to the touching. They were unseeing, unknowing. When he'd had his fill of feeling them up, he'd open their purses and remove the money. Twenties, fifties, the occasional hundred-dollar bill.

When men had their hair cut, he skipped the feeling-up stuff. Usually he just dropped a post-hypnotic suggestion that they should tip really well. Everyone in the chair was hypnotized to some degree.

On July 22, 2003, Murphy was ticketed for "failure to yield right of way," involving a car accident in Hillsborough County. Murphy was driving a 1991 Mercury, which belonged to Dave Gallant. Murphy was cited for a traffic violation in connection with the incident. He did not contest the infraction and was ordered to take a course in driver improvement.

When Murphy moved out of Gallant's apartment, he moved to a dilapidated but homey mobile home in Gibsonton. He wanted a place of his own, where there was plenty of room for his "spiritual images." He had progressed past the Ouija board. He could summon even larger and more sophisticated images from the souls and spirits without a planchette. He invented a new contraption, cutting the bottom out of an empty butter bowl. He would turn the bowl upside down and insert as many as a dozen different-colored felt-tip markers into the hole. He'd set the bowl on a piece of folded fabric, which served as his canvas. He would then summon a soul and walk away. After a couple of hours he'd return to look at the completed image. He would slowly unfold the cloth to reveal the spirit world's latest creation. They were phenomenal. Making the images consumed his time; soon the walls of his new home were covered with them.

On September 2, 2003, Murphy pawned a Weller soldering gun and two knives at the Universal Jewelry and Pawn on West Brandon Boulevard in Brandon. He pawned a Samsung color TV and an auto battery charger at a second pawnshop, also on Brandon Boulevard, on September 23, 2003.

Around that time he stole a nice bicycle. He checked it out on the Internet. It was worth almost $3,800.

During 2003, Murphy's art also consisted of paint on plates, creating images that only he could see. He wanted his brother and sister-in-law to sell the plates in their gift shop, but they refused, frightened at this new level of delusion. (Eventually, when Murphy said he would be moving to Sarasota in December of 2003, they were glad to give him a ride.)

Chapter 29

Shade Avenue

During the final months of 2003, Murphy lived at a series of Florida addresses, in St. Petersburg, St. Pete Beach, and Oldsmar. By the December holidays he lived on Shade Avenue in Sarasota, near Bee Ridge Road, in a rooming house, in one of six single-room, low-ceiling apartments. He found the place by answering an ad in the *Sarasota Herald-Tribune*. His room, known hyperbolically as "apartment B," had "immediate access to the bath and kitchen."

Like most digs for transients, the place was a madhouse. Transients, after all, rarely count stability among their strong points. But the house did have one thing going for it, from Murphy's point of view: a great landlady!

Kit Barker, the owner, had gone out of her way to

give the place homey touches, like the white picket fence that opened up to allow access to the front walk leading to the door. There was a carved flower at the top of each freshly painted picket.

Just in front of the door was a round garden, walled off from the walk that surrounded it by bricks. It was covered with mulch and featured a combination of interestingly shaped large rocks and plants. There were lights set up so that the garden (and, importantly, the front door) was illuminated at night.

Murphy thought it was a nice place, even before he entered the building. Right away, the landlady charmed him. Barker told Murphy that she was a former Hollywood stuntwoman. She showed him a newspaper clipping, an article about the lady daredevil and her Hollywood exploits with glamorous movie stars. She had an office in the back of the first floor, but she wasn't there all the time because she had a second home in North Carolina.

Murphy's rent was $100 a week, and he paid from the end of December until the middle of February. Kit Barker remembered Murphy as a guy who caused little trouble. "He said he was a hairdresser and an artist," the landlady recalled.

Cops were *always* being called to the Shade Avenue address—before, during, and after Murphy's time living there. But the calls almost never involved him.

The house was like a soap opera. Tenants stole stuff from one another—a TV, a cell phone—and the super, a guy named Albert Sanchez (pseudonym), collected the rent but failed to give it to the landlady, resulting in a charge of grand theft.

The TV was taken by a tenant calling himself John Hughes, who took off and, as far as Murphy knew, was never found. Hughes was also suspected of stealing the license plate from the landlady's Cadillac, which was parked in a locked garage at the residence. He'd stopped by to "get his things."

The landlady told police that when an apartment owner rents out rooms by the week, she didn't expect to get the best citizens as tenants. Everyone was of sketchy repute.

Barker said that during the first few months of 2004, she rented a room to a suspected cocaine addict who drove on a suspended license.

She didn't compile detailed information on her tenants. Just as long as they paid cash, they were fine with her. She didn't need or want anyone's whole biography.

After Sanchez was incarcerated, his mother came to the rooming house to get his stuff. She found that the door to his room had been pried open and his "entertainment center" was missing.

Police were yet again called to the address when an anonymous informant reported "heroin use" going on in the building. The responding officer found everyone sober, and was told by the Shade Avenue tenants that it sounded to them like mischief from a hostile ex.

Another visit involved a man named Jones, who

was overdosing on alcohol and drugs. The man was transported to the hospital, where his stomach was pumped. There was no evidence that the man was attempting suicide.

So the landlady had problems, and Murphy wasn't one of them. She thought Murphy was one of the better citizens to pass through. She recalled that the only less-than-perfect thing about Murphy was that he was "grabby." On a couple of occasions he had inappropriately touched her buttocks. The first time occurred when Murphy complained to her that there was something wrong with the toilet, which was between apartments A and B. When Barker bent over to take a look at the commode, Murphy grabbed her ass from behind. She felt he was somewhat strange, not crazy—a big man with big hands, eager to use them. The touching all occurred when he was brand-new in the house, late December maybe, before the holidays. (Murphy remembered the ass-grabbing incident as well. He said this was during his "touching period," and added that the landlady didn't seem too put-off by it—which was the impression Barker gave as well.)

The one time the cops did come to the Shade Avenue house about Murphy, Barker recalled, it was about inappropriate touching at work. The landlady correctly assumed that during this period of Murphy's life, he had to work to keep his hands off women. Poor impulse control.

He was always on his bicycle, she later recalled.

"Some kind of ten-speed," she said. He didn't have a car, and she never saw him get in a car.

Murphy showed Barker some of the eating plates he had painted. He gave her one as a gift, but the painting, she thought, was too dark and scary. She kept it on a kitchen shelf, not wanting to throw it away because it was a gift, but not wanting to look at it, either.

Murphy told her that some of his painted plates were on display, on consignment, in Sarasota art galleries, but he was never specific about which ones.

Scott Richards (pseudonym) was another tenant of the Shade Avenue place when Murphy was there. He remembered that Murphy usually wore khaki pants and a collared shirt, usually a button-up style. Richards said Murphy's mode of transportation was a rather nifty "mountain bike."

Murphy, for his part, had blurred memories of his experiences in the Shade Avenue house. He had other things on his mind. He didn't befriend any neighbors. He did, however, remember a little Spanish guy in the front apartment—Victor, Hector, something. He knew the guy because they shared a bathroom, and each had to make sure the other wasn't already in there before entering.

He remembered that a guy who cleaned carpets for a living had moved in about a week before Murphy left. He just knew him to say hi to. Talked to him for a few minutes, maybe twice.

He remembered a guy named Clive. It was Clive

who fixed his toilet when Sanchez wouldn't or couldn't.

The only problem Murphy had with theft involved food. "I had food disappearing all the time. I would put things in the refrigerator and then they'd be gone—mustard, bread. A few times," Murphy said.

Despite Barker's observations, it seems certain that for the first couple of weeks that Murphy stayed on Shade Avenue, he did have a car. He didn't give the Geo back to Dean until January 8. After that, he rode his nifty bike all over Sarasota—exploring neighborhoods, scouting interesting locations like a movie director—a filmmaker with larceny on his mind.

In his free time he frequently went to the beach, and made many all-day trips to Venice Beach and back. As he pedaled, the voices urging him to rape and kill were almost a constant in his head. He could put his fingers in his ears and shout "la, la, la, la" all he wanted, and it did nothing to drown out those voices. They came through loud and clear, no matter what.

There were many *almost* incidents. Women were almost hurt on many occasions. But conditions were never just right. Circumstances needed to be just right.

"I knew without a doubt that my opportunity would come soon," Murphy said. He still thought he was a god, maybe the God, in communication with other gods: Lord Enki. Marduk. Nergal. And, of course, Jesus. He was Lord God Elton Brutus Murphy, dominant to almost everything, but unadulteratedly subservient to the ever-present female voices nagging in his head.

Chapter 30

To Rape and Kill

On January 16, 2004, *that* day, Murphy was doing most of his talking to Jesus. As he looked back on it, Jesus sounded like Charlton Heston, the way the actor sounded in *The Ten Commandments*. That sounded like a joke, but Murphy couldn't be more serious.

"Jesus said, 'Today's the day. Today you rape and kill,'" Murphy explained. Jesus told him to go to downtown Sarasota because it was there where opportunity awaited him.

It was like that all morning. Jesus was talking to him even as he prepared his breakfast: sausages, eggs, toast, glass of juice, and a cup of coffee.

Murphy quietly chewed a piece of crust and said, "Forgive me, Jesus, if I misinterpret what you are saying. You want me to kill a woman today, right?"

"Yes," Jesus replied. "You are a god like me and you can kill."

Murphy had given up on God twenty-three years before—at age twenty-three—half his life before. Now he was a god among many gods. And he still felt subservient. Now he had to please and appease the voices—whether it be Jesus or the gaggle of crabby gals that usually inhabited his gray matter—just as he had once tried to keep the collective happy.

He had no choice. He had to do what the voices said or they would drive him crazy. So, at about ten-thirty in the morning, he got on his bike and pedaled the twenty-minute ride to downtown Sarasota. He took a left at the end of the driveway, and another left on Fruitville Road, which he took into downtown.

He had only been in that neighborhood once before that he could recall, and he didn't recognize the street names.

"I chained my bike to a pole just a couple of doors away from a combination coffee shop and bookstore," Murphy said. He went in, browsed for fifteen minutes, and had a second cup of coffee.

From the bookstore he walked to the marina and wandered around, looking at the boats. The voices screamed at him, furious now: *"You are stalling, so get on with it!"* Henpecked into action, he walked back downtown to where he'd left his bike. When he first saw his bike, right where he'd chained it, so beautiful, he paused for a moment to admire it. When he looked up, his eyes fell on a place called the Provenance Gallery.

One voice in his head, a solo voice amidst the chorus, said, *"There's a possibility."*

Murphy was dressed in his nicest clothes: a pair of black dress slacks, a green short-sleeved dress shirt, and black leather shoes. He was dressed to go undercover, to play the part of an art buyer in a real-life drama of life and death.

He carried his black backpack, the kind that had only one strap that went over the left shoulder and buckled at the right waist. Murphy walked diagonally across the street toward the Provenance's front entrance.

His memories are like a dream—so vivid, yet unreal. He entered the gallery and there was a woman, in the back, and she started to walk—a little bit jerky like stop-motion animation—in his direction.

Murphy took his attention off the woman for a heartbeat and glanced at the front door's lock. It was his lucky day. There was a dead bolt, with a flipper on the inside, so he wouldn't need a key to lock the door from inside. He was thinking, *How convenient,* when he returned his gaze to the approaching woman.

He remembered her wearing pants, a loose-fitting top, and cloth shoes. He was almost forty-seven, and she seemed a little bit older, he thought. He liked her hair. He liked her build.

She wasn't too fat at all. Or too skinny. She was "shapely in a feminine sort of way"—and he found her attractive.

Murphy's eyes searched the joint. He saw no evidence of other employees. There was good reason to believe the woman was alone.

She could be the one.

The voices said, *"Yes! Yes! This is the one! Time to rape and kill."*

"Can I help you?" the woman asked. Her tone was so pleasant. She never did give him her name.

Murphy realized right then that the voices, for all of their pestering, had never been specific about what his victim should look like. They hadn't specified a particular age, build, or hair color. The only specification was that she be an "attractive woman." Other than that, Murphy felt free to pick and choose.

Yes, this was the one.

"Yes, you may," Murphy said. "I'm interested in buying some art, perhaps a painting, for my new home."

"Is there anything in particular that you were looking for?" She was perfectly charming.

"No, not in particular," Murphy said. "If you'll show me around, I'd appreciate it. If I see anything of interest, I'll let you know."

"Okay, let's look around," she said.

She showed him around the gallery, discussing pieces of art that she found interesting, or perhaps thought he might like. They began to tour at the front of the gallery and worked their way back. At last, they were just about all the way back, in an alcove off to the side, where they couldn't be seen from the street.

Murphy thought, *If I do kill her, this is where I will do it.* It was not a voice in his head that said this. He was thinking for himself here.

Another factor to his advantage. Inside the alcove there were paintings that weren't hung on the wall, just sort of stacked up, so he had to follow the woman deep into the alcove to look at the art that was on the floor.

And Murphy did . . . nothing. He wasn't ready. He needed more time to build up his courage. And that meant a drink. He decided to go to a bar and get half wasted, then return to the Provenance.

He told her that he liked one painting, a nude of a lovely blond woman, but he was still undecided. He was going to continue his tour of the area's galleries. If he didn't see anything he liked better, he would return for the painting.

The woman said that would be fine. "We're open till five," she said cheerfully.

As Murphy exited the gallery, he became extremely excited. He finally had found someone, an opportunity!

* * *

In part, he'd been telling the woman the truth. He really did want to tour the other galleries, but he wasn't shopping for art. He was shopping for opportunities even more desirable than those presented by the woman in the Provenance Gallery.

He visited every gallery on the strip, and he failed to find anything that came even close. The lady in the Provenance was uniquely vulnerable.

As Murphy put it, there was only one "open invitation to murder." There it was: the future title of the movie about his life.

With his tour of galleries complete, Murphy retreated to a small tavern only a half block from the coffee shop/bookstore.

"I was there for maybe an hour and a quarter. I had a cheeseburger and french fries, three beers, and a scotch on the rocks," Murphy remembered. He was feeling better, but still not good enough to murder.

He skipped out on the bill, easy to do as they were changing shifts, and walked to another bar on the next block. He had two more beers.

After his second beer, the bartender asked him to leave. Murphy didn't remember the specifics, just that he was feeling pretty good, half wasted, and said something the bartender found offensive. It could have been *anything*.

It was going on five in the afternoon and Murphy was ready to return to the gallery. He concluded that closing time was the best for making his move. If his gods were with him, maybe no customers would show up. He waited until the appropriate moment and entered the gallery.

The woman was in the back again, and Murphy took the opportunity to flip the flipper on the front door's lock. The door could no longer be opened from the outside. He flipped the flipper, using only the sides of his fingers so as not to leave identifiable prints.

He walked to the back of the gallery, anonymous. The woman was almost in the perfect position, just outside the desirable alcove. If he could get her to move just three feet into the alcove, they would be invisible to outsiders.

"I'm back!" Murphy called out. "I came to buy the painting."

"Great," the woman replied. She stepped into the alcove to retrieve the nude of the blond woman.

Murphy followed her in. He had his backpack over his left shoulder, with the zipper partially open for easy access to his combat knife. The woman smiled as she lifted the painting and held it up for her customer to see.

He didn't even like that painting. It just seemed like a painting that a guy might like if he wasn't part God. He thought the painting was amateurish. He didn't like any of the paintings in the entire gallery.

But she believed he loved the painting, and that was all that mattered. The ploy worked perfectly. "She fell for it . . . literally," Murphy recalled.

Later he would suppose that there must have been classical music playing, since the music was playing when the body was found, but he didn't remember hearing it. He only remembered the sounds the woman made.

Murphy pulled the knife out of his backpack. He stepped forward and held the knife in the woman's face. Her smile was replaced by a taut grimace of terror.

He could see the panic in her eyes.

Chapter 31

Pornographic Rapture

"Do as I say or I will kill you," Murphy said. "Drop the painting to your right."

She did as she was told. He pushed her back and shoulder blades into the gallery wall. They were now in the perfect position, invisible to the outside world.

"I held the knife to her throat. I didn't say a word as my left hand first found her left breast and then her right," Murphy recalled. He thought how good those breasts felt, even through her clothing.

Years later, Murphy still lapsed into a pornographic rapture as he recalled the details of the sex attack, how he forced a hand inside her pants and vaginally penetrated her with a middle finger. He liked the feeling that gave him.

He withdrew, removed his hand, and grabbed

her by her right arm. With the knife still to her throat, he directed her to move forward a few feet away from the wall.

Murphy reached inside his backpack with his left hand and removed a long men's stretch sock.

"Put your arms behind your back!" Murphy said, using his command voice.

She complied and he attempted to tie her wrists together with the sock.

"You can't do this," the woman complained. "It hurts my shoulders."

For some reason that statement made Murphy extremely angry. He cursed her. A voice in his head said, *"Kill her!"*

"Without a second of hesitation I lifted the knife away from her throat, stepped to her left side, and drove the knife very deep into her back between her shoulder blades." He pulled the knife out and then stabbed her again, just as deeply, very close to the first wound.

She began screaming loudly, so he threw her once again into the wall, where she hit her back. He must've tried to stifle her screams with his hand; because the next thing he knew, she was biting down hard on a knuckle on his left hand, drawing blood. He already had a cut on that finger from a haircutting incident a few days earlier; the old wound opened, along with the new, until he was bleeding pretty good—spilling key evidence onto the scene.

The bite to his knucklebone made Murphy berserk with rage. He stabbed the woman repeatedly on the top of her head. He put her up against the wall again and let go, so that she slid downward. He continued the attack, with her on the floor.

"I knew that she had to give up her soul," Murphy commented.

He had an "overwhelming sense of immortality and exhilaration." Never before in his entire life had he felt that way. (And never would he again.)

He saw her eyes go vacant. He grabbed her by the feet and adjusted her, so that she was just right on the floor.

"Well done," said the voices in his head. *"Now rape her! Rape her!"*

He pulled off her shoes; as he did so, he noticed that his finger was still bleeding. In the bathroom he washed the blood from his hands.

There was a fax machine on a desk in another of the alcoves. He used his combat knife to cut the cord so there would be no interruptions.

He returned to the woman, grabbed her pants legs and pulled down her pants. He removed them. He retrieved scissors from his barbering tools, which he had in his backpack, and used them, expertly snipping away like the professional cutter that he was, opening up the woman's shirt and bra.

"Her breasts were nice and shapely, among the best I've ever seen," Murphy commented.

He used the scissors to cut off her panty hose.

He remembered that sex lesson from so many years before, when he lost his virginity on a picnic table at the Fisheating Creek Campground.

You can't do it with the panties just pulled down. They have to come all the way off.

He pulled her legs open until they formed a right angle on the floor. Murphy gazed happily at her "womanly place."

The woman's voice in his head said, *"You have conquered her. Now you can do whatever you like to her. Go ahead. Taste her!"*

He did.

"Rape her!" the voices said. He pulled down his own pants and he tried, but "my body wouldn't cooperate." He shouldn't have had those last two beers. There was a time when he could drink all night and still get the job done with a woman, but age had taken its toll.

He had just managed to get his pants back up, when the voices in his head let him know how unhappy they were. He wasn't through with the woman yet.

"Cut off her head! Cut off her head!" the voices echoed urgently.

He tried to comply, and again he failed. He cut at the neck, deeper, deeper, until he hit the spine. Then his knife would go no farther. His knife was sharp as a razor, too, but not a match for bone. Her head wasn't going to come off. He gave up.

"Cut her between her legs," the voices commanded. *"Cut it out and take it with you."*

Murphy went to the very back of the gallery and found a plastic bag.

"I returned to the woman and I removed a pizza

pie–shaped section of her womanhood and placed it into the plastic bag," Murphy recalled.

Police would later put forth the theory that the body was posed. That it was supposed to represent a work of art, that there had been an attempt to make the body resemble a framed piece that was nearby. He laughed every time he heard that.

"The police have been reading too many crime novels," Murphy theorized.

Police would one day say that he purposefully placed her hand so that it was indicating a copy of *Sarasota Magazine,* to an article called "A Fine Madness." Murphy would like us to believe that was another coincidence, or perhaps the mad part of his brain operating without the sane part realizing it. (He insists that he wished he *had* done it on purpose, because the article's title magnificently described his state of mind on January 16, 2004.)

If it was art, and Murphy was willing to consider the possibility, so be it. It wasn't him creating it. There was this and other reasons to believe Murphy's gods were overseeing these events. How else to explain one physical improbability?

"Throughout the stabbing and the cutting of the woman, not once did I get any of her blood on me anywhere, not on my hands, not on my clothes," Murphy said.

Was it a miracle? Murphy said he didn't believe in luck. "Let's just say I was *fortunate.*"

He put the plastic bag containing the woman's flesh into his backpack. He found the woman's purse and dumped out its contents. The only money she

had was in her wallet, and there wasn't much. Maybe
$50 in all.

"I looked at her driver's license and that was the
first I knew her name, Joyce Wishart. Now I had a
name for the woman I had been so intimate with."

He swiped her wallet and an expensive digital
single-lens reflex (SLR) camera. The wallet and
camera went into his backpack. Murphy claimed he
took the victim's keys, which had spilled from her
purse, but police reports seemed to indicate he left
the keys behind. Perhaps the victim had her office
keys and her car keys on separate chains.

For reasons he didn't understand, Murphy
grabbed the OPEN/CLOSED sign that went on the
front door and he ripped it, and threw it onto the
bathroom floor. He unlocked the front door from
the inside, making sure that no one was coming,
and stepped outside. He went through the woman's
keys until he found the one for the front door; then
he locked up.

He put the keys in his pocket and walked casually
across the street to his bicycle. He unlocked it and
rode away. He was surprised to learn that he'd only
been inside the gallery for about a half hour.

He took Cocoanut Avenue north to Fruitville
Road, took another right and rode all the way to
Shade Avenue. In twenty minutes he was home.

Murphy put the bagged wedge of vagina flesh in
a second plastic bag; then he put the whole bundle

in the rooming house's freezer. He planned on keeping the flesh as a souvenir.

Then, with disappointment, he realized it wasn't going to work. Someone had been stealing food from him out of the refrigerator, and a communal freezer might not be the safest place for his treasure.

He removed the bag from the freezer. It wasn't as messy as you might think. Murphy said there was no blood on it.

"It was just like a fish fillet," he said. "A flat piece of flesh."

Using a pair of his barber scissors, he cut the flesh into small pieces. "I did it in my room, over a paper plate and a piece of paper towel," he explained.

When he was done, he took everything—plate, towel, and chunks of flesh—into the bathroom and flushed it down the toilet, the same toilet that his landlady had been bending over when he goosed her.

In his room he cut up the contents of Joyce Wishart's wallet, cut all of her credit cards, cut her driver's license, cut up the wallet itself.

He went for a ride on his bike and threw away all of the items that might connect him with the Provenance Gallery. He tossed the bits and pieces away, one at a time. He even took the keys off the key ring and threw them away, one at a time.

With that done, he wrapped up his combat knife in a piece of newspaper and threw it into the bottom of a nearby Dumpster. He hung on to the camera.

For the next few days after the murder—it was the long weekend with the Martin Luther King Day holiday—he was glued to the TV, watching the news. He read the newspapers, cover to cover, looking for an article, a mention, something regarding Joyce Wishart and the Provenance Gallery.

It seemed like a full week went by before the story finally made the news—and when it hit, it hit big!

Chapter 32

Flight

On January 23, 2004, one week after the murder, Murphy filled out an application for a haircutting job at the Great Clips Salon in Bradenton. He was hired two days later. The manager of the salon was Monique Santiago (pseudonym), and it was owned by Joanne Terefinko.

His coworker Cindy Keenan (pseudonym) at Great Clips said that she remembered thinking Murphy was a nice guy at first. But then he started speaking of the "spiritual arts" and Keenan decided to give Murphy some space.

She didn't remember the specifics of his beliefs, but she got the impression that Murphy thought he could "see the future." He'd only worked at Great Clips for a couple of weeks, and she never saw him outside the salon.

For the most part he was okay with the customers, engaging them in normal conversations about the weather, their careers, whatever. Only once in a while did he bring up his odd beliefs—people who live in the walls and stuff like that.

When his manager told him to knock off the alien talk, Murphy lost his temper and "got in her face." After that happened, Murphy gave off "a very bad vibe."

Murphy sometimes discussed his artistic pursuits; a couple of times, if someone expressed interest, he showed some of his art to the customers. As far as she knew, he never tried to sell any art. He did give some away, though.

Keenan said the artist gave off bad vibes, but the art did not. Murphy's artwork was *happy*—colorful, maybe watercolors, "splashes of stuff," with lots of bright blues and greens, maybe some yellow.

"Happy" was not the first word that sprang into Murphy's mind when asked about his art at that time. "The artwork I showed to clients at Great Clips was supernatural in origin," he explained—multidimensional supernatural, at that. "These were pictures of spirits *created by spirits*," he explained.

From his viewpoint it could hardly have been any other way. He was *so* involved in the spiritual world. The spiritual world was much more Murphy's world than the real world was. He'd crossed over.

The spiritual world, like a good lover, could be either dominant or submissive. Luckily for him, every time he summoned up a spirit to create a piece of art, the spirits accommodated him. He never knew what to expect. The results were eclectic—and, yes, some of the results looked happy, he admitted.

"Even whimsical," Murphy added.

The incident that made Keenan feel most uncomfortable was when Murphy grabbed her hand and wouldn't let go.

"I really had to back off," she recalled. "He was a strong guy and I made a mental note to never be caught alone with him."

Murphy started hypnotizing the customers again so he could feel them up and no one would care. Predictably, the end for Murphy at Great Clips came when a client accused him of inappropriate touching. The incident occurred on Saturday, January 31.

Murphy left and never again saw the people at Great Clips. He stayed in his apartment on Shade Avenue until February 16. His behavior at his last haircutting job was so bad that cops were called and advised Murphy to hit the road, and soon.

So he disassembled his bike, boxed it up, and carried it out the door. His next stop: the Sarasota bus terminal—less than a mile west, northwest from the murder scene. Under an assumed name he purchased a Greyhound bus ticket to Jacksonville.

He stayed in a nice two-story motel in Jacksonville for a few days. Although he didn't dwell on it, part of him understood he was no longer just "moving on." He was no longer freedom personified. He was no longer an aimless, wandering sort of fellow.

He was *fleeing*. He'd done something bad and it wasn't a good idea to stay in one place for very long.

Although the hotel was extremely comfortable, he didn't stay in his room much. After reassembling his bike, he pedaled around Jacksonville for hours, looking for stuff to steal.

His days were so filled with healthy outdoor activity that he slept like a log at night. And he was falling asleep by early evening, experiencing a "good kind of tired."

He tried to stay focused. He was no longer under the delusion that he was gathering materials for his art, or cleaning up because his life was a never-ending battle against litter. He knew he was stealing for profit, and he tried to keep his mind from wandering.

The occurrences in the Provenance Gallery crossed his mind occasionally, as one might expect. That was all. He was untroubled by feelings of guilt. He felt that his paranoia, his mental illness in general, was much milder than it had been a year earlier.

He wasn't looking for communications centers and surveillance teams as much as he was looking for fancy houses with no one home to break into.

There was one aspect of his time in Joyce Wishart's art gallery that was sticking in his craw—

the camera, his lone remaining souvenir from the Provenance. It bothered him. He couldn't use it, because he needed a computer to get the pictures. It had value, but he couldn't hock it. There was a chance it could be traced back to Joyce Wishart.

When he'd had his fill of Jacksonville, Murphy rode on his bike forty miles to the southeast to St. Augustine. On the way he disposed of the camera—he threw it into a lake. Now all of his murder souvenirs were gone. He only had his memories.

Murphy pedaled into the beach town around midnight or one in the morning. It took him an annoyingly long time to find a place to stay. When he finally did locate a room to check into, it was in a hole-in-the-wall hotel, not nearly as nice as the place in Jacksonville.

Not that he was difficult to please. "It was still comfortable," Murphy said of the accommodations. He was so tired from his bike ride that he was asleep the instant his head hit the pillow.

In the morning he engaged in some early criminal activities. He liked to think of himself as a one-man crime wave. Ever since he left Sarasota, there had been crime after crime. He was a breaking-and-entering machine.

And it wasn't just burglaries, either. There were a couple of purse snatches, too. One woman's wallet had $400 in it. Another had $300. One burglary netted him $450 in cash. He was traveling around Florida, leaving a trail of broken windows and pried-open doors.

Back at the hole-in-the-wall, he again disassembled his bike, but this time he took the parts outside, a few at a time, and threw them in a Dumpster.

That afternoon he took a Greyhound to Tallahassee under a different alias. He stayed in Tallahassee for only a few hours before taking another bus to Mobile, Alabama. He spent the night in a motel; the next day he caught the bus to Houston, Texas.

The bus stopped for a leg-stretching break at the New Orleans terminal, which was huge, with many, many busses parked side by side. The most busses he'd ever seen in one place. Plus, a lot of hustle and bustle.

It was past ten at night when the bus pulled into the Houston terminal. The Houston bus station was not nearly as busy as the one in New Orleans. Still, there was a moderate level of activity—it wasn't deserted or anything like that. Plus, the Houston terminal was a well-lit location. Murphy liked that.

Murphy set off into the city, "looking for a motel"—walking straight or making turns, without rhyme or reason—but he never made it.

Chapter 33

The Dentist's Office

Murphy didn't know why, but he had always been attracted to homes that were converted into businesses. It was that very attraction that—on the evening of February 25, 2004—led Murphy to break into Midtown Dentistry on Westheimer Road in Houston.

It wasn't just any dentist's office, either. It was the office of Dr. Jonathan Penchas, a so-called "superdentist," with an expertise in maxillofacial prosthodontics. The building was a two-story framed structure, with yellow lap siding.

"I entered by smashing out a rear window with my hatchet," Murphy said. "The alarm went off immediately." He climbed through the window, found the alarm panel, and turned off the alarm. He found and pocketed $60 in a desk drawer—his final act as a free man—and was standing in the reception area when he knew the jig was up. Flashing lights, screeching brakes. When he looked out the front window, he saw a policeman approaching the building, with his gun drawn. Then there were two more. Murphy threw his hands up in the air.

Murphy was caught red-handed. The first responder to the alarm was Officer Shawna Hampton, who found the dentist's front door locked. However, there was a broken window on the building's south side. Officer Hampton saw a light go on upstairs just before fellow officers arrived on the scene. Houston police officers J. J. Garcia, a field training officer, and Jaclyn "Jackie" Clark, a probationary officer in field training, made the bust. When arrested, Murphy still had the hatchet. He also had on his person a jackknife and three different prescription narcotics (fifty-three Valium pills, seven Tylenol with codeine, and forty-nine Darvon).

He did not resist.

Murphy was plenty mad at being caught—but there was evidence that he was an angry man before that, too.

One cop observed, "The suspect was found inside the business, which was ransacked with property destroyed."

The alarm panel was destroyed, apparently smashed with some sort of object. The dentist had a small living space above his office. The burglar had gone up there as well, opened the refrigerator, and helped himself to a couple of cans of beer.

When Dr. Penchas arrived at his office, Murphy had already been apprehended, his hands still up in the air. The dentist had never seen the man before. The burglar was dressed all in black and was wearing a headlamp on his head. Dr. Penchas recalled thinking that this guy was like a "Hollywood burglar," straight out of central casting.

There's something to be said for "Texas justice." It's quick. In a month Murphy was assigned a public defender, quickly tried, convicted, and was sentenced to a year in jail.

Pow!

He was sent to the Pam Lychner State Jail, forty-five minutes outside Houston, which was for prisoners who were serving terms less than two years.

"Even though they still called it 'jail,' it was really prison," Murphy observed.

And it was hot—the hottest cell he'd ever been in. "Luckily, they gave me lots of paper and pens and colored pencils so I could be creative. I dripped sweat onto the many drawings I drew," he said.

Just as before, the drawings were all spiritual in nature, "loaded with spirits."

He was in that Texas jail for at least two and a half months. His job while there was cutting the other inmates' hair, which one might think would be Murphy's dream job.

"I hated cutting inmates' hair," Murphy said, still angered by the memories. "They always wanted haircuts I wasn't allowed to give."

It was always something. They wanted it longer on top than he was allowed to do, or they wanted shorter on the sides than the rules allowed. No one was happy.

He requested a transfer, which was granted, and joined a small group of inmates that cleaned up the outside visitation area. He also was allowed to step outside the jail's fence momentarily when he took out the trash.

Then he got in trouble. Murphy didn't want to talk about what he did, but it was bad enough to land him three months of solitary confinement in the summer, miserably hot, soaked with sweat all day and night.

During his incarceration Murphy gave authorities a sample of his DNA.

While in jail he wrote letters to his brother and sister-in-law. The letters contained now familiar bragging. He said he had a calling, that he was strong and "getting stronger by the minute." He said that he was drawing and coloring pictures and sending them to his kids. His fellow inmates were "amazed" and respected him because of his artistic brilliance.

The letters were filled with racial hatred, as Murphy reacted to the fact that his new jail home was not segregated. Murphy wrote that he didn't need for them to send him any money. He had plenty of money on him when he was arrested, more than enough to last him the year he'd be in jail. He wrote that he knew he seemed crazy sometimes, but they had to trust his instincts.

The DNA match between the Murphy sample in Texas and the one left at the scene of Wishart's murder took longer than it should have because of a glitch in the FDLE database.

PART III

JUSTICE

Chapter 34

Good Old-Fashioned Police Work—Building a Case

Suzanna Ulery had just told Detective Jim Glover that a match had been found for the DNA that was foreign to the victim's found at the Joyce Wishart crime scene. The DNA sample that matched, Ulery said, had come from the State of Florida's Convicted Offender DNA Database. Ulery said, "Elton Brutus Murphy's DNA was obtained as a result of his burglary conviction in Leon County."

The matching samples were those taken from skin found on the alcove carpet under the body, blood found on a copy of *New Magazine*, and blood found inside the victim's right shoe.

The name rang no bell. It hadn't come up once during the Sarasota Police Department's exhaustive investigation. *Thank God for science,* Glover thought, *or this bastard would have gotten away with it.*

Murphy was not going to be difficult to locate. He was housed at that moment in the Pam Lychner State Jail in Humble, Texas, where he was serving a one-year term for burglary. Murphy had been in that jail since February 26, 2004, about five and a half weeks after the Sarasota murder. He was tall, with brown hair and green eyes. When free, he cut a well-groomed appearance, wearing Dockers most of the time and neatly pressed shirts.

Captain Tom Laracey and Sergeant Norman Reilly were informed of the match. Laracey called a meeting for the following day in the CID's conference room. Also at that briefing were Detective David Grant and Bruce Steinberg, a criminal analyst.

Detective Glover contacted Lieutenant Danny Billingsley at the Harris County Sheriff's Office (HCSO) in Texas and made arrangements for a couple of Sarasota investigators to go there and interview Murphy. They would need a Texas bench warrant. The interview could not take place at the state jail, so the prisoner would need to be transported to the county jail facility. That would take some time; but, in the meantime, the Sarasota investigators could go to Houston and examine the items that were found on Murphy's person at the time of his Texas arrest.

This was done on July 28, 2004. His items held in the Houston Police Department (HPD) evidence room included a backpack, a fanny pack, a hatchet, two cordless drills, red gloves, clothes, tin snips, and a set of keys with a dog tag (with the name *Edward A. Dupuis*), two books, and a folding knife in a leather pouch. Inside the backpack Detective Grant found batteries wrapped in a black sock, an apparent improvised blackjack.

Waiting for the Texas bench warrant and the transfer of the prisoner also gave the SPD an opportunity to talk to some of the people who knew Murphy the best, to get an idea what he was all about before plotting their interrogation.

Florida law enforcement started with Murphy's first wife, Elaine Crabtree, who had changed her name to Margaret Towne. She told Detective Philip DeNiro that during their three years of marriage, Murphy had frequently discussed his dream to become a minister.

"He had at least two bisexual relationships before we were married," the woman said. It turned out that this meant he'd been a third bedmate for swinging couples.

She was twenty-two, and was named Elaine Crabtree, when she married Brutus. He was twenty. They lived in Pensacola and Bermuda on a naval base, and they spoke in tongues.

"He wanted very much to be a preacher, and I wanted very much to be a preacher's wife," she said. He had been very religious when they first met.

They broke up because he fooled around with other women. He picked them up in bars.

Asked about Murphy's dad, Towne said she knew he was abusive and died drunk. "When they found him, he was surrounded by, like, thirty empty bottles," she said. He hadn't just died drunk; he drank himself to death. The mom remarried.

What did she know about his other women? Not much. She assumed that he'd gotten married a few years after they split up, because she'd received an annulment form from the Catholic Church, which she signed.

"Any abuses during the marriage?" Detective DeNiro inquired.

"He became abusive and tried to kill me about three times," she said. One time he put a towel around her neck and tried to choke her. "He was in some kind of trance and I had to slap him out of it."

Another time, in Bermuda, they were riding on a motorcycle and he became very angry with her. He began pounding on her head. "If I hadn't been wearing a helmet, I probably would have died!" she exclaimed.

The third attempt came when they were renting canoes, not far from where his mom lived. He took the paddle from the canoe and struck her over the head with it. They were divorced soon after that, and she hadn't seen him in years.

The police wanted to know more about Murphy's mother. Anyone who had witnessed the Provenance crime scene had to conclude that

Murphy had oedipal issues. The woman said Murphy's mother was a hard woman; she had no choice but to be hard because of the man she married. She'd died just a few years back, following a fall in her home.

She concluded the interview by saying that Murphy had had many affairs with other women during their marriage, and that he enjoyed being in the woods.

On July 30, 2004, Detectives Mike Jackson and Anthony DeFrancisco interviewed Dave Gallant, the man Murphy met in a bookstore and went on to share alternative beliefs with. Gallant told them he met Murphy around Christmas, 2002, in the Barnes & Noble in the Brandon Town Center. The fast friends had gone for coffee together. Gallant ended up giving Murphy his phone number. After that, Murphy called every once in a while at night and they would chat about religion. Murphy came over to his place a few times and told Gallant he was a hairdresser for women. He said he got into an argument at the salon, lost his job, and was about to lose his apartment. Gallant invited him to move in with him, and Murphy did—for three or four months, starting April or May 2003.

On July 22, 2003, Murphy borrowed Gallant's car with permission and totaled it. Murphy suffered a broken collarbone in the accident and was "laid up for a while." After the accident Murphy stayed in

his room a lot. He and Gallant didn't talk much.
Murphy still went to work, however.

"He was a big, strong man, and he was powering
through the pain," Gallant commented.

It wasn't that he got mad because the guy totaled
his car, but they didn't chat quite as much after the
accident. Murphy borrowed the car because his red
Geo was broken, and Gallant loaned him $500 to
have it fixed. He never saw that money again.

Then came a time that summer—August,
maybe—when Gallant spent the weekend with his
girlfriend. When he returned on Sunday, Murphy
and his belongings were gone. No note, nothing.

Murphy left some stuff behind, in a storage shed
in the back: two pairs of shoes, several computers,
a hot plate, and a roll of metal, which he had
picked up somewhere to make a sculpture with.
Murphy himself had put that stuff in the shed when
he moved in. There was a combination lock on the
shed, and Murphy knew the combination. It was
not uncommon for him to go out to the shed. Gallant had no idea what he did back there. Gallant
said he didn't know where Murphy lived before he
became his roommate. At one time he knew where
Murphy worked, but he'd forgotten. He had
Murphy's business card at one point, but he was
pretty sure he'd thrown it away.

Gallant saw Murphy once after that. It was winter
and Murphy showed up, unannounced, and stayed
for maybe an hour. It was cold out and Murphy
wasn't dressed for it, just a T-shirt and pants. He

was carrying a gym bag, which he put on top of Gallant's freezer during the visit. They talked religion, and Gallant passed on some "new information" he'd learned. Gallant was under the impression that Murphy had just gotten fired from a job. Gallant assumed that Murphy would spend the night, maybe move back in with him, but Murphy left without saying where he was headed. Gallant looked out the window and saw Murphy leaving in a car, and that was the last he ever saw of him. Gallant noticed no injuries. Murphy seemed fine—relaxed, casual. He was usually kind of a stressed-out guy, but not on that last visit. It was strange.

When asked if anything was missing after Murphy took off that one weekend, Gallant thought and said yes, the license plate from the totaled car. He'd had it on a table out in the shed after the accident and then it was gone. He assumed that Murphy took it. It had to be him. No one else knew the combination for the lock. It was odd. Gallant had thousands of dollars' worth of tools back there and Murphy just took a license plate. That was all he knew about Murphy. Gallant concluded by saying he was done with Florida. Gallant's plans were to sell his house and head west, maybe to New Mexico.

Detectives Glover and Grant interviewed Albert Sanchez, the super of the transient rooming house on Shade Avenue in Sarasota, where Murphy had been living at the time of the murder.

Sanchez said he remembered four things about Murphy: He drove a Geo Metro for a time. He rode a bike after that. He was a good cook, always cooking stew. He wore a backpack sometimes.

Any recollection of when Murphy cooked stew? No.

The detectives were struck by two facts that just might fit together: First, Murphy stole his victim's vagina from the murder scene. Second, Murphy cooked stew.

What Sanchez didn't know wouldn't hurt him, they guessed—and they couldn't help but wonder if Murphy's stew contained a secret ingredient.

Murphy's second ex-wife, Paula, spoke to Detectives DeNiro and Carmen Woods about her ex-husband. Paula provided the investigation with useful dates. They were married in 1987, divorced 1996. They lived in Tallahassee, where they ran a haircutting place together. They had two kids, who were ages fifteen and eleven in 2004. She was Catholic, and Murphy had been adamant that he did not want the kids raised as Catholics. She told police that Murphy had a short temper—he yelled at her and the kids too much—but he had never been violent with her. She remembered him as a bit of a hoarder, collecting magazines and newspapers. She didn't recall him being artistic when they were together. (Amazingly, it seems, Murphy kept his artistic feelings internal. His gathering of art materials translated to Paula as hoarding, his "gallery" in their haircutting shop was, to her, storage.)

Regarding his religion, Paula said, "He kind of didn't believe in God, but he was looking into several different religions before we got together."

She told police about the time she had sex with another man while Murphy watched. "I wasn't thrilled about it, but I did it," she said. Murphy, she added, was merely a spectator at this event and was in no way a participant.

After the divorce, she said, Murphy went to Tampa and moved in with his mother, Betty Jo. He was distraught over the breakup and began to act out. He paid child support until 2002. He took each child for two weeks every summer. He called every Sunday. Then it all stopped. That was the same year he went to jail, and also when his peculiar behavior worsened.

In the recent past—sometime in January 2004—Murphy showed up at Paula's house to see the kids. This troubled her, because it was the first time he'd ever just shown up without calling first. He arrived right at dinnertime, driving his little red Geo. He brought a used computer, which he gave to Trevor. The car appeared to be in good condition, and it didn't look filled up with stuff.

He stayed for three or four hours—had dinner, spent time with both children—and as he left, he told Paula that he "had to get back to Tampa." He drove off in the tiny red car.

Other than its unexpected nature, Paula could recall nothing unusual about the visit.

"Wait, there was one thing," she said. "He had bruises on his arms," she said.

They tried to pin down the actual date of that visit. She knew it had to be before January 19, because that was her son's birthday and Murphy came before that. It was the week before, in fact, and it was a weekday. She finally concluded that he showed up unexpectedly between January 6 and January 10.

"How did he have money for a car?" Detective DeNiro asked.

"As far as I knew, he was cutting hair. As far as I knew, he was still working for his brother at the Solomon's Castle restaurant," she said.

"Was there any conversation about his mental state?"

"I asked him if he was taking his meds. He said he didn't need them anymore." She'd talked to a doctor about him once and was told he was bipolar. She knew he was supposed to be on meds, because she took him to the drugstore once to pick them up.

But the big reason she knew something was wrong with his mental state was that she could see his behavior. It had changed. He'd grown yet flakier.

When they were together, he might say a wacky

thing every once in a while, but it was just a facet of his quirky personality. By 2004, he was acting wacky all the time, discussing aliens every other sentence.

Back in 2002, after his arrest for criminal mischief at the apartment complex, Paula cleaned out his apartment. There was evidence of madness there as well.

"You said he was a bit of a hoarder. Was it cluttered?"

"It was more than just clutter," she said. "There were maybe a thousand wire hangers. He was collecting hangers."

She mentioned that she'd heard that, in more recent days, he'd been eating out of Dumpsters.

While Murphy was in jail, Paula had occasion to speak with his brother Dean's wife, who said that Murphy's breakdown was all Paula's fault. She said that his troubles started when Paula left him and broke his heart.

"Back in the day, you two ever go camping?" DeNiro inquired.

"No," she replied firmly. "I didn't like it. He could do it, though. He could fend for himself."

Asked about Murphy's military record, she got some key facts reversed. She said he was given a dishonorable discharge the first time he was in, because he'd gone AWOL, and he'd signed up a second time so that he could be discharged honorably, to right the wrong and remove the blemish on his record as an upstanding American. In reality it was his first stint that went well and his second was a mess.

"What kind of schooling did he have?"

"High school. No college. Went to hair school."

"Any abuse in his upbringing?"

"His dad was an alcoholic. Abusive. Pointed a shotgun at the mother in front of the kids."

"Did he have friends?"

"He was kind of a loner. He didn't have best friends."

"Did you have friends as a couple?"

"Yes," she said. Barbara and Mark Brindley from the apartment complex when they lived there in the 1990s—the same couple that Murphy wrote the obscene graffiti about on the pool patio years later. "Barbara told me about the graffiti, and about the note he'd pinned up in the laundry room."

Paula was asked about the other women in his life, but her knowledge was limited. He'd been engaged to Mary before they got together. There'd been a woman named Jane.

"Do you know a Margaret Towne?" That was the name being used by Murphy's first wife.

"No."

The detectives wanted to know if she'd heard from Murphy since that visit, and she said she received letters from him, the first dated March 29, 2004, stating that he was in jail.

In the letter he wrote how he understood how difficult it was for his family to understand him. He said that he was sorry about that, but it was probably going to be true for all of "our earthly years." He stated, quite rationally, that a psychologist would have a "field day" doing a "case study" on his mind. He explained that he'd caught a year in jail, and was, as he wrote, in his fifth week. He told them he loved them, and would "until Eternity." God had put him in jail to teach him things. That was what God did with his "copartners." He was happy to report that God told him that Paula and the kids were going to have a prosperous year, so they had that to look forward to. They didn't have to believe in the magic for it to happen. It was going to happen no matter how skeptical they were, and it was all going to be great.

Although the March 29 letter was odd, it was clearly written and its emotional tone, regarding his love for them, and all of the good things he was going to make happen for them, had an emotional truth that led Paula to believe that the old Elton Brutus Murphy was still in there someplace. But, by the time of the second letter, the letter of July 13, that was over. He wrote that he "admired" Paula and the kids.

The letter began: *I have a GAME PLAN. The Plan is Real. I have it in my GRASP. It will not elude me. I have money waiting. I will have More. I will make it happen. I have a mission. I have Rank. I have Power. I have followers. They have rank.*

Less weird was his equally clipped message to his kids. To Darcie, he wrote, *Feed your horse. Groom and respect it*. To Trevor, the message was: *Work, study, learn, help*.

Paula said she did not answer either letter, and she hadn't tried to call him or get in touch with him in any way.

DeNiro's next line of investigation was the Great Clips Salon, where Murphy had worked briefly after the murder and was quickly fired for inappropriate behavior. The detective spoke to Murphy's only male coworker at Great Clips, Bill Overstreet. Overstreet said that he only worked one day with Murphy, but that Murphy seemed like an ordinary guy, maybe a little bit timid or shy. Although the salon's owner said that Murphy's arms were covered with "rashes and sores," Overstreet told DeNiro he noticed nothing unusual about Murphy's arms or hands. Another Great Clips employee who was briefly Murphy's coworker was Jamie Hazelbaker. She remembered that Murphy said he rode his bicycle to work, but she never saw the bicycle.

An idea flashed in DeNiro's brain. Bike Man! The killer was Bike Man.

The manager of Great Clips in Bradenton was a woman named Monique Santiago, who told police she remembered Murphy well. Murphy had no car, just a bike, and he carried his own haircutting tools in an over-the-shoulder tote bag. Murphy came in on January 23, 2004, and started to fill out the job application right there in the shop. But he left before finishing and returned the following day with the application completed. He dressed neatly, and he cut hair well.

He did have what appeared to be a nasty rash on both arms. His coworkers described his skin as "nasty, scabby, scaly." His first day of work was Sunday, January 25. That was the day the register came up $40 short. Murphy and the other employees all denied taking the money. The police were interested in whether or not Murphy carried a straight razor in his tote bag. If he did, no one in the shop saw it. Straight razors were illegal in Florida.

Murphy left the salon on January 31.

"I'm gonna leave," Murphy said at that time. "There is a black cloud in this salon."

On July 28, 2004, Detectives Mark Opitz and Sensei DelValle interviewed Alane Solomon, Dean Murphy's wife, at their home, near Solomon's Castle, in Ona, Florida. They lived in what had once been a mobile home, but it was considerably larger after remodeling and a series of additions. Construction was ongoing and the place was busy when the detectives arrived.

When the detectives found Alane Solomon, Murphy's sister-in-law, she had just picked up the phone:

"Solomon's Castle. Hey, Brent, how are you?

You're looking for somebody? Okay, hang on just a minute. Bob, would you take my golf cart and go tell . . . who do you want? Ernesto? Would you tell Dean that Ernesto needs to come and call Brent. My golf cart is there by the truck." Alane turned toward the detectives and asked if she needed a lawyer. "Be careful on the steps, Bob," she added.

The detectives explained they were there only to ask about Dean's brother, and that she and her husband were in no trouble. Dean Murphy was in the room briefly and asked that the men not show their badges, because he feared his wife would be frightened by them. Then he said to Alane, "Go ahead and answer their questions." So she did. Dean left, after being informed that the investigators wanted to question them separately, if that was okay with them.

Alane started: Brutus had severe mental problems. She believed him to be a paranoid schizophrenic. Dean and Brutus came from such a sparse family. They really only had each other.

"When did you last see him?"

Sometime in the middle of January. He'd returned his brother's car, the red Geo, and had only stayed for about six hours. He said he didn't need the car anymore because he was going to get a van. That car had since been sold to a Tory Fenimore, although it sat parked at their house for a couple of weeks in between. She appreciated it if the investigators did not speak to Fenimore, as she hadn't told her about the previous owner.

"How would you describe his behavior?"

"Clean, orderly. He liked to clean and organize things." When he visited, he liked to help around the kitchen. If he made a mess, he would always clean it up. Sometimes he even wiped up behind her.

Alane believed that a lot of Murphy's problems stemmed from his failure to become a Navy SEAL. He'd told her that he got close to qualifying, but he had developed hypothermia and had to drop out.

"That sat hard with him," she explained.

Many years later he claimed that he had pretended to be a Navy SEAL, and they hated that. He'd been picked up by a van and beaten by the men inside to punish him for falsely claiming to be one. Who knew what really happened? He was paranoid.

He had a rap where he was walking the earth cleaning up, picking up people's stuff. He would remove the towel from the top of the fence, or pick up the air filter some kid left on the lawn. But everyone saw through his game. By his own way of thinking, he could never be a thief or a burglar. He was just cleaning up.

He'd been on a "God kick." Somebody taught him deviant religious lessons and now he preached the same nonsense. Alane and Dean had tried to pry details of his life out of him, but he was close-lipped. Brutus told them that the less they knew, the better off they'd be.

She discussed his plate art. He painted plates.

Just a mishmash, but he always wanted to know if she "saw pictures" in his plates. She did not. Sometimes it looked like he'd scribbled with three or four different-colored Magic Markers. Sometimes it was worse, scary bad.

"Just like smear smear" was how she put it.

It upset her on a couple of levels. He had been a talented artist at one time, and now it was gone, clouded over by his mental illness.

"My father knew Brutus when he was a little boy, like fourteen years old. And when he was in his twenties, he created many pieces of art that were exceptional," Alane said.

It seemed like she could see the deterioration of her brother-in-law's mind or psyche or whatever when she looked at those plates.

He had wanted her to sell his plates in the castle's gift shop, and it was impossible for her to either sell them or tell him they were crap.

There were times when she had to resist the urge to grab him by the shoulders and give him a good shake, screaming into his face that the plates were "just awful!"

She gave in and did try to sell some of the plates. Not all of them. They went through the plates together and decided which ones she would sell and which he had to keep.

She remembered giving him long speeches about the clientele at the castle. They tended to be low-income people, taking an economical vacation— low-income families, seniors who are downsizing,

et cetera. She explained that she wouldn't be able
to charge very much for the plates, which irritated
Murphy. He suggested that he might be better off
selling the plates on eBay.

"Do you still have any of those plates?" Detective
Opitz asked.

"Threw them out," Alane replied. "They looked
like something a kindergartner might do. They
were scary. I don't believe in spirits or anything like
that, but they gave me a creepy feeling."

Brutus had plans to sell the plates for twenty
dollars apiece on eBay.

He was more successful with sculpture, she
thought. He'd made her an airplane made out of
various items, and she had it hanging in her house.
Her father had bought a couple of them; although,
as she recalled it, Brutus had come back six or eight
months later and bought the sculptures back.

"Did he ever mention anything about the end
of the world, a day of reckoning or anything like
that?"

"No."

"Did he have collections?"

"He collected forks. He thought it was a message
from God when he saw a fork on the ground. I said,
'How many forks can you possibly see on the
ground?' And he said, 'You'd be surprised. I know
the god put them there for me to see.'"

The god. She didn't think that could possibly be
the same as *her* notion of God.

There had been a time when she convinced

Murphy that he needed professional help, and she was proud of that.

It was when the movie *A Beautiful Mind* came out. She was reading the reviews in the paper, and this was one of the times when Murphy was staying with them, sleeping on their couch. She told him he should read the review of the movie; he might find something worthwhile in it. "I know you've got some pretty heavy-duty problems going on here, and I know a place over in Sebring that could probably diagnose you and help you."

Murphy's first reaction, of course, was: "Oh no, I'm not going to do that."

Alane left for a couple of hours. When she came back, she found Murphy's attitude had changed.

Murphy said, "You know I read it and it all makes sense, perfect sense to me, and you are right. I need help. That's why I am going to move to Tallahassee, because my kids are up there. I can see my kids, and I can get help at the University of Florida, and whatever is up there. I'm sure I will need the support of my ex-wife and my kids. Having them around would be helpful."

Alane was thrilled. "Sounds good to me!" she said.

Her happiness was short-lived, however, as Murphy "went downhill fast" after moving to Tallahassee. That was when he started camping out in the woods and stuff like that. "He'd throw a tarp over some bushes and that was his shelter," she explained.

"Do you think he continued living outside after he went to Sarasota?"

"I don't know," Solomon said. The next she heard, he was in jail in Houston.

Alane said, "Dean was always extremely patient with his brother. He had a river of patience." But her husband had his limits. Dean would say, "Please stop talking about God!"

Brutus would reply, "They've chosen me to make a list of all the people who are protected." Brutus would become excited and warn Dean that thinking he was crazy was a mistake, because this was real and some "very big things were going to happen." Brutus was never agitated, just excited. As far as she knew, he was not a violent man.

Did he keep any of his things at their house?

No, when he stayed, he just brought a small bag, an overnighter—a backpack, she thought it was. "It was smaller than a suitcase, smaller than a carry-on piece of luggage."

"This last time he visited, he returned the car, so how did he get back home?"

"Dean and I drove him," she said. The detectives wanted to know where she dropped him off, and she wasn't sure. They all looked at a map together. It didn't help. She thought it might have been on Fruitville Road or Bee Ridge Road.

"Did he say he was camping in the woods?"

No. He gave her the impression he had a room somewhere in Sarasota.

When they dropped him off, he told her he was

going to be on the move, but he didn't tell her where he was headed. He gave her the impression that the less she knew about his whereabouts and activities, the better off she would be.

He had to be where the gods wanted him to be. If he wasn't, there was going to be *hell* to pay. By that time Alane allowed Murphy's words to flow in one ear and out the other.

She said that he sometimes cut her hair. He would come over with a box that had his cutting tools in it. He cut everyone's hair, except for Dean's.

Had her brother-in-law mentioned anything about his job history in Sarasota?

"Yes," she replied. "He said he had worked for an older lady who had an art gallery in Sarasota. He said she had adult children."

"Anytime, recently—that you know of—did he give anybody a camera? There is a camera that we are trying to locate."

"No."

"Not as a gift or in lieu of payment, or anything like that?"

"Nope."

The investigators next interviewed Dean Murphy.

What was the oddest thing about Brutus? His coolness. Chilliness. He didn't seem upset when either of their parents died.

Had there been occasions when Dean gave his

brother a ride to Sarasota? Yes, he'd dropped him off near Fruitville Road, in an office complex parking lot near apartments.

There was a time when he seemed normal most of the time and stupid at others. But, as time passed, the stupid part of him was taking over. The doctor said he was bipolar.

What about his plate art?

Dean said it looked like a first grader had painted the plates. There was a time when his brother was a guy with artistic talent, but it had eroded, along with his mental state.

When Brutus owed his brother money, Dean gave him a job at the restaurant so he could work it off. Since January 2004, Dean hadn't seen his brother, although he did get a letter from him in jail. Brutus wrote about his plan: get a van and sell painted plates on the road. He said he already had the van.

Detective DelValle asked if Brutus had any items in storage anywhere. Dean said he didn't believe his brother had possessions, or close friends. Or even acquaintances. His mental problems had isolated him.

"Did he have any barber tools with him?"

Dean, who still didn't know what all of this was about, became particularly uncomfortable when the questions were about sharp tools. Dean said, "It was common for him to carry his haircutting tools with him. He kept them in a bag. I cut hair, too. We each have our own tools. I don't remember what the bag looked like."

"Your brother violent?"

"Never known him to be. No, I don't believe he is."

Dean described Brutus's delusions: the aliens, the followers, the big payday right around the corner. The deterioration came after he broke up with his wife, and his two teenaged children lived with their mother.

"That shook him up," Dean said.

DelValle and Opitz wondered what religious stew had resulted in Brutus's peculiar beliefs. Dean said they had grown up Baptist, but his brother was influenced by Seventh-Day Adventists while in the navy. He stayed at a religious halfway house after he was released from jail. The investigators didn't hear anything odd in that mix.

Opitz asked, "When your brother is acting like God, does he ever make sacrifices or hurt any animals?"

Dean was firm: "No." His mind was briefly invaded with an image of someone slitting a lamb's throat on a stone altar. Again, like the questions about tools, the fact that the investigators asked the question made Dean uneasy.

"Brutus was wacky, but he was great with computers. He could even build computers. Anytime he was in the vicinity of a computer, there was a chance he used it. He was athletic, too. He ran and took vitamins, enjoyed lifting weights."

They asked Dean about his parents. Dean said his dad was an alcoholic, but there'd been no abuse problems in the house. (On this point, Dean disagreed with Brutus, who recalled his father pointing a shotgun at his mother.)

Were there any abuse issues with any of his brother's ex-wives? No, not that Dean knew of.

Weapons? Dean said his brother might have owned a small-caliber pistol at some point, but he suspected it was long gone. He didn't collect guns or knives or anything like that.

Dean never knew his brother to be a consumer of pornography, although he supposed he looked at *Playboy* every now and again. Every guy did.

On their way out the detectives were stopped by Alane Solomon, who said she had reconsidered something she'd said earlier. Looking back at it, she did not think Murphy had ever borrowed or used any of hers or Dean's computers. She was 99 percent sure that Murphy never used their computers, especially not during his most recent visits.

After they had spoken with Dean and Alane, the investigators interviewed Howard Solomon, who'd owned the land around Solomon's Castle for the past thirty-two years. Solomon said he'd known Brutus and Dean since they were teenagers—and he'd never had problems with Brutus.

Solomon demonstrated a remarkably open mind. He thought Murphy had some artistic talent; and if he wanted to believe in aliens, that was okay. Solomon had a lot of friends who were artists, and Brutus was no stranger than a lot of them.

Solomon showed the investigators two of Brutus's metal sculptures that were nearby. Solomon had once owned five of his sculptures, but Murphy had bought three of them back.

"I tried to mentor him, and I believe he admired me," Solomon said. They were not chummy, however. "If you put all of our conversations together for the past four years, they would sum up to less than an hour."

What was Solomon working on now?

The sculptor said he was working on an art display that would be in Naples, Florida. No, he had no art contacts in Sarasota and had never displayed his art there.

"I haven't had a show of any kind since the 1970s," Solomon said, "and that was in St. Petersburg."

Finished at Solomon's Castle, DelValle and Opitz took off in search of Murphy's Geo Metro. Investigators had not ruled out the idea that Murphy was still driving the Geo at the time of the murder.

The cops located Tory Fenimore in Altoona, Florida. Fenimore said that she bought the Geo from Dean Murphy on February 1.

"Go ahead and process the vehicle," she said, signing a form, but she'd appreciate it if they could finish up quickly because she needed to get to work.

Criminalist James Tutsock was sent to Altoona to do the processing. DelValle and Opitz spoke to Fenimore and her sister Karrie Bootsma, who said that they first remembered seeing the Geo on Dean Murphy's property on January 24. Fenimore said she bought the car to save money on gas, but she hadn't driven it much. She vacuumed it out good before driving it. There was a knife in the trunk and a box cutter under the driver's seat, which weren't hers.

"All right if we take the trunk liner with us?" DelValle asked.

"Sure," Fenimore said.

"If we need to take the whole car back to Sarasota, would that be okay?"

"Okay, but I would need it back by October."

"We don't need to take it today, but there's a chance we might later."

Though the DNA identification of the killer was irrefutable evidence that Elton Brutus Murphy had been present at the killing of Joyce Wishart, SPD detectives were not satisfied.

All they needed was one juror who was skeptical of DNA technology, the possibility of contamination, and there went their case. If possible, they wanted to tie their suspect with the crime in another way, verify the scientific with something jurors could more easily grasp.

Taking one of the plates that Murphy had painted his art on, Detectives Jack Carter and Ken Halpin went around on July 31, 2004, to Sarasota's galleries to see if anyone recognized Murphy or his art.

A man named Louis DiVita said he remembered receiving a visit from an artist who behaved oddly in his mannerisms and who didn't have a portfolio. The guy was five-eleven and thin. The detectives showed him a photo of Murphy, but DiVita couldn't identify it. Bill Bowers, DiVita's coworker at the Plum Door Art Gallery, said the photo of Murphy "looked familiar, but he couldn't be sure." Everyone else was pretty certain they'd never seen him before.

Detective Carter was also in charge of pursuing Murphy's credit records to see if he could find any links with Sarasota. He learned that Murphy only had one credit card that was still functional—and it hadn't been used in more than two years.

Carter also canvassed local motels, places where Murphy might have stayed while he was in town during January. Comfort Inn, Quality Inn, Residence Inn, Sleep Inn, Courtyard Marriott, Knight's Inn, Springhill Suites, and so on. The detective always checked under Murphy's real name, as well as under all three of Murphy's known aliases: Moore, Marks, and Dupuis. No luck.

It turned out that one of Murphy's assumed names belonged to a real person: Edward Alan Dupuis, who was in the National Guard. His girlfriend, Nancy, had had her bag stolen from a bus station in Lake Charles on January 25, 2004. She verified that the bag contained car keys, two books, and a Bible—all items found in Murphy's possession when he was arrested in Houston.

Later that day Detectives Rick Lewis and Jack Carter followed up on an incident report from the Manatee County Sheriff's Office (MCSO) from the end of January 2004. The manager at Great Clips on Clark Road claimed that Murphy might have worked there at that time. They spoke with Candia Roberts, who said Murphy worked at her other store at South Tuttle, but his employment only lasted a couple of days. She recalled that Murphy had presented an active barber's license and that she had interviewed him twice before hiring him. During one of those interviews Murphy claimed that he had previously worked at the Great Clips in Tampa, but the location had gone out of business. Roberts tried but was unable to verify that portion of his work history.

"I remember he rode his bicycle to work," Roberts recalled. She found his job application, which listed his address as Shade Avenue.

She remembered telling him he should try the Great Clips in Bradenton. He only worked for a couple of days and his manager was Amanda Noack.

On August 2, 2004, Detectives Woods and DeNiro canvassed Palm Avenue with various photos of Elton Murphy in their hands. The owner of a hair salon, Ana Molinari, said she recognized the man in the photo. He came to her place maybe a month after the murder.

He'd asked for her by name, but she lied and said, "Ana wasn't in." The guy was suspicious and she didn't want to have anything to do with him.

The man said that God had sent him; he was the Chosen One. Everything he did, he did because God told him to do it. God had spoken to him when he was asleep and had told him to go to her salon on South Palm Avenue.

He said he lived at the Salvation Army. Molinari was so upset by the visit that she called the police. By the time the officer arrived, though, the man had already departed down the street on foot.

She described the man as being in his late thirties, about six-one. She told Detective DeNiro that she had a good memory for faces and she was certain the man in the photograph was the guy. He said his name at one point.

"Robert or Cody," she thought he said. "He wasn't right. He scared me," she concluded.

Meanwhile, Detectives DelValle and Opitz spoke to Detective Wendy Davis-Zarvis, who had investigated Murphy after he was fired from his last job. She gave the investigators the address where Murphy had been staying at the time.

"He was tall and thin," Davis-Zarvis said. "Reminded me of a beach bum. He was smart but lazy—eccentric, like most artists are."

* * *

The detectives returned to Sarasota and visited the rooming house on Shade Avenue. The owner, Kit Barker, was away. In her absence Daniel Walker managed the property. He allowed police to photograph and search the room where Murphy had stayed.

"I don't know if you're going to find anything useful," Walker said. "Several tenants have come and gone since Murphy was here."

Walker himself did not know Murphy. He had only been at the rooming house since March 2004, weeks after Murphy left. None of the tenants were the same as those who had lived in the house six months before. The investigators did assemble a list of people who had resided in the house at the same time as Murphy, but they found them scattered to the wind.

When Opitz talked to Kit Barker, she recalled how Murphy had grabbed her butt as she bent over the toilet. She gave the police the painted plate Murphy had given her as a gift. It had always scared her and she was eager to be rid of it. Murphy, she recalled, told her that he worked cutting hair in a place in Bradenton, and he commuted on his bicycle.

Chapter 35

Brutus Talks to the Police

It was the beginning of August, a couple of weeks after he'd been released from solitary confinement at the state jail. Things were going smoothly for Murphy.

Murphy made a friend while in general population. The guy had robbed a bank. He met him in recreation, up on the roof. Murphy was walking laps around the perimeter—the big steel cage all around him, a happy home for pigeons, which took off and landed, took off and landed—when he was joined by another man, a larger-than-average guy.

"Mind if I walk with you?" the guy asked, walking beside Murphy, stride for stride.

"No, go ahead," Murphy replied.

"I just got extradited from the state of Washington."

"What are you in for?"

"I'm accused of robbing several banks."

They started talking and the bank robber told Murphy his life story. He'd been in prison in Washington for robbing banks, and now they thought he robbed banks in Texas, too. His reputation followed him.

"Sounds to me like you've been busy," Murphy said with a laugh. "What's the most money you ever got out of one bank?"

"Eighteen thousand dollars," the guy said, although that one was exceptional. If you averaged them out, he'd netted about four grand per.

The guy taught Murphy the tricks of the bank-robbing trade. Rule One: "Have a home base close to the bank, and escape via bicycle." Rule Two: Elmer's Glue on the fingertips, so you don't leave fingerprints.

A social animal in general pop, Murphy also befriended two other bank robbers. They looked like normal guys and their technique was simple. They walked into a bank unarmed and demanded money.

One of those guys was incarcerated for a different crime, but he had done time in the past for bank robbery, so he figured it all evened out in the end. He said his best friend was a bank robber, and he got arrested trying to board a bus drunk and without a shirt on.

Murphy asked the guy how he had gotten started.

Did he start out robbing banks, or did he work his way up?

"I started out by robbing liquor stores. I'd walk in, grab a couple of bottles of expensive booze, and *dare* the guy behind the counter to do anything about it."

Murphy wanted to know what was the guy's worst jail experience. Murphy's new friend had once done six months in a really rough Mexican prison. Luckily, he got connected with the right guys and they got him through.

Then life changed.

"I was called out of the dorm to meet a stranger from outside the prison," Murphy remembered. The man was a law enforcement officer of some type; Murphy didn't recall which kind. "Before he spoke to me, he looked at a large photograph he had of me, to make sure I was the right guy."

Satisfied that he had the right man, the cop took Murphy into custody and took him *outside the prison* to a waiting unmarked car. In the car was a woman, another law enforcement officer of some sort. They didn't tell Murphy who they were or where they were going. They took him to a sheriff's office in Houston. They sat him down in an interrogation room.

Murphy looked around for a camera and didn't see any. And there was no window, no mirror, no portal for them to watch him. He thought he wasn't being watched, that he wasn't being listened to. Only months later did he realize that everything that happened in that room was recorded. He was still mystified as to how they did it.

Murphy intended to get through the interview—just as he always did when he talked to the authorities. He would just "beat around the bush, be as vague as possible, lie, misinform, and concoct a story or two."

Detective Jim Glover and Sergeant Norman Reilly had made the trip from Sarasota to Texas. Murphy was given his Miranda rights and agreed to speak with them.

The interrogators were interested in Murphy's activities before he got to Houston. Murphy said he'd arrived in the city when a friend of a friend, whose name was either Jim or Dave, gave him a ride. The guy, if Murphy remembered correctly, dropped him off and then continued on to Las Vegas. (All a lie, he'd actually taken a series of Greyhound busses under a variety of pseudonyms.)

Before that, when he was still in Sarasota, during January 2004, he'd lived in an efficiency apartment on Shade Avenue owned by Kit Barker, a sassy woman who spent much of the year living in North Carolina. The house had six rented rooms, lettered *A* through *F*. He stayed there for a couple of months. Rent was approximately $100 per week.

Murphy gave the cops his recent work history, which consisted only of a couple of short-term gigs at Sarasota barbershops.

He talked about his military career and both of his ex-wives. He said he didn't abuse drugs and considered himself sane.

He said he was an *artist.* To kill time in jail he drew pictures. "Fantasy art," he called it.

He acknowledged that he'd seen press coverage of the Joyce Wishart murder. They told him his DNA was found at the scene. Murphy said he understood DNA evidence, that his DNA was linked to God's. It was that very connection to God that gave him his power, Murphy boasted. He could make cars crash just by looking at them. If someone pissed him off, he could give them a headache, "snap, just like that."

Murphy answered questions willingly, but his openness changed when the subject of Joyce Wishart's murder came up. He said, "I've told you all I'm going to about that case. I am not going to fill in the blanks for you."

They asked him to explain his DNA being there. Murphy said it was simple: He was framed. He was a barber, and he used cutting equipment. He cut himself all the time.

Who would frame him?

He had no idea. He had no friends. He was a loner. No one had visited him during his time in the Texas jail. He had "numerous followers," he said, but he was unable to provide the name of a single person he was "close with."

They asked him for a voluntary DNA sample.

Just to confirm the results they already had. He said no.

The next day Reilly and Glover spoke to Murphy's jail warden, who said Murphy had been given no medication since his arrival. He had not been a disciplinary problem. Murphy followed instructions and did not exhibit abnormal behavior.

On August 11, Sarasota detectives Jim Glover and David Grant spoke to Murphy at the Harris County Jail. Before commencing the questioning, a detective named Hoffman came into the room with one purpose only. He told Murphy that he had a court order to take "buccal swabs"—i.e., a DNA sample. Detective Hoffman explained that the long Q-tip he was unwrapping was sterile, and Murphy obediently opened his mouth so Hoffman could rub the cotton swab against the inside of his cheek on either side.

"It's almost as good as going to the dentist," Hoffman joked.

"Even better," Murphy agreed cheerfully.

Hoffman left with the sample, and Murphy was alone in the room with Glover and Grant. They informed him that they were being recorded. After reading Murphy his Miranda rights, they briefly discussed Murphy's living arrangements at the jail, and agreed the place was huge.

"How many people are over there?" Glover asked.

"A few thousand. They keep coming," Murphy

said with a laugh. "The building is wild. There are seven floors underground!" The detectives were impressed. "There are underground tunnels. It's all under the bayou!" He described the jail as a "slaughterhouse." Prisoners were beating the hell out of each other. Guards were beating the hell out of prisoners.

"I got punched in the mouth." He accused a guy of stealing his stuff; and later, while Murphy was headed for the shower, the guy punched him. "I needed four stitches," Murphy concluded.

Glover explained that they had brought with them some photographs of Murphy's art, and he hoped they could discuss it.

"All right," Murphy said.

Glover then looked for the photos of Murphy's artwork, but he couldn't find them. Because of that, he continued the interview without his visual aids.

"If I recall, they were plates with images painted on them. My question would be, what are they supposed to be?"

"That's up to the person," Murphy replied. "Each person can interpret them as they will. The plates want each person to do something, to enjoy the work the way I felt," Murphy said. "I am not going to give them to anyone else. You interpret them your own way, and each person sees something different."

"How many of those plates did you do?" Glover asked.

"About thirty."

"And where did all of those end up?"

"I'm not going to answer that one."

It was true, he added, that he did give some paintings to a girl to sell for him. That artwork had not been plates. The girl's name was Ann Marie. He didn't recall a last name.

Detective Grant asked, "Was the painting you gave to the girl to sell in the same style as the plates?"

"Different. Different," Murphy replied. "The first ones were manipulated. The paint just moved around, so they work two different types together."

"Okay, yeah, but it was all pretty much abstract, right?" Glover asked.

"Interpret what you think. I say you draw your own conclusions."

Glover pointed out that a lot of the stuff was abstract, but he had seen Murphy's artwork done in jail that involved very fine line drawings.

Murphy said he'd been drawing his whole life, although there were gaps, years when he created no artwork at all. There was a gap during both of his marriages, he said, apparently forgetting about the "Boneyard Gallery" that he created when married to Paula. He maintained to the cops that he needed to be *single* to be an artist. He didn't know why that was.

Glover said he knew of both wives, Elaine and Paula, but wondered if Murphy had cohabitated with any other women without being married. Had he ever shacked up?

Murphy said there was one he almost married. He tried to think of her name and either couldn't recall or decided not to say her name aloud, so he moved on to another woman.

"No, I lived with Jane Wingate." He started to tell the cops about her, when Glover interrupted his story to ask if Murphy was right-handed. He was, and he used right-handed shears to cut hair. He could use a comb in both hands, however. "I'm always switching," he said.

Murphy's hairstyling training was not limited to just the course he took at the barber school at Sunstate Academy, but also many weekend seminars. More than a hundred seminars. The seminars were routine when he worked at Regis. They did education classes once a month, so everyone was up on the latest stuff. After a while Murphy taught as many seminars as he attended. He didn't really need the classes anymore, but he went because he wanted to. He enjoyed them. You can't kid a kidder. Murphy knew that many of the seminars were thinly disguised infomercials. The pitch "usually boiled down to a new product you needed to get."

There was also a course regarding AIDS and cutting hair that Murphy had to attend once a year.

Then the lightbulb went on over Murphy's head.

"Mary Border! That's the name of the other girl.

I was engaged to her when I was twenty-two or so."
She was so gorgeous. They'd stand on their balcony
that overlooked the water.

Glover snapped the prisoner out of it with a
question about religion.

Murphy said he hated the word "religion." He
hated talking about it. He preferred the term
"spiritual." To him it was just a quiet thing—no
conversation necessary.

"I can sense people really well," Murphy boasted.
"I know where their spirit lies. I don't talk to people
unless they connect. . . ."

"Where do you see me?"

"You're not here on my level."

"I'm very open-minded."

"Uh-huh. I don't know of anybody who has the
same beliefs as me, to tell you the truth. I don't
know a single person with my exact beliefs, and I've
talked to hundreds of them."

Detective Grant told Murphy that he used to
study religion, and the spiritual part that Murphy
was saying reminded him of Myrtle Fillmore and
the Unity Christian Church.

"I don't pay attention to Myrtle Fillmore. I don't
worry about it. I don't worry about Main Street religions. I don't worry about any of it. It's my own
thing."

Murphy said when he met people—in a bookstore, on the street, or in a gas station—he only
talked to them for five minutes or so. No long

conversations. He didn't believe in them. He very seldom talked to anyone for more than an hour.

Murphy admitted that he met his first wife in church, but he didn't go to church anymore. He didn't believe in any of the "affiliated religions."

Glover asked if his spirituality had anything to do with the Bible. Murphy said part of it, but part of it also had to do with all books. Glover noted that a lot of artwork was associated with various religions. The detective wondered if Murphy had ever studied that type of art. Murphy said sure, he'd studied all art. His favorite religious artist was Michelangelo.

Glover got around to geography. How familiar was Murphy with Sarasota? Had he spent any time there, as a kid or as an adult?

Murphy said not really. He didn't remember ever going to Sarasota before he was old enough to drive. After that, maybe just once.

The detective decided to introduce an element from the crime scene and see if Murphy bit. "There was an artist who had a gallery down on the South Trail in Sarasota and his last name was Stahl."

"I don't know him," Murphy said crisply.

Glover continued, "He painted the Stations of the Cross and they were on display in Sarasota during the 1960s, when they were stolen."

"Too young for that," Murphy said, thinking perhaps he was being accused.

"No, no, we're all too young for that," Glover said, smiling.

"Okay, I just wanted to make sure," Murphy replied. He reiterated that he'd never heard of Stahl and knew nothing of the stolen paintings.

Grant interjected that he remembered the stolen paintings being the subject of a report on *60 Minutes*. Murphy said he might have seen the paintings somewhere, but he was totally unaware of that artist's name.

Murphy admitted to being in Sarasota within the last year and said that he left because it "was time to go." The detectives wondered what he meant by that.

The prisoner said he'd always been that way. His mind would tell him it was time to go and he would up and leave.

Glover said, "You left shortly after the Manatee Sheriff's Department came and talked to you about the [inappropriate touching] incident at Great Clips. Is that what drove you to leave Sarasota?"

Murphy said no, he had other reasons.

"Okay, what were those other reasons?"

"I'm not telling you."

"Okay, that's fine."

"Does that buy me a cup of coffee?" Murphy asked with a laugh. They all laughed and someone brought Murphy a cup of coffee. Murphy said he loved caffeine. They could keep the coffee coming if they wanted.

Glover switched subjects: "A detective talked to Paula. She said at one point when you were living in Tallahassee, she went over and cleaned out your apartment." When Murphy had nothing to say about that, Glover noted that Paula had informed the detective that Murphy was a collector. He was always collecting different things: magazines, coat hangers, for example.

"What are some of the things you've collected?" Glover asked.

"Cameras. I own a lot of cameras. Over one hundred. All antique. I had a fascination with military photography and antique cameras. I never bought a new camera. They were all old."

"What else?"

"Antiques of all sorts. Old books. Bottles I found when scuba diving. Stuff like that."

"I heard somewhere that you collected forks," Glover said.

"Yeah, various silver forks and what have you. I had unique forks."

"Where did you find that stuff?"

"Goodwill, Salvation Army, yard sales. Pay fifteen cents or so apiece." No particular design. Just what caught his fancy. At one point he had thirty forks, and he kept them in a special tray in a drawer.

"I heard you collected keys."

"Not true. I might have had keys, but I didn't collect them. If I had a key, it was because it opened a door."

Murphy said when he was through with a collection, he would just throw it away and move on to something else. Grant found that amazing, but Murphy pointed out that he got rid of collections because he moved so frequently. Transients don't want to lug stuff around.

"I'm not a huge keepsake person," he said. "I don't have anything that I've had throughout my life."

Grant wondered if he ever gave stuff to his brother, Dean, to keep for him. Family photos, photos from when he was a kid, or anything. Murphy said no, Dean had his own stuff. "I have no storage facility of any sort. I have no home. I don't have a place to put anything."

Murphy didn't want the police to know about things he might have stashed and where. Better to tell them he never stashed anything. Glover caught on.

Glover asked, "What did you do with your barber equipment?"

"That's one thing I did stash. I'm not going to tell you where."

"We could retrieve it for you," Glover offered hopefully.

No dice. "I don't intend on barbering anymore," Murphy said. "I hate it with a passion."

"I imagine at the state jail you're going to have to give a lot of haircuts! What? Thirty or forty people a day."

"That's no big deal. At the state jail you get mostly black, you know, and I have to cut their hair. Some Hispanic panic. Maybe ten percent white."

His complaint was not racist, he claimed, but a matter of fashion. Darker-skinned prisoners wanted their hair cut in a specific way, with very precise edging, and he didn't know how to do that.

Plus, the customers were not very nice. "Cut my hair and I'll kill you." Murphy heard that a lot. Usually, prisoners were getting their hair cut on a voluntary basis. However, every once in a while, you got a guy who'd been ordered by a guard to get a haircut, and they were the dangerous ones.

Glover asked if Murphy was in a cell alone. He said he was. Did he have a TV? There was one downstairs, not a big one, but they could see it from their cells, and the guards kept the volume up so they could hear it. Reading material? Some books. Pencils? No.

Glover said that detectives had talked to Murphy's first wife. She said she wasn't upset when they split up, but Paula had more to say. She told the story about his threats, how he requested to watch her having sex with another man, and how she did that for him.

Glover said that detectives had talked to his brother, Dean, and he was *not* upset that Brutus was in jail.

Murphy said he suspected as much. Dean had hung up on him the last time they spoke.

Glover taunted the prisoner: "Dean also said you are a lousy barber, and that Mr. Solomon only purchased your artwork because he felt sorry for you."

"*Pity* money," Grant interjected.

Glover added, "He said the artwork just wasn't—"

"Just didn't turn him on," Murphy finished the thought.

"He said it wasn't marketable pretty much anywhere. You flunked out of the navy."

"The second time. . . ."

"You flunked out of the SEALs first day."

"Not first day. Three weeks into it. Three weeks and change. They might have written first day. They want you to look humiliated on the paperwork."

Glover said, "We pulled all the reports from the Hillsborough County Sheriff's Department. We pulled the report to your mother's death. There was a lot of suspicion surrounding your mother's death at the time."

"All unfounded and stupid," Murphy said with disgust. "Every bit of it."

"A lot of the suspicions were aroused by the actions you took at the time."

Murphy said that those suspicions belonged mostly to Dean. He didn't know why. Dean also thought there was a life insurance policy he didn't know about. Ridiculous.

"Paula says you told her that your mother fell off a ladder," Glover said.

"I did not tell her that. That's stupid."

"There was no ladder in the kitchen when your mother fell?"

"I didn't see a ladder. I don't know what resulted in her falling in her home."

Glover asked, "Where were you at the time of your mother's death?"

"Over in, um, Ruskin. I didn't have anything to do with her death, and that's the God's honest truth. I swear on my mother's grave. I loved my mom more than anybody in this world. I didn't bother her. I did all I could to help her during the last year I was with her. She was good to me. She loved me when she died, very much. My brother might find that hard to believe, but it's a fact." Murphy said his brother only suspected him of killing their mother when Dean was drinking, which he did more than usual during the stressful days after his mother's passing. Dean, Murphy claimed, once told them that if he really thought Brutus had murdered their mother, he would have killed himself. Dean's period of suspicion was brief.

Murphy admitted that he didn't spend a lot of time looking at the future, and he hadn't for years. That was because his dad died at age forty-three, so Murphy figured he would die at forty-three, too. That was a long year—2000—when he was forty-three. He still figured that every day he lived past forty-three was a bonus.

Glover said Murphy had lived a life that one might think was full of regrets. Murphy agreed that was true. If he had to do it all over again, he'd change just about everything—all except having kids. That was a good part.

Maybe he would choose not to live his life over again at all. Maybe he would just "cancel it out," so that he'd never have been born into this life.

Glover said they'd spoken to Dave Gallant, who said he was a religious mentor to Murphy. Gallant said it was he who had taught Murphy that people were on Earth to mine gold for aliens. Murphy acknowledged that this was true.

"He showed me some knowledge," Murphy allowed.

"He said he was your mentor."

Murphy didn't like that: "Everybody's my mentor. He was one of frickin' thousands."

"You said you had a DNA connection with God, that you have followers," Glover said, adding, *"You got no followers!"*

"In your opinion. The thing is, I connect with my people immediately. . . ."

"Connect with them now and have them meet me in the lobby," Glover said.

"That's not going to happen."

"Of course not, because they don't exist. Even your family isn't behind you. If you have followers, they would know you were in trouble and they would rally—"

"I told them not to."

Glover decided to continue his efforts to make Murphy face facts. He was a sex criminal with an *inadequate* personality. Paula had said so—and she wasn't alone. Both the Regis in Tampa, where Murphy had worked, and the Great Clips, where he briefly held his last job, were being sued because Murphy—word was—

couldn't comb a woman's hair without touching her breasts.

"We talked to a girl at the Great Clips on Bee Ridge Road and she said you worked there for three point eighty-three hours. Three point eighty-three hours! A nineteen-year-old woman customer said she had to repeatedly shift her position in the chair because you were trying to rub your penis up against her as she sat there. You never went back there. You never bothered to pick up your check, so you are very complicated."

"Extremely," Murphy concurred.

"People might say you have an impulse-control problem," Grant said.

"I'm very impulsive," Murphy agreed. He didn't care what people thought. "It's just my thing," he added.

"If you don't care, then why don't you tell us the truth?"

"I like to play a little game with your head. People fuck with my head. I fuck with their head. Every time."

"You say you don't care about yourself, but you *love* yourself. That's why there are things about your time in Sarasota that you don't want to tell us."

"If my intuition tells me not to tell you things, I won't tell you."

"Tell us about Sarasota. . . ."

"I refuse to tell you because I'm fuckin' with your head, that's why."

"At some point, are you going to tell us the truth?"

"Probably not. I'd rather leave you hanging. You can think I'm the worst person on the planet. When I leave this planet dead as a doornail, you can say, 'That crazy, stupid motherfucker never told me whatever I wanted to know.'"

"It's not important to me that you tell, it's—"

"I don't give a damn about anyone's family, none of that shit."

"Obviously. If you cared about their family, you wouldn't have hacked up their mother."

Mother. That got Murphy's attention: "What are you talking about? Whose mother are you talking about here?"

"The family of Joyce."

"Who are you talking about? Joyce. Joyce who?"

"Wishart."

"Oh, oh. That one. That Joyce. I don't know anything about her. Never met that woman in my life, as far as I know."

"You cut her," Glover said.

"You cut her," Grant echoed.

"I might have cut her hair" was Murphy's perfect reply. "I don't know who she was."

Glover said, "I don't know if you cut her hair or not, but you cut her. How is Elton Brutus Murphy going to be portrayed?"

"It doesn't matter. They could paint me as a beast with ten horns and ten dragon heads, and it would not matter."

"Well, do you have ten horns and ten dragon heads?"

"I might have. It was my destiny, predestined thousands of years ago."

Grant said, "Everything you've done, you've pretty much messed up. . . ."

"Always," Murphy concurred.

"The only thing you managed to do with any degree of success was kill this woman, and that's the one thing you won't talk about."

"Umm-hmm," Murphy said. "It's none of your business. It is only the business of those who are blessed."

"Are you among the blessed?"

"Yes. That is why I have the authority to say what I say."

"And that's why you can decide who lives and dies?"

"If need be."

"A blessing is supposed to be something good. This blessing you've acquired is kind of like the plague."

"Yeah, a plague and a curse. A blessed curse."

"You said you had the power to cause people to have a heart attack. When you were cutting hair in jail and afraid of getting beat up, why didn't you just give those guys a heart attack?"

"Once, in a Tallahassee jail, one person pissed me off and he died in his cell that night."

"Was that your will?" Grant asked.

"I didn't wish it, but it happened. Pretty much

every person I ever cursed in my mind, things happened to. If I want, I can take your soul."

"Is that what you did to Joyce?" Glover asked.

"Joyce who? Who are we talking about?"

"You are bad with names?" Grant asked.

"What's your choice, and Joyce *rejoicing* about? Are we rejoicing today as somebody's heaven?"

"Why don't you want to talk about that?"

"This is my way of talking. Jesus talked in riddles."

"Are you equating yourself with Jesus?"

"Well, I'm just using him as an example."

Murphy said he believed in chaos circles, like Ping-Pong balls bouncing around. One second here, the next there. Pattern-free. Purely random. No way of knowing where it would be next. Mortals could guess all they wanted, but they could never be right.

Glover noted, "Charles Manson used to talk a lot about chaos."

"Oh, how ironic," Murphy said.

Glover pointed out that Murphy had had his first marriage annulled by the Catholic Church, and Murphy said that was because Mary Border was a Catholic. The annulment was so he could marry her.

That pissed him off. The idea of other men deciding whether or not he could marry a Catholic girl. He got so fed up with everything Catholic that he ended up not marrying the girl at all, in the long run.

Murphy explained that Catholics and Baptists

weren't in God's family. To be in God's family, you
have to be born into it, to have the correct DNA.
And if you had it, you had it. It didn't matter what
you did in life—you still received your reward.

Just another reason why Murphy didn't have to
follow rules, why Murphy could hurt people without conscience.

Glover became impatient with the rhetoric. He
asked when Murphy was going to get around to
telling the whole story. Murphy said that wasn't
going to happen. There were just going to be more
"riddles and games."

After more sparring regarding Murphy's inco-
herent philosophy, Grant said it reminded him of
reincarnation mumbo jumbo.

"Well, that is part of the program," Murphy said.
"I've lived many lives."

Glover asked if he'd been successful in any of his
lives.

"Oh yeah. I killed Julius Caesar," Murphy
boasted. He didn't remember why, but he did it.

"That's why you like the Brutus thing," Grant
said.

"That's why I was given that name," Murphy
replied.

Grant added, "And that's why you like knives."

"I use steak knives to cut steak," Murphy responded.

"You like collecting stuff. What are you collecting
in jail?"

"You would be surprised. It might be souls."

"You got some of them before you came here."

"I might be harnessing yours as I speak."

Glover asked, "Where do you want to see this go?"

"I don't give a damn. I'm going to wind up dead."

"Do you think you are going to die while in prison?"

"Certainly a possibility. It's a big possibility."

"Elton, what would it take to be truthful about the Joyce Wishart case?"

"Joyce who? Who in the hell is Joyce Wishart? Brutus doesn't know who Joyce Wishart is."

"Sure, he does. Brutus is the knife guy."

"He doesn't give a damn about Joyce Wishart—just as much as I don't give a damn about Joyce Wishart."

"You want more coffee, Elton? Anything else we can get you?"

"A flight to Hawaii?" the prisoner joked.

Glover returned to the DNA. He told Murphy he had an FDLE report. The State of Florida's Convicted Offender DNA Database indicated a match between Murphy's DNA and that found at a murder scene in Sarasota.

Glover said, "That match would indicate that Elton Murphy killed a defenseless sixty-one-year-old woman. That's the Elton Murphy that I'm seeing here. You pick on people smaller than you."

"The weak," Grant added.

"And now you tell us that due to your spiritualism, none of this is going to be explained until sometime down the road. Truth is, you attack the weak and meek, and you can't even bring yourself to talk about it. It's ridiculous."

"I know," Murphy said with a laugh. "It's awful, isn't it?"

The detectives made it clear they found nothing funny. At least Murphy had stopped claiming he'd been framed and that his DNA was planted.

Glover said, "Elton, Elton, what would be your reasoning for rubbing your penis up against a woman while you're supposed to be cutting her hair?"

Murphy was silent.

Glover continued his questioning. "What would be your reasoning for killing a sixty-one-year-old woman in an art gallery?"

"I haven't a clue."

"What would be your reason for removing a body part from that woman?"

"I don't know."

"You don't have the balls to talk about it."

"Oh, I have a couple of them."

Grant said, "He can't talk about it. He's too scared to talk about it."

"I'm not afraid," Murphy said.

"You are double-talking."

"It triggers a fatality in the future," the prisoner said. "You're going to have nightmares because of me. Just you wait." Murphy again laughed.

Grant said, "You can't even think of a decent explanation why your DNA is at the crime scene. You can't handle the memory of what you've done."

"Yes, I can. Sure, I can. I laugh about it."

"You laugh about what you did?"

"I laugh at what you say I did."

"Face reality," Glover said. "The reality is that your DNA is in that gallery."

"Match up another hundred DNA from somewhere while you're at it. Connect me to another three hundred murders. I don't care."

Grant said, "You don't have enough balls to commit three hundred murders, but nice try."

Glover added, "You know how this is going to play out in a courtroom?"

"I don't give a damn. I already told you, I don't give a damn."

Grant said, "I thought you would stand behind your work, but you can't even speak about it. You probably sleep in a fetal position."

"I sleep very well," Murphy said.

"Tell us what happened on January sixteenth."

"I don't even remember January sixteenth."

"Sure you do," Glover said. "You killed Joyce Wishart."

"Joyce who?" Murphy said.

"You're scared," Grant said. "You can't bring yourself to say it. You're scared of a sixty-one-year-old dead woman. Good God, man, get ahold of yourself."

"I'm not afraid of Joyce Wishart or any other Wishart."

"So, why don't you tell us what happened that night?" Glover asked.

"I refuse to tell you anything that I don't want to tell you."

"Tell me what it was like after she was dead, with her lying there in the gallery?" Glover prodded. "The lights are on. It's dark outside. You have her back there in that little alcove. You start doing what you did. Didn't you worry about somebody walking by and seeing you?"

"I don't know what you are talking about, first of all. What art gallery?"

"You know damn well. You were in the same place your blood and skin were," Glover said.

"You're scared," Grant added. "You want someone to come in and hold your hand? You need a pillow? What do you need?"

"I need you to bring me some beautiful chick. I'll hold her hand," Murphy said. "It's a damn shame somebody killed that woman. I don't give a shit about Joyce whoever. All I'm saying is whoever killed her, she deserved it." He laughed.

Glover asked why she deserved to be killed. Murphy said he didn't know. Glover asked who told him to kill her. Grant said Murphy needed to be strong enough to face the things he'd done.

"I hear ya," Murphy said.

"I got your DNA," Grant stated.

Murphy shot back, "Why you asking me questions, then? You got DNA. Conversation over. Pack your bags and go back home. You said I could end this conversation whenever I want. I'm ready to go back to my facility."

* * *

That ended that interview. Murphy, however, was
not taken to his old facility, but rather he was taken
to a different jail in Houston. He was locked into
a one-man confinement cell—a cold room with a
concrete bed. After a few hours he was given a
mattress and a blanket. He was there for a week.

The SPD wasn't through with Murphy, however.
Not by a long shot. They were just resting, getting
in a week's worth of investigation—coworkers,
Shade Avenue tenants—before starting in again.

Murphy was again pulled out of his cell so he
could be questioned by detectives. Same interrogation room. Detective Grant was back, but this time
with Detective Opitz rather than Glover.

Grant apologized for the redundancy before informing Murphy, yet again, of his Miranda rights.
Grant wanted to fill out the bio and asked Murphy
about his life. Murphy discussed growing up in
Hardee County; how his dad had died when Brutus
was twenty or twenty-one; that he grew up in the
country woods on account of his daddy having an
"acreage" with an orange grove and ten acres of
swampland converted into pastureland. His childhood had been one of hard work. No play. The
second he got off the bus, he went to work in the
fields. His mom and dad ran a nursery business,
growing shrubs and palm trees. Daddy drank a bit,
but overall a solid, normal, happy childhood,
Murphy said.

"What was the best part of your childhood?" Grant asked.

"Being exposed to the country, away from the city."

"I've seen your school records. You were a pretty good student."

"Except for math," Murphy said, and everyone shared a laugh.

"And what was the worst part of your childhood?"

Dad drank; Mom and Dad fought; they divorced. Dad, who had been on the wagon and was doing good, started drinking again. A year after that, he was dead.

Murphy told the detectives about scuba school and going into the navy for the first time to be a photographer. Served five years, was out for a while, re-upped to become a SEAL. The second time he only served a year and a half. He skipped the messiness of the AWOL and court-martial.

"They, uh, let me out early," Murphy said.

His first marriage took place during his first stint in the service. They lived in Bermuda and then split up. After they broke up, she once called collect with a new name. He didn't accept the charges. Once, after he was out of the navy the first time, she called or wrote a letter. He couldn't recall which. Other than that, there had been no contact since the breakup.

Murphy burned through this part of his bio: cut hair at Gateway Mall, met Paula, became a haircutting team, owned his own barbershop, moved to a worse location, went to work for Regis for seven years, had kids, broke up with Paula. . . .

Grant asked why his marriage to Paula broke up. Murphy explained that it was his fault. He spent too much time "doing stuff." They got into a habit of not listening to each other.

Grant wondered whose idea it was to go their separate ways, and Murphy admitted it was hers. But he blamed the metal sculptures, his obsession, for making him a bad husband. Paula was pissed off because he was so busy tinkering that he couldn't go with her and the kids to the beach, or talk to her and her girlfriend.

Did he make any money on his sculptures? Murphy bragged that he had a little display area built in his hair salon and sold a few small pieces. Said he sold them for $300 apiece, but Grant made it clear that he didn't believe him. Murphy then admitted that he gave most of them away. "You like it? It's yours," he would say.

He had a big-time case of the blues when he and Paula broke up. He moved away, an attempt to remove himself physically from the painful memories. As if . . .

Grant asked, "How close did you and Paula stay in touch after that?"

"Well, we really didn't have a relationship after that," Murphy replied. When he came to see the kids, it was just "hi and bye" with Paula.

"How often did you visit your children?"

"Not that often. Three, four times a year."

"Did you guys have a child-support agreement?"

"I paid her more than she asked for. I went way overboard. It was supposed to be six-fifty a month, but I paid seven hundred fifty dollars for four years. I always made sure the kids got a lot of extra money."

He paid as long as he could. After he fled Tallahassee, he lived in Brandon for five years. He stayed there until 2001. His job at Regis was very stressful, a demanding job. He was their "master stylist" and their "highest moneymaker."

He cut the hair of the biggest clientele, and a lot was expected of him. So he went back to Tallahassee and worked at the Seminole Barber Shop, where work was easier. He wasn't in Tallahassee for long before he got arrested for some "little stuff" he did. Trespassing. He was scrounging one day for metal to supply his welding habit. He was near Florida State University and saw some metal scrap he liked. He picked that up and was in the process of checking the Dumpster for anything else interesting when the cops showed up and arrested him for being on some company's property.

There had been another trespassing arrest, something about being on a roof, Grant noted. Murphy told the story. He was just trying to help the guy clean his roof. Cops were called.

Grant thought that was pretty interesting and wanted to hear about some of the other good deeds Murphy might have done while in his Good Samaritan phase.

"I'd rake a lawn, pick up garbage, stuff like that."

"Was there an event in your life that led to you becoming a Good Samaritan?"

Murphy said no, it was just "spiritual awakening." It was also around that time, he volunteered, that he'd spent about four months in jail on trespassing and burglary charges.

Grant asked what he had burgled. The actual items had slipped Murphy's mind, but it was probably just some garbage or "some metal shit." Supplies for his art.

Grant asked if, maybe, Murphy had ever gone through somebody's *house* in search of supplies for his art. Murphy agreed that could've happened.

Murphy admitted that his art was suffering during those days. Not only did he lack supplies, but equipment as well. He had gotten rid of his welding equipment. He was collecting equipment and supplies for his art. That might have been why he was going through a house.

"You did four months in Tallahassee?"

"Uh-huh."

"Probation or anything?"

"One-year administrative probation. I had to let them know when I moved. I also had to go to counseling," Murphy said.

"Mental-health counseling?"

"Yeah." Murphy found the counseling unfulfilling. So much so, that in retrospect he wished he had served an extra couple of months in jail and skipped the counseling. First he went down south; then he started counseling. He liked the guy— White, Waite, he forgot his name. But nothing ever happened. His counselor never made a diagnosis; he never said Murphy was okay.

(Grant came to learn that when Murphy lived in Tallahassee, he'd received mental-health treatment from a provider known as Personal Growth and Behavioral Health, Inc. His counselor was Dorothy Hahn. Later, while on probation, Murphy received mental-health counseling from Michael White.)

"Did they try to put you on meds?" Detective Opitz interjected.

"No," Murphy said.

At the time he was living in a "a place near the water, Port of Tampa. Stayed there for a few months." It was a little house, to begin with, and had been walled up into a duplex. He had a little red car, a Geo Metro, and still worked sometimes at Regis, cutting hair.

After that, he moved in with Dave Gallant, a guy he'd met in a bookstore, Barnes & Noble, Brandon Town Center. They had a common interest in books and started talking.

"He told me his story and about his mental—not mental, spiritual—stuff that he had an interest in, and he said he had all of these books I should see. He invited me."

The detective noted the Freudian slip.

The bookstore guy told Murphy he had people

in and out of his house all the time, renting space, cheaper than what he was paying, so Murphy moved in with him.

Murphy was still being the Good Samaritan. A large reason he moved was because he could tell this guy needed the rent money. Normally, Murphy wouldn't have gone for such an arrangement.

"I don't do well living with guys. I'd rather it be a woman, you know?" was how he put it. "I might be in jail with 'em, but I don't like living with 'em."

Grant asked if the man he was living with was into the alien thing.

"Yeah," Murphy replied, "which I thought was interesting, but it's not something I'm following, certainly."

He only stayed for a month or so. Grant asked if anything "happened, or kind of felt uncomfortable." Murphy said no. He just "preferred women."

Grant asked if he preferred living with a woman to living alone. Murphy said he did. He didn't mind living alone, but he really enjoyed being married— both times.

He admitted to regrets regarding his first wife. He sent her home to her mom so he could screw around. Looking back, he wished he'd been married longer to her.

After living with Gallant, Murphy moved down to Inglewood Drive, in the town of Gibsonton, where he lived for three months.

"It was a shit hole little trailer I found for rent in the newspaper." Rent: $100 a week. There were some positives: "It was peaceful, and right on a little creek. You could see the creek right outside your window."

The landlord lived next door. Murphy worked just a little bit, just enough to get by. Cutting hair was "getting old." So it was a stressful time. He was a middle-aged man thinking about changing careers.

Murphy decided he couldn't afford the car anymore, so he gave it back to Dean. He used it for the last time to see his kids and visit his brother. When the visit was over, Dean and Alane drove him back home. Dean had told police that they drove Brutus back on a Thursday. Murphy said that sounded about right—although he was just guessing. "I don't know what day it is right now," Murphy quipped.

For the first two months of 2004, Murphy lived in an apartment on Shade Avenue in Sarasota. He answered an ad in the paper. It was okay, but Murphy didn't make any friends there. He didn't have a chance because of the rate of turnover, in and out, in and out, like a revolving door. The owner was a *strong* woman. The super was an old Spanish guy. The landlady didn't trust the super, he remembered that. There was drama over getting Murphy's toilet fixed.

Police were familiar with the Shade Avenue address. Cops were called to that location many times. There had been many calls even during the time

Murphy was living there, but Murphy's name hadn't come up in any of them.

"Remember a guy named Albert Sanchez?" Grant asked, referring to the Shade Avenue superintendent who was arrested for stealing rent money.

"I remember an Albert."

"Guy says you cooked dinner for him," Grant said. The detective sounded nonchalant, but he was actually eager to discuss the meat that Murphy had cooked during January 2004.

"Well, I'd be cooking and I'd give him some. I don't cook good."

"He said you were a good cook."

"He'd smell it and say, 'Umm-umm, something smells good!'" Murphy laughed. "I only had a hot plate, but once I boiled pork."

"Boiled pork?"

"Yeah."

If Murphy was aware of the reason for the food questions, he didn't let on—and Grant moved off the subject.

"He said that you gave him a gift," Grant said.

"A knife. I gave him a knife," Murphy said, looking pleased that he'd remembered.

"That's an unusual gift," Grant commented.

"Yeah, well, there's nothing wrong with it," Murphy said, sounding defensive.

Detective Opitz chimed in. "What kind of a knife was it, Elton?"

"It had a curved edge on it, and I don't know what you would call it. . . ."

"Do you remember when you gave Albert the knife?" Grant asked.

"Sometime in January. Third, fourth week in January."

"Why a knife?"

"Oh, I was just cleaning house. I started getting rid of everything I knew."

"Did you get rid of the knife before or after getting rid of the car?"

"After."

Opitz asked, "Where were you planning on moving to?"

"I was going to go to California eventually," Murphy replied. "Actually, I had Oregon in mind, but I was going to spend some time in California first."

He had a license to cut hair in Oregon. He flew out west and got it sometime in the late 1990s, when he was living with Jane.

"We talked to her," Grant acknowledged. "She said she called you once and you said that you'd quit Regis and had become a day trader."

"Yeah, I did that for a while."

They took a break. Murphy was allowed to use the restroom. His right ankle cuff was loosened after he complained it had been digging into his anklebone since he was transported.

Opitz returned the questioning to when Murphy got rid of the red car. What day had he arrived?

Murphy didn't remember what day exactly, but it wasn't a Monday because that was the only day Dean's restaurant was closed. The place had been open for business when he got there.

What were Dean and his wife doing when Murphy arrived with the red car?

"Dean was in the restaurant when I got there," Murphy recalled. After a brief visit they left. He didn't even stay a day. He asked Dean right off to drive him back; soon thereafter he did.

At the time of Murphy's Houston arrest, he had been in possession of prescription bottles with a Bradenton man's name on them. Grant asked if Murphy knew that guy, and the prisoner shook his head no. He didn't know how he came into possession of those bottles. Prescriptions were for a Craig Hoffman. Murphy didn't know the guy. After a moment he decided that he did remember picking up those bottles. He'd found them by the side of the road when riding his bicycle.

"What kind of prescription was it?" Opitz asked.

"There was Valium and Tylenol 3."

Grant said Murphy must have realized the seriousness of the crime for which he was being interrogated. He didn't have to worry about talking about prescription bottles.

"Did you take any of the pills?" Grant asked.

"Yeah, well, I had never tried Valium in my life, and I wanted to try them for the heck of it. And, to be honest, I tried them and they didn't make me feel good, so I just held on to them. I thought somebody else might want them, or I might try them again someday when I was stressed out."

"When did you find the bottles?"

"February." Not long before he was arrested in Houston, and that was February 25. He had decided to leave Florida only a few days before that.

"It was just time to go, man," Murphy explained. "I was gearing up for getting rid of all my stuff."

Opitz asked, "What'd you do with all of your artwork and stuff?"

"I just kept giving it away. I threw a bunch of it away." A lot of it ended up at a flea market in Bradenton, but there were two flea markets: the Wagon Wheel and the Big Top—and he didn't remember which one.

"What do you remember?"

"It was the one with the red barn. I gave it to a woman named Ann something. Ann Marie, maybe." He was just there and she was smiling at him, and he thought this looked like a good home for his stuff.

Grant asked what sort of stuff she sold. Murphy said she sold freaky stuff. Gothic. He told her his name was Brutus, no last name, and the stuff was hers. She'd probably never see him again and that was cool because he didn't want any money.

Grant produced Murphy's business card and asked him about it. Murphy said he'd had them printed himself—not many, fifty maybe—just to give out to people who might be interested in his artwork. He didn't hand out many and ended up throwing most of them away.

Still, Grant noted, Murphy was making an effort to sell his art, which meant he was going to places where selling art was possible, such as flea markets and galleries.

Murphy said he didn't go to any galleries—just flea markets. And he didn't sell any art—just gave it away. To Ann Marie, and to some other chick at the flea market near Gibsonton and Ruskin. That was the place where he handed out about twenty business cards and threw the rest on the floor.

Grant asked if he remembered any of the people to whom he gave a card. Murphy said no, except he gave a few to his coworkers at Regis.

He added, "I never called on a single art gallery to try to sell my work." Then he took it back and said he did go into one gallery, in a mall on Route 41, next to the food court. He never did show his stuff to the lady in there, just told her he was leaving town and looking to get rid of some stuff. She wasn't interested. She only wanted local artists. This was Sarasota and he said he was from Bradenton.

Grant asked about Murphy's bicycle. What became of it?

Murphy said it was falling apart, the chain kept jumping, so he threw it in a Dumpster.

"How did you get to Houston?"

"Hitchhiked."

"But—"

"I'm not going to elaborate, but I did indeed

hitchhike." All right, he was at one point in a bus station, where he stole a bag and a bus ticket. "I went to a lot of places," Murphy added.

Grant thanked Murphy for being so honest. Grant said Murphy struck him as a "pretty honest guy," a guy who told the truth until he got to something that might hurt him and then he "kind of backed off."

Murphy nodded his agreement. He admitted that he didn't like to talk about the thefts he'd committed, and there were "more than one of them." When he was on the road, he tended to swipe things along the way. He stole a backpack at a bus station and then filled it with other stuff he stole.

Grant summed it up for Murphy. At that point Murphy's game plan was to go to Oregon and cut hair. Murphy said yes. Grant wanted to know, if that was the plan, why did he stash his haircutting tools? Murphy said they were stashed so that he would have access to them when he got to Oregon.

Grant became blunt: "If your barber equipment didn't have anything to do with our killing, why is it a big secret where it's stashed?"

Murphy said, "The stash contains stolen items."

Grant said he didn't care about the stolen items. In the overall scheme of things, the stolen items were small. He was interested in the stash because barber instruments were *sharp*.

The detective had talked to people who knew Murphy and they said those instruments were special to him. "We don't throw away things that are special to us," Grant added.

"Well, I did," Murphy said, raising his right hand as if taking an oath. The police knew he was lying. He'd already admitted once to stashing the tools, now he was reverting to his earlier lie that he had dumped all of his belongings.

"Would you dump them if they had evidence on them?"

"Not at all," Murphy said, shaking his head with sincerity.

"Then you wouldn't mind telling us where you dumped them."

"I dumped them, piece by piece, a little here, a little there, down the road. . . ."

"Where?"

"In the garbage at a bus terminal in Tallahassee, on Tennessee Street, to be honest with you."

"You went from Sarasota to Houston via Tallahassee?" Opitz asked.

"Yes."

"And why did you get rid of the stuff piecemeal?" Grant asked.

"I got tired of carrying. I was getting my load lighter and lighter as I went along."

Grant asked Murphy to itemize the things he got rid of. Murphy said all of his clippers, and maybe eight to ten pairs of scissors.

"Uh-huh. According to Dean, you had another item you're not mentioning."

Murphy said, "Straight razor."

"Yeah," Grant replied, with a raised eyebrow.

"It was just a little thing for giving shaves," Murphy explained. It would have made a lousy weapon because the blade was so thin and easily breakable.

Grant said, "You know there are some tough questions that I have to ask you."

"Ask away," Murphy said.

Grant shifted the subject away from the razor to Murphy's apparent need, in later years, to molest his clients as he cut their hair.

Murphy said he thought the touchy-feely behavior was part of the spiritual process he was going through. He'd touched many more than the ones he had gotten caught touching. "I've touched hundreds," Murphy bragged.

The sexual touching was done after placing the subject in a hypnotic trance. The touching itself was *so subtle* that the great majority of them never realized they were being touched. He was a "master hypnotist."

And that wasn't where his powers ended. He was able to amplify the hypnosis with his spiritual connection. People said that you couldn't hypnotize a person who didn't want to be hypnotized, but that wasn't true, according to Murphy. The spiritual connection allowed him to overrule that so-called rule. Unfortunately, his powers were just shy of being perfect. Once every 150 times or so, the person realized they were being touched.

"When you touch them, what do you do?"

"I feel up their titties. I even kissed some of them on the back of the neck."

He got to the point where he could hypnotize more than one person simultaneously. "I could put a whole room out," he bragged.

He could feel up titties right in front of people, but they wouldn't be able to see him do it. One woman, he recalled, didn't go under. She put up with the touching at first, like she was paralyzed, but then she ran out of the shop.

"I saw her crying, out in front of the shop," Murphy added.

"That was in Sarasota?"

"Brandon. I said to myself, 'Uh-oh, I got caught.'"

"When did you start with the touching?"

"Autumn of 2003."

He didn't just do it when he was cutting hair, either. He'd do it wherever. He'd feel up the lady in front of him on the grocery checkout line.

"Did you have specific and vivid memories of feeling up the clients?"

Murphy said he did. He was working in a shop at the time in a mall that had a Walmart.

Grant said he didn't like the word, but he thought this act fit in with a pattern of sexual "deviances" that Murphy enjoyed. The various deviances Murphy practiced were known as "paraphilia." It included sexual contact with people who were unaware, wife swapping, voyeurism.

"Was it your ultimate goal to be able to hypnotize

people to the point where you could secretly have sex with them?"

The question caused a short surge of energy in the prisoner. Murphy said yes. "That's my goal, my *dream.* I got to where I was very good at it. I'm not going to tell you how good."

In the long run it was his spiritual connection more than his hypnotism skills that allowed him to get away with what he did. It was a God-given thing. He liked to call it "the Power." He'd gotten to the point where he could "pretty much do anything" sexually.

"Kind of like being a pickpocket," Grant said—and Murphy liked the analogy.

Murphy admitted he was a voyeur; it was true. "I watched another guy fuck my wife and it turned me on," he said. "And I've watched other guys fuck their wives as well."

"What are your other interests?" Grant asked.

"I'm pretty straightlaced, but I like the gothic chicks—you know, the ones who look like vampires and stuff, dress all in black."

"Are you familiar with necrophilia?"

"Uh, no. I heard that name, though."

"It means someone that derives pleasure from sex with people that are dead. Ever have any thoughts or fantasies like that?"

"No."

"Because those gothic chicks, they're always, you know, kind of pale. Like they're dead."

"Those girls get a bad rap. I met one once—she was a devout Christian."

"Can't judge a book by its cover," Grant said. "Some people do like sex with the dead, like to have sex in a cemetery, in the back of a hearse. I'm not judging them. Whatever floats their boat."

Opitz added, "Some of them just have their sexual partner lay there still and pretend they're dead."

Murphy was silent, just taking it all in.

"What about bondage?" Grant asked.

Murphy responded quickly: "I'm not so much into that, and I'll tell you why. . . ."

His wife Paula had had a bondage experience before they met. She had gotten drunk with a guy and went home with him. He tied her up and said he was going to rape her.

"Maybe, I'm not sure, he told her he was going to kill her. She got away from the guy. I don't know if he passed out or what. Short time after that, this guy did rape and kill a girl, and Paula testified against him at the trial, put his ass away," Murphy said.

"You have any personal experience with bondage?"

"I only allowed one person to handcuff me, if you don't count cops," Murphy said. "It didn't do much for me."

"You ever use bondage on anyone else?"

"No. Well, one time, sort of."

He met this girl and she went into the bathroom. She came out with a little body outfit on and dangling handcuffs. She tried to handcuff him, but he turned the table on her and put them on her, just one of them on her leg. He wasn't sure that counted as bondage.

"I've never fantasized about handcuffs, if that's what you mean," he concluded.

"What kind of fantasies do you have?" Grant asked.

"Multiple partners. Wives. I love doing other people's wives."

It was two pleasures in one, Murphy explained. First of all, it was sex, but it was also the joy of *taking a sacred object,* something that is sacred to someone else. He was turned on both by other men's wives and by watching other men with his wife. "I'm no hypocrite," he added.

Grant wanted to know how Murphy went about recruiting a man to have sex with his wife so he could watch.

Murphy said the first few guys he asked said no. Then one day he was cutting this guy's hair and he asked if he'd like to come home and have a three-some. The guy said sure. Then he called Paula, told her he'd gotten a handsome guy to do it. The guy ended up turning Paula on; they had him over two, three times.

"When you say 'threesome,' does that mean that you participated as well?" Grant asked.

"Oh yeah, we doubled. I would do her some, and then he would do her some."

"From the way you talked before, I thought you just sat there and watched."

Murphy shook his head. Sometimes they would take turns having oral sex with her. Sometimes Paula would give Murphy oral sex, while the other guy was having vaginal intercourse with her.

Grant asked if Murphy had contact with the other guy during the threesome.

"Uh, yeah, but it was just random. I never actually, you know . . ."

He put a condom on one guy once, but that was earlier. Back when he was in his twenties, he had been the third with a married couple in their forties. They had had a picnic; then they went back to the couple's mobile home and got it on. That time the husband gave Murphy oral sex. But he didn't feel like a guy with bisexual tendencies. It was more just a means to the end, to the real fantasy, which was to have sex with the guy's wife.

"Do you ever have sexual fantasies about possessing someone totally?" Grant asked. "What would you consider the ultimate?"

"I guess the ultimate would be to have that individual anytime I wanted. I could do it to them again and again, whenever I wanted, and they wouldn't realize it."

"Did you ever get to that point?"

"I haven't. But I have engaged in sex with people when they didn't realize it."

"Did you ever have an occasion when you thought they were hypnotized and you were about to have sex with them, and all of a sudden they said no or something bad happened?" Opitz asked.

"There were times when the hypnotism wasn't working as well as I thought and I had to quickly go back to whatever else I was doing, drinking coffee or whatever."

Murphy decided he'd talked enough on the subject. He wasn't going to give them anything that might result in a rape charge. He explained that this was one of those times when he was "backing off."

At this juncture Grant switched subjects. "Let me take you back to January 16, 2004."

"Okay."

"Do you know where you were that day?"

"I'm not good with dates. I have thought about it, trying to determine my alibi, but nothing specific comes to mind. All I know is that I was following my routine. If I wasn't at work, I was riding my bicycle or taking a walk or eating."

"Where would you ride?"

"Around my neighborhood."

"We've showed your picture around, and people remember seeing you in downtown Sarasota—in places you claimed you hadn't been."

"If they could positively identify me, I might have been downtown," Murphy said with a laugh. Then: "Yeah, I've been downtown. Might've stopped for coffee—coffee shop and a bookstore, right there on the corner."

"You remember when that was?"

"January."

"The sixteenth?"

"Could've been. I don't know. I didn't peddle my artwork."

"Other than haircutting, you work anyplace else in Sarasota?"

"No."

"You tell your sister-in-law you were working for a lady in an art gallery?"

"Right," Murphy said, remembering.

"You said you were helping a lady who had a couple of grown kids, and she was going to help you sell some of your art, right?"

"Yeah, I made a big elaborate lie, said the lady had a bunch of artists working for her, and that I rented space there. . . ."

"She doesn't remember that part," Grant said.

Murphy tried to explain. He said he was telling a lot of lies at that time because he didn't want people to know he was planning major thefts and to leave Sarasota.

Grant said, "You're being inconsistent." Earlier, Murphy had said the reason he was leaving Sarasota was that he was all touchy-feely with the women whose hair he cut, and the sheriff's department had come over to confront him.

Murphy said they were both true. He'd already planned on leaving Sarasota before the lady detective came to visit. That just hurried up the process. He was already getting rid of his stuff in preparation for going mobile.

Grant asked Murphy why he bled so much.

There was blood on his backpack, on his fanny pack, blood all over. Murphy said he had a problem with sores that didn't heal.

"I have wounds that haven't healed in years. They start to itch, I scratch, and pretty soon I'm bleeding again," Murphy said. There was another reason for all of the blood, however. He cut himself while committing a burglary. It happened when he broke the window to get in.

Grant said he'd noticed the scab picking. It grew worse when Murphy was alone, but he could sort of control it when he knew someone was watching. Grant said it seemed like compulsive behavior to him, and Murphy agreed.

"I've been doing this for eight, ten years—picking that same spot."

"I believe you're hypnotizing yourself, because you're touching yourself all the time."

"Well, I don't know about that," Murphy said with a laugh.

Grant said Murphy also had a habit of sticking his hands down into his pants when no one was looking. Murphy said he picked that up in jail because it was cold, and it was a way to keep his hands warm.

"I don't have a hard-on when I do it," Murphy added. "It's just a little nervous habit I picked up."

"It's compulsive," Grant said.

"Yeah, sure," Murphy said, "like people who blink their eyes too much."

Grant shifted suddenly to the crux of the situation:

"In relation to our case, I was wondering if we've gotten to a point in time when we could handle the truth."

"I wasn't going to share this with everyone, because it has to do with my spiritual calling and it's going to turn a lot of people against me. But at the same time it may be time for me to start sharing. I've been forming my own religion, you know. I believe there is a god beyond the God in the Bible."

The cops were impatient with Murphy's evasive jibber-jabber.

"Okay," Grant said, "but getting back to our crime, in the gallery, you said you couldn't handle the truth of what happened there. You said you couldn't tell us everything about that incident."

"I don't recall referring to that gallery. If you took it that way, it's not how I meant it."

"Okay, because you know, we're curious about what happened. We know, because of the physical evidence, that it is true, that it happened. But cops are not always looking for what happened, but also *why* it happened, so we can make sense of the whole thing."

"I'm insisting adamantly today that I was never in that gallery and I never killed that woman. I'm sticking to that story and I'm insisting I'm not guilty." Murphy laughed and said, "I'm also insisting I'll walk away a free man for this."

"We could disagree on that," Grant said, not laughing. "There comes a point when denial is ridiculous. I have a pretty good idea what happened. I'm more interested in the why."

"I am not going to admit to this murder."

"You're doing what you have to do for your protection. But if it gets to the point where denial is ridiculous, I'd appreciate you discussing with me the why."

"I can pretty much promise you that I never will." Murphy laughed again.

Opitz reentered the conversation. He said that Murphy had written a letter to his brother. The letter contained some interesting things. "You said, 'I create life in the missions. I am thankful everything I do will be justified.' What were you talking about there?"

Murphy said he was talking about the hypnosis and touching and things like that.

Grant said, "Every religion at some point has something to do with sacrifice. What happened in the gallery could be interpreted as a sacrifice. Would your god justify what happened in the gallery? Would religious sacrifice be a valid reason for someone to die?"

"'Sacrifice' is your word. I never mentioned that."

"I'm just saying, generally . . ."

Murphy explained his religion. He was the coordinator between his new god—he didn't have a name for the new god yet, and the God of the Bible, and of Jesus, and of Satan.

"I deal with all of them." Heaven and hell had

been destroyed. "All of mankind is in prison in the new hell, including myself."

Murphy's job was to help the inhabitants of the new hell, who had previously been in the old heaven, to be free. "I help in their release efforts."

Grant said it didn't make sense. How could he be serving the same religion one minute by committing selfless acts, and later by committing selfish acts of chaos?

Murphy said it might seem like a contradiction, but—as far as he was concerned—it was all part of the same process.

Grant said that in an upscale neighborhood like downtown Sarasota, a murder in an art gallery could be considered chaos.

Murphy said he didn't kill that woman, but he agreed with the premise that the murder was chaotic. Everything he knew about the murder came from what he'd read in the papers or from video clips on TV. He'd seen pictures of computers being confiscated from the gallery and the body being carried out.

Grant said he knew that the photo of the confiscated computers ran in the paper, because he, in fact, had been the one carrying the computers. "I also know for a fact that there are no photos, no video, of the body being removed."

"Well, maybe I just thought I saw it," Murphy said.

Opitz asked, "Is it possible that you were down there and just happened to see it?"

"No, uh-uh," Murphy said.

Grant said, "One thing I will tell you is that there was a camera that was installed inside the gallery after the murder. Would it surprise you if I told you there is somebody on there who looks very much like you? Did you ever wander by there afterward and look through the window?"

"Nope."

"You know that there is software for facial recognition, right?"

(Grant was bluffing, of course. The recording had been almost useless. You could tell that there was an adult male looking in the window, but that was about it.)

"I used to be a military photographer—Soviet spying and shit. I guarantee you try to match that face in the window to mine, it won't happen."

"We have evidence, we believe," Opitz said.

"And you know what that evidence is," Grant said.

"We're just trying to figure out *how* it happened. One possibility is that it's involved somehow with your hypnosis thing. Maybe something went wrong and she did something that made you strike back at her, and it got carried away," Opitz theorized.

"It didn't happen. No, I never hypnotized her," Murphy said. "I never had sex with her, never hypnotized her. I have never been intimate with her."

"Did you cut her hair?" Grant said.

"It's possible I did cut her hair."

"If you cut her hair, you might have hypnotized her."

"Well, that's possible," Murphy conceded. "How

can I say for certain? Other than pictures in the papers, I don't even know what this woman looked like. Who knows? I find myself fuckin' so many of them. I did them all, yeah."

"Total chaos," Grant said.

Opitz commented, "Let's talk about the artwork you made while you were in jail. Nude women. Legs spread. Demons and stuff all over the place. Looks like a scene you were imagining, something that happened, something you were recalling and drawing later."

"No, the imagery just flows. I make the imagery access a lot of energy through different ways."

"Your art hasn't been widely accepted," Grant said.

"That is usually the case," Murphy replied. "People don't know what to do with my art. They either loved it, or . . . they are scared of it."

Grant said he was going to say something, and it required no response from the prisoner. It was just something for Murphy to file away for possible future consideration: "I believe the whole scene and everything at the art gallery was an art form."

"I hear you. That's fine. But I'm disagreeing with what you're saying."

"I'm anxious to test my theory, because I think you are probably one of the brighter, most articulate, artistic people I've ever met. You are complex. Definitely complex. I think that scene at the gallery featured your greatest fantasy. It was art comprised of somebody totally possessed by art. You know what I mean?"

Murphy said he did. The theory sounded good, plausible, geared for him to appreciate it—but it wasn't true. "My artwork flows from different places. Picasso helped me with one of my paintings."

"As an artist you are not a mainstream sort of guy," Grant observed.

Murphy said he met a chick at a flea market, a tall redhead named Sandy. She said she once worked on a painting so intensely that she went into the painting and finished it from the inside. Murphy said he believed her, and he found that kind of trance or transformation fascinating.

Chapter 36

The Nine-Inch Gash

A few days after the interview with Murphy, Sarasota law enforcement announced their intentions of arresting Murphy and charging him with Joyce Wishart's murder.

Murphy was examined by four psychologists, one of whom worked for the state. Murphy said he didn't need to get up close and personal with other humans in order to kill them. He could kill people by staring at an ambulance or fire truck. He could heal people by touching them. He told the psychologists that he had been in touch with aliens and that he was the leader of a thousand-member cult.

Following up on the lead from Murphy regarding a tall redhead named Sandy, Detectives Glover and Grant went to the Midway Flea Market and searched for the woman with a booth who, according to Murphy, took his painted plates.

They found Sandy Rucinski, who remembered Murphy: "He was very strange. He asked me to coffee, but I declined."

He'd given her a business card, with his phone number and e-mail address. Printed in one corner was *What's real?*

During August 2004, Hurricane Charley ravaged sections of Florida. The detectives wanted to reinterview the folks out at Solomon's Castle, but they had to wait. Murphy's brother and sister-in-law were in the process of having the damage to their home repaired.

When the follow-up interviews were finally performed, Murphy's family had nothing new to say about him—although Alane did have an interesting question for the men: "Was there something ritualistic or satanic about the crime scene?"

On August 18, 2004, the affidavit of probable cause was filed. It argued that a DNA sample volunteered by Elton Brutus Murphy was a match for DNA found inside the victim's shoe at the crime scene. A second match had been made of Murphy's DNA and DNA found on a piece of human skin tissue found on the gallery carpet. And, though

Murphy had not confessed to killing Joyce Wishart, he did admit being in Sarasota at the time of the murder. The affidavit noted that the FDLE forensic DNA analyst responsible for matching the samples was Suzanna Ulery.

The first thing a person noticed about circuit judge Andrew Owens was that he was tall. Six-foot-seven. And, back in the late 1960s, he averaged twenty-seven points per game as the star forward for the University of Florida basketball team.

Instead of taking a crack at pro basketball, he went to the University of Florida College of Law, and received his J.D. in 1972. His first job as a lawyer was with a law firm in Punta Gorda called Farr, Farr, Haymans, Mosely and Emerich.

From there, he worked for a short time with a law firm in Sarasota before being appointed to the bench in 1982 by Florida's then-governor Bob Graham. He filled a newly created judgeship in the Twelfth Circuit, which is a position he has held ever since.

He overcame some rough times during his first few years as a judge. He presided over felony criminal trials and was publicly criticized by defense attorneys because he participated with law enforcement in several undercover drug buys.

In June 1985, a manslaughter conviction in his courtroom was overturned by an appellate court. The case involved a woman who stabbed her boyfriend to death during a fight and was sentenced to five years in prison. The appellate court ruled that Judge Owens had read an incorrect definition of self-defense during jury instructions—and the woman's prison term was reduced to three years.

During his time on the bench, Judge Owens moved around from division to division in an attempt to avoid burnout, and had presided over civil, criminal, and juvenile trials. During that time he helped develop drug and mental-health programs that offered people treatment rather than jail time for minor crimes.

Presented with the evidence against Elton Brutus Murphy, Judge Owens signed the arrest warrant for murder.

While this was going on, Murphy picked at scabs in his one-man confinement cell. Two weeks after his interview with Detectives Grant and Opitz, Murphy decided to end his own life.

"I cut open my mattress with a razor blade. I peeled back the top of it so that my blood would drain into the stuffing of the mattress," Murphy said.

Murphy cut his left thigh, creating a nine-inch gash. It was so deep that it went almost to the bone.

"I was hoping to cut my femoral artery, but I just missed it," he said. He stopped cutting. He thought he might survive, but lose his leg. That frightened him into stopping. In order to stop the bleeding, he stuffed pages from a newspaper into the gash.

A couple of days later, Murphy was moved to Huntsville Unit in Texas. When he arrived, he was strip-searched.

The guard looked at Murphy's leg, saw the newspaper stuffed into the gash, and said, "What the hell did you do to your leg?"

Murphy was rushed to the prison doctor, who had to cut away half a pound of infected flesh before he could sew up the leg. Twenty-nine stitches were needed to close the wound.

"I still have a huge scar on my leg as a reminder," Murphy said years later.

In September, police located Murphy's ex-girlfriend, Jane Wingate, who had remarried and now had a new surname. She remembered, just as he had, that Murphy tried to turn her into a swinger, but she declined.

She told police that he'd confessed to perverse acts as a young man, and that he loved his sharp barber tools. By the time they broke up, all he ever did was weld things together.

Before he lived with Jane Wingate and her seventeen-year-old daughter, he lived with his mother.

In October, Murphy was removed from Huntsville Unit and extradited to Sarasota, Florida, to face the music. This process sounds like something that should have taken a day. But the truth was he was in transit between the facilities for three days.

He was put on a bus, where he was handcuffed and shackled. The bus stopped at many jails and prisons, picking up prisoners and dropping prisoners off. They spent the night at various prisons and jails en route.

Murphy's new home was the Sarasota County Jail, where he was charged with the crime of murder and was put into a cell. He arrived in Sarasota in the middle of the night; the next morning he was again handcuffed and shackled and taken across the street to the interrogation room at the SPD. This room had a big mirror, and he assumed that he was being both observed and recorded.

Detective Grant was again asking the questions. This time Grant tried to come off like he was Murphy's buddy, and Murphy played along.

Grant said they were going to take Murphy for a ride. He wanted the prisoner to visit downtown Sarasota and point out the places where he'd been—such as the gallery where he was trying to sell his work, as well as the coffee place and bookstore on the corner. Murphy said he would be glad to do that if they'd just loosen one ankle cuff, which was bothering him. Murphy said, "My one ankle's swelled up a bit. That's why it needs to be loosened. *Ahh,* that feels better."

Murphy got into an unmarked car with Grant and another officer. They drove him right past the Provenance Gallery so they could see his reaction.

"I just ignored it," Murphy recalled. After the ride he was returned to his cell.

On October 30, 2004, public defender Adam Tebrugge wrote a letter to SPD chief Peter J. Abbott officially informing him that he had been appointed to represent Murphy.

Please consider this letter to require no further contact between my client and anyone employed at your office, Tebrugge wrote.

Tebrugge came to visit Murphy. Murphy liked him. The public defender was lean and tall, with slightly graying hair. Murphy figured he and the lawyer were about the same age, maybe a difference of five years, tops.

"He told me at our first meeting that he didn't want me to think of him as just a guy from the public defender's office. He said, 'Think of me as your private lawyer, and that you retained me for sixty thousand dollars. I will do just as good of a job and put forth just as much effort as if you had paid me all of that money.'"

Tebrugge immediately had Murphy sign an invocation of rights affidavit, instructing authorities that Murphy should no longer be questioned without his lawyer present.

Murphy would be represented well. Tebrugge, an attorney since 1985, was an anti–death penalty activist who frequently argued in public, often at Catholic Church gatherings, that life in prison was a superior, and more just, punishment—even for the worst of the worst. People thought that the death penalty saved taxpayers money because it was cheaper to kill a prisoner than to keep him incarcerated for life. But this was not the case. In fact, the opposite was true.

Tebrugge used the example of Joseph P. Smith, the man who kidnapped, raped, and murdered eleven-year-old Carlie Brucia. If the state had not tried (and succeeded) to get the death penalty in that case, there would have been no trial. Smith would have pleaded guilty, been sentenced to life in prison, no chance for parole, and that would have been that. Because the legal process between sentencing and the carrying out of the death penalty was so time-consuming and complex, costs to the taxpayer exceeded those of keeping a man in prison. Tebrugge argued that the criminal justice system would be better served by allocating resources to help victims and their families through counseling and other support.

Murphy liked the guy.

"After I was there only a few weeks, they moved me into an adjustment cell," Murphy said. The cell was also referred to as "confinement" or "the Box." The official reason for the transfer was "administrative." His new home was a tiny one-man enclosure furnished with a stainless-steel combination sink/

toilet and a steel bunk. That miniature room would be his for many months. That's a lot of scab picking.

"During that time I was alone with my mind twenty-four hours a day," Murphy said. Not a nice place to be. In this fervid, claustrophobic ambiance, Murphy's delusions were malignant, growing and multiplying.

The only way he could tamp down the delusions was by reading a book. It helped to replace the narrative in his head with another. If an author was good, he could shout down the voices in Murphy's head.

Every waking hour during those long days and weeks was a descending trip through a "self-imposed spiritual nightmare." Over those weeks he formulated a new makeshift philosophy, an attempt to answer unanswerable questions.

"I figured out the process necessary to make everything work," Murphy said. The system involved replacing souls—removing the soul from a human being and replacing it with a completely different soul.

He had the power to pull the soul out and plug in the new. It wasn't just a quick switch. It was complicated. Sometimes it took hours, sometimes days. The new soul had to go through an intensive program of "disciplined indoctrination" in order to properly accomplish "transformation and renewal."

He saw spirits and souls as physical entities. They were objects and existed in all living things. Since he was made out of time, he performed the soul renewal process with "everyone I could think of."

The disciplined soul program resembled in some ways the ordeal a candidate must endure to become a Navy SEAL. Murphy perhaps understood the similarity, once referring to soul refurbishment as "virtual boot camp."

The process did not always go as planned. With something that complex, there was always the possibility of something going awry. "Sometimes souls and spirits from different living entities would merge, to form a new solitary soul," Murphy explained. "The renovated souls sometimes flew back into the body that they came from. Sometimes they switched bodies."

Because of the complexity of the transferences, Murphy needed complete concentration—vivid and relentless visualization. And that was what kept him busy during his months in the Sarasota County Jail.

At least, that's Murphy's version. Jail records indicate Murphy was not being a good boy. At one point he was on the receiving end of a stun gun, held down by a couple of deputies and stunned repeatedly on the backs of his legs.

Hurt like hell, Murphy recalled. But, he claimed, he was not incapacitated. They also pepper-sprayed him. It wasn't gross police brutality. Murphy admitted that he deserved the treatment, for he had just attacked a deputy with a mop bucket wringer.

Murphy offered as an explanation that anyone would be cranky, given the circumstances. He had endured months with no window, no TV, no radio. He only left the cell for twenty minutes a day to walk down the hall to a shower. The leg wound still looked nasty.

As he was taking the stun gun, trying to show heart, he recalled the time, three years earlier, when he had owned and used a stun gun. He knew the one that got him on the legs was top quality, leaving a huge welt each time it struck, probably tons more powerful than his own. He felt he could testify to the weapon's ineffectiveness. Stun guns were useless. Now a Taser, on the other hand, was very effective. He'd seen them used in the jail a few times, and he was impressed. They would knock a grown man to the ground and, yes, incapacitate him.

On November 10, 2004, Detective Glover received word that an African-American inmate named James Franklin, doing a seven-month stretch in the Sarasota County Jail for selling cocaine, had something to say about Murphy. He claimed Murphy made several admissions to him regarding the murder of Joyce Wishart.

Franklin said he'd been taking a shower when he met Murphy. The name was familiar and Murphy said he'd probably heard about his case on the news. Franklin made the connection.

"I said to him, 'You the man that killed the lady on Palm Street? At the art gallery.' He said, 'Yeah, they say I did that.' I asked him why he did it. He said he didn't mean to do it, but she had pissed him off. It wasn't supposed to happen that way."

Franklin recalled that Murphy liked to clean and spent a long time cleaning in front of Franklin's cell. It creeped Franklin out, and he told Murphy to clean someplace else.

According to the jailhouse snitch, Murphy replied, "Fuck you, nigger. I wish I could pluck your eyes and kill you the way I did that lady."

Later, Franklin saw some sketches Murphy had drawn: woman-like demons, one of a dead lady with her tongue hanging out. Murphy said he was drawing his nightmares, drawing the "shit I see every night."

Franklin said Murphy told him he'd been in a Texas jail since February. Franklin asked him how he knew the lady in the art gallery. Murphy told him he "used to do odds-and-ends work for her, like handiwork or whatever."

Franklin apparently didn't know about the stun gun incident. Franklin noticed that Murphy had marks on the backs of his legs. He asked how he'd gotten them. Murphy refused to answer, telling him he was asking too many questions, and adding that he'd "said too much already."

Murphy never said how he killed her or what she'd done to irritate him. After that, all he heard Murphy talk about was "being a hybrid, an alien."

Franklin said that on the day before, he had told Murphy that he hoped Sarasota gave him one hundred years. Murphy replied that he would kill Franklin if he got the chance.

Chapter 37

The Lord God
Elton Brutus Murphy Speaks

The investigation into Joyce Wishart's murder and Murphy's background continued for many months, although new info came now in dribs and drabs.

During the spring of 2005, in compliance with the rules of discovery, Assistant State Attorney (ASA) Debra Johnes Riva officially authorized Murphy's attorney, Adam Tebrugge, to make copies of all written and audio/video recordings pertaining to the case.

By 2006, prosecutors were plenty pleased that the DNA match was so positive, because other elements of the case against Elton Brutus Murphy were not up to snuff. There were problems matching Murphy's prints to those found at the crime scene.

The grainy surveillance recordings of the front of the Provenance Gallery from the days and weeks after the murder were sent to the Federal Bureau of Investigation (FBI) Technology Services Unit in Quantico, Virginia.

A man had come and looked in the front window. If a viewer were to judge from his size and shape, the man could have been Murphy, but there was little facial detail. The state attorney's office sent a copy of the surveillance tape to the FBI, but the Feds rejected it, saying they would need the original in order to do their thing. The original was sent then, processed by Amanda Broyles, of the FBI; facial recognition, however, was still impossible. There was "insufficient image detail."

Murphy claimed that he never visited the scene of the crime; and despite modern science the prosecution would be unable to prove otherwise. Sergeant Jack Carter maintained that the man looking in the window was Stephen Garfield, the Bay Plaza security guard.

During April 2006, the SPD's Criminalistics Lab examined the items found in Murphy's backpack when he was arrested in Houston. It was discovered that the keys Murphy had on him did not fit the Provenance's lock. The purse Murphy had apparently stolen was checked inside and out for fingerprints, again with negative results.

But, while fingerprints were getting the authorities nowhere, DNA matches kept coming. A second set of swabs and samples, originally confiscated by technician Valerie Howard, were now sent by Howard via FedEx to LabCorp. Though they already had enough to place Murphy at the scene of the murder, testing continued. The DNA found in blood samples from the interior lock and light switch of the art gallery matched that of Murphy's DNA.

Plus, blood found on the gallery's fax machine by technician James Tutsock had a profile consistent with a mixture of Murphy's and Wishart's blood.

So the physical evidence was both sparse and conclusive. This wasn't going to boil down to whether or not Murphy did it. He did it, all right. But was he criminally insane when he did it? That was the question that needed to be answered.

For months at a time, the presumption was that there would be no trial. The presumption was that Murphy would always be unfit to stand trial.

The only time Murphy was allowed to get out of confinement for any length of time was when a shrink needed to talk with him. The state was trying to figure out how nuts he was, and if they needed to try him for murder—a big expense to the taxpayers that would be unnecessary if he was deemed criminally insane.

The first shrink Murphy remembered speaking to was Dr. Wade C. Myers III, who was both a college professor and a forensic psychiatrist. He had an office in Tampa and had been a shrink for more than twenty years. "He was tall and had movie-star good looks," Murphy said. He showed up wearing an Indiana Jones hat. Murphy told him about his powers.

In his box Murphy built a noose and hung it from the vent in his ceiling. For three days he stared at it, "trying to build up the courage to use it." Then a jail deputy saw it; that finally got Murphy some new digs. He was moved to a cell that had a deputy and a desk located right outside, so there would be someone keeping an eye on him twenty-four hours a day.

On May 5, 11, and 19, 2006, Murphy was evaluated by Dr. Mary Elizabeth Kasper, who specialized in psychology and clinical psychology. She earned her degree in 1996 from the University of North Texas Health Science Center. He found her attractive and intelligent. She later recalled that she thought she and Murphy developed a "rapport."

Dr. Kasper later said, "I spent many, many hours interviewing him, as well as countless hours reviewing and memorizing his background. His case is an excellent study of a descent into madness."

The third mental-health professional to poke around Murphy's screwed-up psyche was Dr. James McGovern, who found Murphy delusional and schizophrenic. Murphy liked Dr. McGovern's military bearing, his crew cut, and neatly trimmed moustache.

On July 31, 2006, Murphy's barber's license expired. He didn't apply for a new one. He didn't even know it had happened, locked as he was in a ward for violent mental cases.

Murphy passed the time by trying to remember all of the girls he'd had sex with, in chronological order. There were many. He'd been quite the hound in his day. He didn't remember all of their names, but he recalled more than sixty lovers.

On August 4, 2006, the court hearing was held to determine if Murphy was competent to stand trial. Presiding over the hearing was tall Judge Owens.

Murphy's defense not only argued that Murphy shouldn't go to trial, but if they did, that tapes of police interviews with the defendant should not be allowed in as evidence. Tebrugge filed a motion that argued that Murphy's bizarre statements to police—while being interrogated by the police about the murder—were not admissible at any upcoming trial because they were irrelevant, and because they were made without Murphy understanding his rights.

On those recordings Murphy could be heard to say: "What's your choice, and Joyce *rejoicing* about? Are we rejoicing today as somebody's heaven?"

Judge Owens decided that the best way to judge a man's mental capacity was to talk to him directly. He asked the defendant to state his name.

"I am the Lord God Elton Brutus Murphy. The Joyce Wishart murder trial must not be delayed," Murphy said. The courtroom attendees could hear the scratching noise as reporters simultaneously jotted down that quote.

From the prosecution's standpoint, however, the cause was not hopeless. Two psychologists who'd examined Murphy testified at the hearing that, given the proper medication and education, Murphy could be made competent to stand trial. Murphy, the psychologists noted, already understood the court system and was able to talk about it.

Dr. James McGovern said Murphy understood how the court system worked for normal people. The problem was that Murphy did not consider himself a normal person. He believed he was god-like and therefore the rules of the court system did not apply to him.

Dr. Mary Elizabeth Kasper testified that Murphy understood that if he was convicted of first-degree murder, he might be subject to the death penalty. This did not concern him, however, since he knew he could never be convicted. "He told me he had the power to control the people involved in the process," Dr. Kasper testified, adding, "That is not rational."

In addition to the results of the exams by the two psychologists, Murphy's mental history was taken into account: He had been diagnosed with a bipolar disorder before the murder; and at the time of his arrest, he had engaged in behavior that was characterized by the investigating detectives as "bizarre."

Judge Owens found Murphy incompetent to stand trial, despite the defendant's protests. The judge ruled that Murphy lacked a rational understanding of the factors of the law.

After Judge Owens's ruling, Murphy was ordered to a state mental hospital in Chattahoochee, where attempts would be made to restore his mental capacity so he could stand trial.

That transfer didn't happen immediately, however. The Chattahoochee facility was full and Murphy remained in jail for two months waiting for a bed to open up.

During the wait Murphy was examined by the jail psychiatrist, "a brief evaluation," Murphy called it. For the first time in years, Murphy was put on "psychotropic medications": Vistaril for anxiety, Depakote for mood swings, and an antipsychotic called Geodon.

The drugs didn't have an immediate effect on Murphy's psychosis. However, after using them for a couple of months, he stopped having hallucinations for the first time since 2001.

In December 2006, the jail deputies drove
Murphy to the Florida State Hospital in Chatta-
hoochee, about a five-hour drive from the Sarasota
County Jail. He was back in the "crazy house," the
state mental facility, the place everyone just called
Chattahoochee.

Unit 25. Ward G. His new home. The first thing
he noticed was that the place was coed! There were
even opportunities to spend time with women. Not
necessarily quality time, if you catch his drift, but
time nonetheless.

Some of the females were good-looking, and
they got to eat meals together and have recreation
together. Usually, instead of any vigorous recreation, Murphy and the women just talked.

Chattahoochee food was both nutritional and
delicious. Murphy put on forty pounds. The phar-
maceutical cocktail Murphy received in that facility
may have had something to do with his weight gain
as well.

Chapter 38

Arend Goes for It

Forensic psychologist Dr. Joseph D'Agostino came to Chattahoochee and evaluated Murphy during the spring of 2007. Murphy remembered him as a giant Ivy Leaguer, tall and hefty, maybe 270 pounds, with a full beard and a shrubbery of unkempt curly hair.

While at Chattahoochee, Murphy took classes on courtroom and trial procedures. The classes lasted for several months. When it was over, he was given an oral exam, which he passed.

In September 2007, deputies from the Sarasota County Jail arrived and took Murphy back to jail. Murphy didn't want to go. The whole five-hour ride he figured he was going to get his old adjustment cell back.

"I had a big surprise," Murphy recalled. "They

placed me in general population, a six-man cell."
He had constant company. The prisoners lived in
eighteen-man dorms, with a moderately big day-
room and a TV. Since he behaved himself, that was
where he got to stay during the remainder of his
time in Sarasota County.

He received second evaluations from Dr. Kasper
(who came twice) and Dr. McGovern. Murphy said
he was feeling much better, thanks.

Assistant State Attorney Lon Arend had done his
undergraduate work at Florida State; he earned his
law degree at the University of Florida. He'd been
a prosecutor for fourteen years, including eight as
chief prosecutor in the DeSoto County Office, and
was reassigned by the state to be the Sarasota
region's chief homicide prosecutor, replacing
Debra Johnes Riva, who had become a judge.
Arend reported to his new office, and the first case
thrown on his desk was the Joyce Wishart murder.

"At first blush I looked at this case, and a lot of
Murphy's behaviors, and I thought, 'This guy is
insane,'" Arend recalled. Even later on, Arend
never stopped believing that Murphy was mentally ill. "The argument wasn't whether he was
mentally ill or not. The question was 'What are we
going to do with him?'"

Even though the Elton Brutus Murphy case lingered and lingered because of competency issues,
it was never far from Arend's thinking. He wanted

to put Murphy in prison—even if it meant butting horns with a formidable insanity defense. Arend looked at the facts of the case and the psychologists' reports and concluded that Murphy, although seriously mentally ill, was not legally insane. He was fairly certain a jury would see it the same way, too. In the state of Florida, a killer can be schizophrenic and still be able to tell and appreciate the difference between right and wrong. Many of the things Murphy had done at the crime scene—cleaning up, locking the door in a special manner so as not to leave fingerprints, and his other attempts to avoid detection—could be used to argue he was sane.

As he prepared his prosecution, Arend read *Whores of the Court: The Fraud of Psychiatric Testimony and the Rape of American Justice* by Dr. Margaret A. Hagen, a professor in the psychology department of Boston University.

The book made many points that Arend took to heart. One thing, for instance, Hagen pointed out that the world of psychology and the world of the criminal justice system are mutually exclusive. There was very little overlap.

"It is a fascinating book that dissects what psycho-expert testimony is doing in our court system. I read that book, cover to cover, and outlined the whole damn thing while getting ready to prosecute Murphy."

Hagen's book put forth the theory that a prosecutor should not have to hire his own expert to refute defense expert testimony supporting insanity—

that a lawyer should be able to refute that testimony himself, just by asking the defense doctors the correct questions.

"Forget the man on the street. Forget the folks in the jury pool. You'd be surprised how many Ph.D.'s don't know what 'insanity' means," Arend said. "They don't get it, because they live in their own world, a world in which insanity equals mental illness. In common usage 'insane' and 'crazy' are synonyms. But in a legal sense they are very different."

Teaming up with Arend for the eventual prosecution of Murphy would be Karen Fraivillig and Suzanne O'Donnell. When Lon Arend replaced Riva as lead attorney on the Wishart case, Fraivillig asked if she could stay on as part of the prosecutorial team. Arend said sure.

Fraivillig was a large woman, with long blond hair, who moved regally, deliberately, and erect—as if balancing an invisible book atop her head. She completed her undergraduate work at New College of Florida; then she went to Stetson University College of Law in St. Petersburg. She graduated in 2002 and had been prosecuting cases ever since. She enjoyed taking on the bad guys. Sometimes she wondered about the human condition, but she felt better when tenaciously combating its darkest corners.

Arend believed that there was room for three

attorneys on a prosecution team. Spreading out the tasks was better because it allowed each attorney to focus on one subject for longer, and that brought the best results. Having two assistants would allow Arend to concentrate all of his attention on the insanity issue. Arend wanted to do most of his prep work on cross-examining the defense's medical experts, and in methods of educating a jury as to what "insanity" is and how it is different from "crazy." His expertise would need to be plenty sturdy, especially since the state was having a hard time getting their own shrinks to say Murphy wasn't insane.

"I knew those issues were going to be a full-time job," Arend concluded.

So Suzanne O'Donnell became the third member of the prosecution team, handpicked by Arend "because she is just so stinkin' smart." O'Donnell was a graduate of the University of Florida College of Law and, unlike some lawyers who'd seen things from both sides of the courtroom, O'Donnell always wanted to be a prosecutor. After school in 1999, she started as a prosecutor in St. Petersburg, Florida. Shortly after that, she came to Sarasota. Her forte was forensic evidence. For four years O'Donnell had been the state attorney's specialist in sex crimes against children.

During the trial the defendant was never sure which one was Fraivillig and which one was O'Donnell, but he found them both attractive.

They were attired like they were in a fashion show, he remembered, in "very nice dresses."

What Murphy did distinguish was the common voice he heard from the prosecutors. Murphy said they were all "desperately aggressive." One wonders if Murphy comprehended the meaning of his words when he said, "They triple-teamed me, as if with a vengeance." He came just shy of calling them mean.

At the trial Fraivillig and O'Donnell would present the *evidence* for the jury. He knew they would be good at it. Arend would focus on the *doctors*.

During the fall of 2007, circuit judge Deno G. Economou officially declared Murphy was now fit to stand trial. Judge Economou was a thin man, with salt-and-pepper hair that grew in thick waves.

The same psychologists who had ruled Murphy incompetent to stand trial had reexamined him. Now they said that, due to the proper medication and education, he was competent.

There was testimony to the effect that Murphy had received instructions in courtroom and trial procedures and had passed the oral exam with flying colors.

Murphy came away from the hearing with the impression that it mattered little what his state of mind was, as long as he could correctly answer what role the judge played during a trial and how many people served on a jury.

* * *

Now that there was going to definitely be a murder trial, Adam Tebrugge announced that he was stepping down as Murphy's counsel to tend to other matters, most urgently his new role as counsel for the man who had killed little Carlie Brucia.

Tebrugge was replaced as Murphy's attorney by another specialist in capital murder—Carolyn Schlemmer, of the public defender's office.

Tebrugge and Schlemmer came to the jail together to see Murphy and explain the switch. Murphy found Schlemmer to be an attractive blonde. He learned that she was a recent widow. Murphy saw a photograph of Schlemmer's late husband on the cover of one of her notebooks, and he sensed she was still mourning his loss.

She was a mother, too, a factor that affected Murphy's future in the sense that court hearings and his eventual trial could never go too late into the afternoon and evening because Schlemmer had to leave to pick up her children at a child care center. (Although it was agreed that if the court's schedule was very tight, co-counsel might carry on in Schlemmer's absence.)

Schlemmer attended Stetson University College of Law. Her career had not turned out at all as she anticipated. When she was attending law school at Stetson, she had wanted to be a prosecutor, but fate pushed her onto the other side of the aisle.

"I had to take the public defender clinic while in law school because the prosecution clinic was full," she once explained. She graduated in 1991 and began her career working for a friend's firm in St. Petersburg. After that, she worked as a public defender in the traffic division in Tallahassee. In 1993, for the first time, she defended a client facing the death penalty; capital-murder cases became her specialty.

How did she handle defending the worst of the worst?

"I do feel that, no matter guilt or innocence, everyone is entitled to good representation and a fair trial," she said. "Maybe that is why I can so easily represent the people accused of the worst crimes. I have a knack for separating feelings and work. You either have it, or you don't."

With Tebrugge off the case, and Schlemmer on, Murphy's co-counsel became Jerry Meisner, another assistant public defender. One notch on Meisner's belt was that he had a few years earlier accomplished something very rare: He'd successfully argued that a client was not guilty because of insanity. Jurors rarely buy insanity defenses; they don't like them. However, in February 2005, Meisner's client Larry Smith, of North Port, was acquitted of second-degree attempted murder charges because a jury found him insane. Meisner sold his theory that Smith was temporarily insane due to "involuntary intoxication," an adverse reaction to a prescribed antidepressant.

It was during that initial meeting with Schlemmer that Murphy finally admitted that he had, indeed, killed Joyce Wishart.

"I confessed because I realized that an insanity defense was my best opportunity for eventual freedom," Murphy said, "even if it meant a stay of a half-dozen years or so at Chattahoochee." That was a hell of a lot better than prison.

"I did it," he now said. "But I was *insane* when I did it."

At first, prosecutors included capital murder among Murphy's charges. However, during October 2008, they announced that they had changed their mind. They would not seek the death penalty. The switch came in anticipation of an insanity defense that might have been more apt to sway a jury if the death penalty remained on the table.

During February 2009, Detective Ken Halpin was contacted by a small group of jailhouse snitches. One was Jack Cash (pseudonym), who had been Murphy's cell mate in 2008. He said Murphy asked him: "Could you help me beat my case by playing the psyche card?"

Cash said sure, and gave Murphy advice as to

how to pull it off. "Act crazy and do stupid stuff," Cash told Murphy. "Tell them you hear voices. Sit around. Talk to yourself. Stare at walls."

A second jailhouse snitch, Dave Stauss (pseudonym), told Detective Grant that Murphy told him that insanity was the best chance he had of avoiding the death penalty or a life sentence.

Other men in Murphy's cell block described a quiet prisoner, who kept to himself, and took a compulsive pleasure in cleaning. Murphy, the snitches agreed, often could be seen cleaning the community section of the block.

Murphy soon learned that many of his cell mates had been interviewed by the police. According to a new snitch, inmate Ralph Faye (pseudonym), Murphy said, "Fuck those cops. That bitch deserved what she got, and I wish I could do more."

Chapter 39

Trial

The murder of Joyce Wishart was almost five and a half years old by the time the trial of Elton Brutus Murphy commenced in the Twelfth Circuit Courthouse on Ringling Boulevard in Sarasota during the spring of 2009.

The location was convenient for Murphy. It was right across the street from the jail, which was next to the police station. And, for further convenience, they had a holding cell with his number on it right in the courthouse so they could efficiently keep him under lock and key when the court was in recess.

Murphy never got to see much of the outer building. It wasn't like they cuffed and shackled him and walked him across the street so he could have a look around.

He was cuffed and shackled, but he was taken from the jail into a garage, where he was put into a car. After a short drive he found himself in another first-floor parking lot. He was led through a side door, then another door, to his first-floor holding cell.

When it was time for Murphy to be in court, he was taken from his cell, marched down a hallway to an elevator, then up to the floor where his trial was being held. (There was even a courtroom holding cell where he could remain jailed during short breaks.)

Murphy thought the courtroom looked small—smaller than they appeared on TV. Trying to stare holes through him from the courtroom's spectator section were friends of Joyce Wishart, who were there every day, sitting directly behind the prosecution.

The defendant saw other familiar faces. Detective Glover was there, who had investigated the murder so hard and had questioned Murphy during one of his first postarrest interrogations. Also there was Mark Klothacus, best man at Murphy's first wedding. Klothacus sat directly behind Murphy, and Murphy even had an opportunity to talk to him for about a minute.

During jury selection Lon Arend asked the same question to every prospective juror: "When you think of 'insanity,' do you think of 'crazy'?" If he or she said yes, Arend would say, "Would it surprise you to know that 'insanity' means 'crazy' *and* 'not able to distinguish right from wrong'?" If they didn't get it, he rejected them. No one was going to sit on that jury without understanding what "insanity" was. Even crazy people were accountable for their actions under the law.

Judge Economou, who had presided over the preliminary hearings, recused himself from the case. He stated that after reading the doctors' reports on the defendant, he felt he'd already made up his mind about whether or not Murphy was insane.

On the bench for the trial was the Honorable Charles E. Roberts, who had served on the circuit court bench since January 2003. He earned his B.A. at Duke University, and his J.D. at the American University Washington College of Law. Judge Roberts gave the jury a brief course in how trials worked.

The judge's job, he explained, was to determine how the law was to be applied, and to see that everyone understood those applications.

On the other hand, it was the jury's job to determine what the facts were and to apply the law to those facts. They were a team. The jury was to base their opinions solely on the evidence—which consisted of the witnesses' answers, not the lawyers' questions—as well as any physical items that might be introduced by either side. It was entirely up to the individual juror as to how much weight he or she should give each piece of evidence. The words of a sincere-sounding witness would outweigh those of one who seemed insincere, and that was perfectly understandable. It was *forbidden* for jurors to come to any conclusion regarding the defendant's guilt or innocence until they had heard all of the evidence. Jurors were not to discuss the case with anyone, even fellow jurors, until the trial was over and it was time for them to deliberate.

The defendant, Judge Roberts noted, had a right not to testify on his own behalf; and should that happen, the jury was not to hold the decision against him.

Sometimes the jury would be asked to leave the courtroom and there would be some chitchat with them out of the room. Despite this, the jury would miss *no allowable evidence.* First they would hear opening statements, then the prosecution's case, the defense's case, and closing arguments.

Sitting in the journalist section of the courtroom during the trial was Jackie Barron, of WFLA-TV, who had been covering the Sarasota-Manatee area for quite a number of years.

She was a third-generation Tampa native, with roots that could be traced back to when her great-grandmother rolled cigars in Ybor City. She was a local—through and through—a factor she felt gave her an edge when reporting for her hometown station.

Barron earned her degree at the University of Florida, and it was there that she began her career reporting news and weather for the college station. Her first job out of school was out of town, anchoring and reporting for WHAG-TV in Hagerstown, Maryland.

She returned to Florida, reporting and anchoring at Sarasota's WWSB-TV, before joining WFLA, and thrice won awards: Outstanding Excellence from the Society of Professional Journalists in Spot News, the 2004 Green Eyeshade Award, and the Jack R. Howard Award for Best Investigative Reporting from the Scripps Howard Foundation.

Barron noted that there were far more spectators present for the victim than there were for the defendant, but Murphy did have his supporters, most notably Mark Klothacus.

In his opening statement Lon Arend said that Joyce Wishart was chosen as Murphy's victim because of her convenience and vulnerability.

"She was alone in the art gallery, offering privacy," Arend said. "It was not a spur-of-the-moment attack. Murphy came prepared, carrying with him a knife and a 'stretchy sock,' which he used to bind her."

Arend warned the jurors that they would hear a lot about Murphy's mental illness, and urged them to think only in terms of what was and wasn't criminally insane.

"In order to be criminally insane, the defendant would have to be unable to distinguish and appreciate the difference between right and wrong, and this defendant's actions prove conclusively that he could make that distinction," Arend said.

In Florida, insanity followed the so-called M'Naghten rule, which stated that two conditions must be met for a person to be ruled legally insane so that he or she cannot be guilty of a crime: First, if he suffered at the time of his crime from a mental disease or defect; second, if he did not understand the nature of his act, or, if he did understand, he did not know that it was wrong.

"Murphy planned the crime and planned to get away with it," Arend said. "When he left the gallery after the murder, he managed to lock the door behind him in such a fashion that he left no fingerprints."

If Murphy hadn't been able to distinguish and appreciate the difference between right and wrong, he would not have told his victim not to scream, or, when she did scream, put his hand over her mouth.

It was probably at that point that the victim bit the defendant, so he bled at the scene, too—blood that eventually led detectives to their man.

Here was a man who stole his victim's wallet and keys. To cover up his crime effectively, he did not do the simple thing, which would have been to throw away the keys and wallet in the nearest receptacle. "Instead, the defendant threw each key away individually, and cut up the contents of the wallet before throwing these pieces away in a variety of locations," Arend noted.

Arend described the scene—a ghastly scene created by a wannabe artist—how Wishart had been left posed on the gallery floor to resemble a nearby piece of art, how a magazine article called "A Fine Madness" became part of the "scene" the defendant created.

There was really only one thing the jury could do. Find Murphy guilty of murder. Arend thanked the jury for their time and had a seat.

The defense's opening statement by Carolyn Schlemmer emphasized the more bizarre aspects of his personality. There might have been times when Murphy wasn't insane, but he most certainly was when he killed Joyce Wishart and brutally mutilated her corpse.

On the day of the murder, the defense argued, the defendant was "the Lord God Elton Brutus Murphy," which was a manifestation of his mental illness. The defendant believed that this entity had a DNA link with God, had thousands of followers, and had killed Julius Caesar. When he killed Joyce Wishart, he did so because he believed God had told him to do so.

The defense promised the jury that they would hear from a quartet of psychologists, who would detail Murphy's extensive history of mental illness.

Here was a man who once lost a job because he

insisted that God was telling him what to do. He claimed to be able to speak in tongues, although those who heard him only heard babble. He'd been known to stare at scrambled television screens as a method of communicating with gods. He believed he was an alien and had been known to hide in trash bins. He once put a line of tomatoes across a parking lot.

"What you will *not* hear during this trial," Schlemmer said firmly, "is an expert take the stand and say Elton Murphy was sane on January 16, 2004."

Bottom line was, he was nuttier than a fruitcake—a sick, sick man, who needed to be in a mental institution receiving treatment, not in a prison being punished.

On the second day of the trial, the jury watched the nearly eight hours of interview by Detectives Grant, Opitz, and Glover.

Murphy, in retrospect, thought that those tapes were what hurt him the most during the trial. He was heard sparring playfully with the investigators, treating the murder of a living soul as if it were some kind of joke.

On the third day, as the jurors heard for the first time the graphic details of Joyce Wishart's murder, Jackie Barron watched the defendant carefully. At first glance Murphy appeared to be sitting motionless. Upon closer scrutiny she noticed that there was a slight tremor in his hands and a rhythmic rocking motion in his legs.

As would be the case throughout the trial, Wishart's friends and family sat in the front row, immediately behind the prosecution table. When the testimony got rough—and it was plenty rough on the third day—family members would clasp hands for support. Those hands were clasped particularly tightly as crime scene technicians described Wishart's remains as they were found on the art gallery floor: nearly decapitated, disfigured, partially nude, posed. No mention of missing flesh.

Also sitting in the audience that day was the writer of "A Fine Madness," Marcia Corbino, Sarasota's premier art historian. Corbino was also coauthor of *The History of Visual Art in Sarasota* (with Kevin Dean and Pat Ringling Buck, University Press of Florida, 2003). The book was her idea and its intent was to tell everyone about Sarasota's rich artistic past, something a lot of locals didn't know about because they were new.

Originally, Marcia Corbino had planned on writing about Joyce Wishart's murder journalistically. After she ran into official roadblocks between herself and the details of the crime, she decided, instead, to write about the murder in a fictionalized way.

Corbino was frustrated by the experience of

attending the trial. When it came time for the jury to see photos of the crime scene, and the images had been blown up and mounted on large pieces of cardboard, the exhibits were always held so that the press and spectators could not see.

"It was annoying," Corbino later said. She tried to chase down the person whose permission she would need to view the photos, but she received the runaround.

"I got the impression that they'd never received a request like that before," she recalled.

In hindsight, though, it was probably the offensive and unpublishable nature of the photos, rather than the request, that had officials nervous.

One thing was clear to Corbino. From what she knew about the crime scene, as an art critic she could tell the murder had been committed by a frustrated artist.

Marcia Corbino got some of the crime scene details she'd yearned for with the testimony of Valerie Howard. The criminalist stated that there could be no doubt that the attack had a strong sexual component.

"Some of the wounds were on her chest," Howard said. She quickly added, almost as an afterthought: "And part of her groin area was missing."

ME Russell Vega testified that the cause of death was twenty-three stab wounds. He had counted them all, adding, "I've never seen a case like this before."

On Friday, May 8, 2009, the defense put on its case. With the jury outside the courtroom, Judge Roberts noted that in order to put forth an insanity defense, the defendant had to admit that he had committed the crime. There could be no such thing as "if I did, I was insane." Judge Roberts wasn't sure that Murphy had ever officially confessed, so he straight-out asked Murphy, "Did you kill Joyce Wishart?"

Murphy's words were loud and clear. "Yes, Your Honor, I did."

"Bring the jury back in," Judge Roberts said, and the defense was allowed to proceed. The first defense witness was a coworker at the Regis salon in the Brandon Town Center.

"I had problems with staff being afraid," said Sylvie Tarlton, the salon's former manager. "They didn't want to work with him."

Frank Burns testified that Murphy placed a ladder up against his and his wife Stephanie's house in Tallahassee. By way of explanation Murphy said that aliens had led him to do it. Murphy recognized the guy as the one with the baseball bat who'd refused to let him down off a ladder until a sheriff's deputy arrived.

According to Burns, "I approached him and asked what he was doing, and he said he was sent there to fix my roof. I asked him who sent him and he said people from another planet."

The prosecution's cross-examination made it clear that Murphy might have merely been pretending to be crazy, that this was his standard method when he was caught trying to rob a house. If you get caught, act crazy—that was just part of Murphy's method, right?

The defense then called four psychologists who had examined Murphy. The psychologists said Murphy was psychotic and had convinced himself that he was related to God, that he was part alien, and that he had acted with God's grace on a mission to find believers. Murphy claimed to have more than a thousand followers who were under his control. He told one psychologist that he had replaced the soul of one of his lawyers by surrounding him with books and magazines—a line that tied in with the murder because Murphy had indeed left a magazine under Joyce Wishart's left hand.

First up was Dr. James McGovern, who had originally been asked to evaluate Murphy's competence to stand trial by the state, but was now appearing as a defense witness.

"In the construct of his universe, everything he did was acceptable," said Dr. McGovern. "Anything he did to hide his action was aimed more at continuing his mission than on evading responsibility," the psychologist testified.

Lon Arend argued that yearning to stay free so Murphy could continue his mission—that mission being to kill and rape women—was hardly a heart-warming defense.

Arend was going to agree with everything the doctors said, as long as it concerned Murphy's mental illness. But he was going to disagree with just about everything that dealt with insanity.

Psychologist Mary Elizabeth Kasper said, "He felt the laws would not apply to him." Murphy, for example, felt that he had gotten permission directly from God to rape and kill Joyce Wishart.

Arend hammered away. The only thing that mattered, when it came to Murphy's mental state, was if he could distinguish and appreciate the difference between right and wrong.

Everything else was irrelevant.

Arend was particularly effective when cross-examining Dr. Kasper. One spectator in the courtroom recalled Dr. Kasper flailing her arms and growing uncomfortably loud as she tried to answer his questions. She was so *annoyed* with Arend, and—according to eyewitnesses—she had difficulty maintaining her composure. (Her performance was so dramatic, and helpful to the prosecution, that one juror remarked upon it after the trial.)

"What is the definition of 'wrong,' Dr. Kasper?" Arend asked at one point.

There was a pause as the question caused the witness to temporarily tilt.

"Not right?" was her eventual response. Arend was making her look bad. She was furious.

When the lawyers were through questioning the psychologists, the jury was allowed to submit questions. The jury asked, "What is psychosis?" They were told that it was a loss of contact with reality. They were told that no, there were no brain scans or biological tests that could prove insanity, and that at no time during his examinations did Murphy show remorse.

Dr. D'Agostino was the state psychologist who'd evaluated Murphy in Chattahoochee when he was deemed incompetent to stand trial.

Arend asked Dr. D'Agostino about Murphy's social skills: "Could he follow the rules if he were in a school or something like that?"

"If there were rules in place, the defendant would follow them," Dr. D'Agostino testified.

Arend thought that was a powerful response. One of the symptoms of knowing right from wrong is the ability to follow society's rules. To know right from wrong, you need to know what the societal norms are.

"That was the key point," Arend later said. "You can talk all you want about hearing voices. I wasn't arguing against mental illness. I conceded to the fact that the guy had mental problems."

Arend impressively cross-examined all four doctors, made them admit that Murphy could distinguish right and wrong, but didn't care.

Still, the prosecutor was kind to the doctors: "I thought they all did a good job. They discussed mental illness, which was their expertise. When I asked about the legal definition of insanity, they recognized that the jury was going to have to make that call."

Arend believed that psychologists, especially forensic psychologists, should better gear their examinations of defendants with the law in mind. If they were going to say someone didn't understand the difference between right and wrong, there should be a baseline for comparison purposes, a test featuring questions such as "Is this right? Or is this wrong?" A test of the defendant's scruples. There should be a way, Arend believed, for the shrinks to *quantify* insanity as a measurable entity, based solely on questions relevant to insanity. The four doctors spent many hours with Murphy and there was little or no discussion regarding "What are the rules? And why don't they conform to you?"

Looking back on the trial, despite Arend's effective cross-examination, Murphy felt that the mental-health professionals were still the strongest part of his defense. Despite the prosecution's negative spin on everything, the shrinks—Dr. Kasper in particular—testified that Murphy didn't really understand the difference between right and wrong. He could distinguish it all right, but he didn't get it. It wasn't so much that he didn't know the difference, but that he didn't *appreciate* the difference. Dr. Kasper held on to her opinion that Murphy suffered from a severe schizophrenic disorder and was criminally insane at the time of the murder. All of this might have been more valuable to the defense if she'd better composed herself during Lon Arend's frustrating cross-examination.

The doctors' consolidated message to the jury was that Murphy had been schizophrenic when he killed Joyce Wishart. And during subsequent questioning, he was not malingering. He was not exaggerating his symptoms.

After her day in court Marcia Corbino had nothing but nice things to say about the prosecution. The way Lon Arend handled the defense psychologists was masterful, she said.

The defense psychologists, Corbino noted, all had similar opinions as to Murphy's insanity, but they didn't have any proof. They hadn't taken a brain scan. They hadn't given him a lie detector test. They sat on the witness stand and relied just on the notes they had taken. She found it strange.

She also didn't have many nice things to say about Murphy's defense.

"It was like they weren't really trying" was her assessment.

The following day closing statements were delivered. Both sides claimed victory. The defense acknowledged that Elton Brutus Murphy knew the difference between right and wrong, but that did not necessarily make him legally sane. The law said that the defendant needed to both know and appreciate the difference in order to be sane. Murphy showed every sign of *not* appreciating the difference. He believed that the laws were all fine and good for mere mortals, but that those same laws did not apply to him. His DNA was different, he said. He was a god.

Lon Arend had an answer for that. If Murphy really believed that he was above the law, and the laws did not apply to him, then there was no point in him cleaning up after himself. If he really believed that he shared DNA with God, he would not have hidden the victim's flesh in a plastic bag when he left the Provenance Gallery. He would have held that bloody human flesh in one hand and the knife in the other and he would have proclaimed for the world that he was the Lord God Elton Brutus Murphy. But that wasn't what he did. He covered up. He fled. He was afraid that something bad would happen to him—just like a sane man who both knew and appreciated the difference between right and wrong. He didn't just dispose of evidence. He disposed of it in a wide variety of locations, just to further befuddle investigators. He locked the gallery door with the edges of his fingers so he wouldn't leave fingerprints!

Would a god hide anything? No, a god would have walked right out that gallery door without a care in the world for what other people, including law enforcement, thought.

Arend went over the recordings that they had heard of Murphy being interrogated in Texas. "'Joyce? Joyce? Are we rejoicing?'" He thought he was funny. Again and again those recordings showed that Murphy was sane, proud of his perversity. It wasn't that this creepy man didn't understand the law; it was that he thought he was *above the law.*

Following closing arguments, Judge Roberts gave the jury their instructions. He thanked the alternate jurors for their time and dismissed them.

He told the remaining panel that the first thing they needed to do was elect a foreperson, whose job it would be to supervise deliberation. All of their deliberation needed to take place in the deliberation room, which had its own bathroom.

A bailiff would be posted out in the hall, right outside their door, at all times. If a juror had a question, he or she was to write it down on a piece of paper and then knock on the door. The bailiff would open the door, take the written question, and Judge Roberts would determine if he was allowed to answer it. If he could, he most certainly would. All of the evidence would be sent back to the jurors' room. They had a right to see all of it.

The jury room was theirs. No one who was not a juror could be allowed inside ever. Some people worried about surveillance cameras. There were none in there, he could assure them. It was time for them to retire to their duty and return a verdict. The jury solemnly filed out the nearby door.

They were assured utter privacy. When it was over, those who chose to identify themselves to the press and make statements had every right to do so, as did those who wanted to remain anonymous and wished to return home the instant the verdict was read.

That jury deliberated only one hour before returning with a guilty verdict.

At the subsequent sentencing hearing, Murphy noticed something missing in the courtroom. The usual people were all in their places, but there was no Mark Klothacus. Murphy's former best man attended the entire trial, but he would not be there for the sentencing.

Murphy didn't like to think that his friend might have given up on him. Later, Murphy noted that the sentencing hearing was very brief. Mark wasn't always the most punctual guy. Maybe he'd simply missed it.

At that brief hearing, Elton Brutus Murphy was sentenced to life in prison without the possibility of parole. If he had been found not guilty because of insanity, a second hearing would have been held to determine if Murphy should be committed to a mental hospital, given outpatient treatment, or released. But that was a moot point now.

Only once had the trial gone late into the afternoon, so late that Carolyn Schlemmer had to return to her full-time job as a mother, and in that case Meisner took charge of the defense seamlessly.

Murphy recalled, "Even though we lost the trial, I told both Schlemmer and Meisner that I was pleased with their performance and I thought they had done their best."

ASA Lon Arend thought that despite his victory the Murphy trial had raised an issue. It was a shame that Florida did not allow a verdict of "guilty but insane."

"Under the law," he explained, "you are either sane, and you are convicted and go to prison, or you are insane, and you go to a hospital. Which means that the second you are deemed cured, you can be released and would be free to repeat a violent crime. If Elton Murphy had been found not guilty by reason of insanity, this very, very dangerous person, who had committed the most heinous of crimes, might have spent five years in a mental hospital and then been released."

That was especially true, Arend noted, because of the budget cuts of recent years and the closing of several state mental hospitals.

Arend said, "There are some states and some countries that have this other verdict, guilty but insane, which would then allow the defendant to be sent to a mental hospital for the rest of his or her life." In that system mentally ill killers could receive the treatment they needed, but society didn't have to worry about them being released back into the population. "I think the fact that we did not have that option is too bad," Arend concluded, "because that's what I believe it would have been."

Chapter 40

Cannibal Killers
and Art World Murders

Because of the research efforts involving this book, we now know more about Elton Brutus Murphy's behavior than did the principals at his murder trial. Though Murphy still will not address the subject, there were elements of his behavior on January 16, 2004, that smacked of cannibalism.

Murphy says he stole Joyce Wishart's vagina and put it in his rooming house's freezer to keep as a souvenir, but his acts mimic those of men who have dabbled in eating human flesh. And we do know that at least on one occasion during that time period, Murphy cooked stew and shared it with another man living in the boardinghouse. According to Murphy, the stew was made of "boiled pork" and he admitted that it was the only time he cooked a meal while living at that address. (Incidentally, he also admitted to tasting the vagina while it was still attached to the victim's lifeless body.) Even if Murphy didn't put some of Joyce Wishart into his stew, who is to say that while he sat in his Shade Avenue room, cutting up the vagina into little pieces that fell onto a paper plate and paper towel, that more tasting did not occur?

It is no longer considered rare for murderers to cannibalize their victims. There is a theory that killers believe, as do some primitive cannibal tribes, that consuming human flesh releases black magic that can, in turn, provide the killer with tremendous power—that a "life force" can be consumed, as well as the flesh. Considering Murphy's belief system, this notion must have appealed to him.

Belief and execution of cannibalism go back to the very prototype of the modern psycho killer, to "Jack the Ripper," who, in 1888, murdered and claimed to have eaten parts of at least five prostitutes in the Whitechapel section of London.

Murphy did not steal just any body part. He took his victim's vagina. Necrophilia and cannibalism have been known to go hand in hand. The serial killer Jeffrey Dahmer, who killed at least fifteen male victims in Milwaukee, Wisconsin, during the 1980s, performed sexual acts upon and ate parts of his victims. When he was arrested, body parts were found in his refrigerator and freezer, being kept fresh for future consumption.

The most famous of the recent cannibal killers was Arthur Shawcross, "the Genesee River Killer," who killed at least twelve women in and around Rochester, New York—primarily prostitutes—during 1988 and 1989. The bodies were found, usually in an advanced state of decomposition, with various sex organs removed. He was arrested in January 1990 after aerial surveillance caught him masturbating at one of his dump sites. While he was in custody, Shawcross claimed to have eaten parts of three of his victims. He said that he became aware of his desire to consume human flesh only after he *accidentally* ate the nipple of one victim. During interrogation by a psychiatrist, Shawcross switched to a woman's high-pitched voice and claimed he had once been a cannibal in medieval England.

Long a staple of murder-mystery fiction and board games, murders in the art world are very rare, but not unheard of. Perhaps the most famous one was the 1985 murder of twenty-six-year-old Eigil Dag Vesti, a Norwegian male model and Fashion Institute of Technology student, on an estate in New York's Rockland County.

The victim was found shot twice in the back of the head, wearing only a leather mask. The murder was committed by twenty-two-year-old Bernard J.

LeGeros, whose father owned the estate that was the crime scene, and who worked at the Andrew Crispo Art Gallery in Manhattan.

The murder weapon was recovered in the Crispo gallery.

The story became headline news and the subject of a best-selling book because it revealed a dangerous sadomasochistic sexual lifestyle among the Big Apple's cultural elite.

Crispo had a rags-to-riches bio, having started out as an abused child in a Philadelphia orphanage, and working his way into New York's high society. Among his friends was Deborah Harry, lead singer of the pop band Blondie. He developed a serious cocaine habit and a bizarre, sadistic homosexual lifestyle. Among his assistant LeGeros's duties were the picking up of men for his boss to abuse and then the disposal of them after his boss was through.

One such sex slave was Vesti, who was bound and beaten by Crispo before LeGeros "took him for a ride." Causing somewhat of a furor, LeGeros alone took the rap for Vesti's murder.

In January 2011, thirty-one-year-old Tajeme Sylvester, a master carpenter, was found murdered—shot twice, once in the head, once in the torso—inside the psychedelic Lotus Temple of Visions Gallery in Brooklyn, a gallery that the victim had been renovating. Police recovered nine-millimeter casings at the scene, but no firearm. The gallery existed to "promote all facets of conscious or cultural visual and living art expressions." Neighbors, who said the gallery had a reputation as a crash pad for traveling artists, heard gunshots in the early evening. There were no signs of forced entry. After hours, the victim was a fixture on the party circuit, dancing to house music. He had also been an activist for environmentalism and holistic health. The gallery's owner—Divine Elohim, a self-described "Space Age herbalist"—was out of town when the murder occurred, and the case remained a mystery.

Afterword:

A God Has Become Man

As autumn approached in 2011, Elton Brutus Murphy was the most polite murderer ever. He never failed to thank the author for the supplies he sent, or for the attention he gave.

"It's been a privilege and an honor working with you. Do you already have another murderer lined up for your next book?" he asked.

The answer was no. The author's next investigation was to be a reexamination of an icy cold case, a double sex murder near the author's home when he was a child.

Murphy said he was doing well. "Considering where I am," he added, which was the Northwest Florida Reception Center prison facility in Chipley.

Murphy had a reason to feel good. After more than a year in prison, he'd received his first visitor, his seventy-two-year-old aunt, Thelma Prance, from Cartersville, Georgia—his father's sister.

She had not been around much when Murphy was a boy and asked him to fill in the blanks for her. What was her brother—dead now for more than twenty years—like at that time?

Murphy told her that his dad beat his mom and "aspirated on a severe drunk."

Murphy's time went through a rough patch in 2010 when, after years of taking the same antianxiety, depression, and psychosis drugs, he began to have bad side effects. But eventually his meds were changed and the side effects smoothed out.

Murphy still thought in terms of how much better society would be if he were within it rather than outside it. He could be a teacher. During his life he had taught an amazing three subjects: photography, scuba diving, and hairstyling.

Some people complained of stage fright and dreaded situations where they had to speak in front of groups, but not Murphy.

"I'm comfortable," Murphy said, "as long as I know the subject matter reasonably well."

Murphy thought it was funny, but his best friends in prison were all bank robbers. He'd always been drawn to bank robbers, all the way back to his days in the general population in the Texas jail. All of the bank robbers he'd befriended had one thing in common: the guts to do it.

"When I was free, I was successful at stealing small amounts of money. I never once contemplated robbing a bank," Murphy said. He recalled a day twelve years past, when he was cutting hair in a Regis shop, and one of his favorite customers came in and told him that her boyfriend just got arrested for robbing a bank. Maybe being a bank robber was a destiny that had gone unfulfilled, Murphy realized with a sigh.

After a lifetime of being in near-peak physical condition, Murphy, at age fifty-four, was letting himself go for the first time ever. "I simply can't exercise to the extent that I used to," Murphy said. He injured both of his arms a while back and this hindered his ability to exercise. The guy who once did eighteen hundred push-ups in one day, while in the Leon County Jail, now could do none. When the injury occurred, it felt like the bones in his upper arms had cracked. His arms never healed, never got back to anywhere near what they used to be.

"Now I mainly walk for exercise," he said.

Regrets? He had one. He hadn't raised his children in a Christian home. He'd never taught them about Jesus or taken them to church and Sunday school.

Other than that, no, not really. He was satisfied with the way his life had turned out: "I've lived a full life and I've had many unique experiences," he said happily.

He was thankful that he'd gotten away with so much before he was finally caught and put away. True, he had to pay the piper for going AWOL; but other than that, he'd gotten away with a lot—and without consequences.

Murphy now believed that the seed had been in him for a long time, that he was destined to do something very, very bad—and he had.

"The seed was there, but I didn't nourish it." But he could only keep Mr. Hyde caged in Dr. Jekyll's psyche for so long. Something had to give. "If I'd nourished it, I probably would have become a serial killer."

He would admit it now. When he did finally kill, it was such a rush. Big-time thrill. And it stayed in his mind vividly, like a movie that he could play for himself inside his head, again and again.

"After the kill, during my time in the Texas state jail, all I thought about and planned for was my next kill. I was hooked on murder. I was a murder junkie," he said. "I tried it one time and I was destined to do it again and again, until I was stopped."

He felt absolutely no remorse for the kill. No guilt! To this day he *still* felt no remorse for the murder and mutilation of Joyce Wishart.

"I do, however, have feelings for the family," Murphy quickly added. He remembered them in his daily prayers.

"I also have regrets about not putting my own

family first when planning the murder." He hadn't completely thought through the possibility that he could spend the rest of his life in prison. He was sorry for the hardship and pain his act caused Dean, and ex-wife Paula and the kids. "I neglected my own family in pursuit of pleasure," he said, "even though the murder was a result of my extreme schizophrenic promptings.

"During the act there was extreme pleasure," he said, but that didn't change the fact that the murder was a manifestation of his "complete psychological breakdown."

He did feel like there was injustice in his spending his remaining years in prison. What should have happened was he should have been committed to Chattahoochee for a few years, give the shrinks a chance to get his meds right so that sanity returned, and then he'd be good to go.

Murphy knew his own mind better than anyone else would, and he could vouch for the fact that he'd been "normal" since 2008. No hallucinations, no paranoia, no grandiose feelings of being God. All of that was before 2008.

Prison, however, was his destiny. If nothing else, he'd become a man of routine—a man who lived life at a lackadaisical pace, day after day, week after week, all very much the same.

He woke up at four-thirty in the morning when the lights went on, shaved, brushed his teeth, and prayed for his extended family and others. After prayer he read the Bible, two to four pages, which always offered him pleasure and comfort. On April 18, 2011, he completed reading the entire Bible for the first time. He immediately went back to Genesis and started reading again.

Just like the days, he would repeat.

Sometime between five-thirty and seven in the morning, no set time, he went to breakfast. After that meal they had "first count," to make sure all inmates were present and accounted for.

After first count Murphy cleaned his cell, every day—took him about fifteen minutes. "Then comes what I like to call 'my time,'" he said. He usually read, maybe a novel. He read several times throughout the day between the counts and the meals.

Occasionally he had to work. His job was called "inside grounds." He walked around the grounds and picked up trash. (Ironic, right?) And he pulled weeds. On the days that he worked, he finished up around 2:00 P.M.

He went to the prison library once a week and picked out three books. Another once-a-week activity was recreation. "All I ever do is walk four miles around a huge dirt track," Murphy said.

Group Bible-study meetings were twice a week, and lasted about forty-five minutes apiece. Every once in a while he got to go to the chapel for a concert. The most recent concert was by Young Isaac, a coed sextet of college students. They were very good.

"I lead a very quiet, reserved, most-of-the-time peaceful life—considering I'm in prison," Murphy said, but he added, "There is a lot of noise and sometimes not-so-peaceful things happen around me."

He said he lived a Christian life, "as much as my personality will allow. And, believe it or not, I am content."

His contentment had nothing to do with the quality of the prison he was in. The inmates all claimed that the Northwest Florida Reception Center was the worst prison, and Murphy was inclined to agree. He was more content than the others for the simple reason that, no matter what the situation was, he could make the most of it. That wasn't true of a lot of guys. Take his best friend, for example. He'd been in this prison for about six months. He'd been in plenty of prisons, he said, and this one was the worst. "The prison is really starting to get to him," Murphy said, "and his mood has been a downward spiral ever since he arrived."

Murphy liked to play devil's advocate when it came to the worst-prison argument: "At least here, the officers don't carry clubs like they did in Texas," he would say. In Texas, Murphy had had a cell mate who one day threw water on an officer. A few minutes later the officer returned and took the guy out of the cell. Thirty minutes later, when the water thrower was returned, he'd been severely beaten: big knots on his head, eye and mouth busted open.

Murphy didn't have any groupies, but he wouldn't mind a few. Back when he was in county jail, he'd had four women at once who wanted to be his pen pal. But he was so psychologically screwed up at that point that he couldn't appreciate how much those women could have helped him combat his loneliness. He had refused to write them back. He wished he had that many women who wanted to be pen pals with him now, but no such luck.

If Hollywood made a movie of his life, who would star in the picture? "Keanu Reeves or Russell Crowe as me," Murphy said. "Katy Perry could play the girl I almost kidnapped—but she would have to put some blond highlights in her hair. And Demi Moore as Paula, the mother of my children."

Keanu Reeves was the star of one of Murphy's two favorite movies of all time, *The Matrix*. His other favorite film was *Contact*, with Jodie Foster. Murphy commented, "Both movies provide real escapism from our everyday reality."

Truth was, TV had become a bore. He'd rather pray or watch a Christian movie. He never watched news that much, and crime news wasn't an interest.

He did, however, admit that—as a "wannabe

serial killer"—he did have some knowledge of the serial killers who'd come before him.

"If I had to pick one, the serial killer I find most interesting is Ted Bundy," Murphy said. "I found him fascinating. The thing wrong with Bundy was he was cruel in the way he killed those women."

What advice would he give to people who, as he once had, heard voices ordering them to do ugly things?

"If you wake up and find your world seems too surreal, it probably is!" he said. "Seek professional psychological help immediately before it's too late. Even if your intuition tells you that nothing is wrong with you."

Did he ever get down in the dumps because his days of freedom were forever behind him?

"They've taken away my freedom, but they can't stop my dreams," he said—and at night, asleep in his cell, he dreamed of those sixty acres behind his house when he was a kid, the ill-fated orange grove and the dense woods, and how he wandered for hours, alone and free.

Murphy remained a reader in prison. Beggars couldn't be choosers, for sure, and he'd read just about any crap. But every once in a while, he would read a book that struck him as pretty good. He recently enjoyed *The Last Juror* by John Grisham,

Digital Fortress by Dan Brown, and Tom Clancy's *Shadow Warriors.*

Noting that the author of this book had previously coauthored a book about submarines, Murphy explained that one of his favorite books of all time was *U.S.S. Seawolf* by Patrick Robinson.

As a kid he loved books about boys who visited faraway planets in rocket ships that they built themselves, but as an adult Murphy read almost exclusively nonfiction. He loved books about the military or scuba diving, or how-to books. It wasn't until his incarceration that he read his first novels for grown-ups. He enjoyed mysteries.

He enjoyed a photographer's autobiography. Surprisingly, he enjoyed the "Christ Clone" trilogy, by American novelist James BeauSeigneur, about the end of days. He didn't think he was going to like it because he assumed it was anti-Jesus, but he was pleasantly surprised to find that it was done with skill and brought the New Testament to life. He would recommend those books to Christians and atheists alike.

He had never been a big James Patterson fan. *You read one; you've read them all,* he thought—until he read *The Murder of King Tut.* It blew his mind. He could hardly believe Patterson wrote it.

But his favorite book was the Bible—and his favorite book of the Bible was the Epistle of Paul the Apostle to the Romans. "The theme of Romans is the gospel," Murphy said. "That is the Good

News, that salvation from sin is available through Jesus Christ. Romans teaches us how to deal with our sinful attitudes and behaviors and how to get back on the right track. I have turned my life and will over to God so he can transform me into the godly person he wants me to be."

Maybe. A better bet is that Elton Brutus Murphy, a unique fiend and ghoul, has a special spot reserved for him in the deepest, hottest ring of hell.

Postscript

Karen Fraivillig said she hoped she would never have to work on a prosecution team on a case as disturbing as this one again, but unfortunately that was not the case.

On January 17, 2008—on a dim, drizzly day in North Port, Florida—an unemployed loser named Michael King abducted a young mother of two named Denise Amber Lee. He took her to his home, where he repeatedly raped and sodomized her, drove her into a desolate area, put a single bullet through her head, and buried her in a shallow grave.

Fraivillig, again teamed up with Lon Arend and Suzanne O'Donnell, prosecuted the case. There were familiar faces on the other side of the aisle at the King trial as well: Carolyn Schlemmer and Jerry Meisner were defending King.

King's defense team claimed that a childhood

sledding incident had left King with a damaged frontal brain lobe, which resulted in him being criminally insane. King was convicted on August 28, 2009, and now resides on Florida's death row.

That case became the subject of this author's book *A Killer's Touch*.

In March 2010, Judge Andrew Owens, after many years of dedication to the First Step program—which helped provide substance-abuse rehabilitation and counseling to pregnant women—was honored as the "Caring Heart of the Year." Judge Owens, who presided over many of Elton Murphy's first court hearings, founded the "Drug Court" programs in Sarasota and Manatee Counties in 1997, which each year led to the substance-abuse treatment and counseling of three hundred individuals.

In 2011, Michelle Andersen, of Admiral Travel on North Palm, said it was funny the author should call, because she'd been talking to someone about Joyce Wishart just the other day. There were still enough old-timers on the block, and they remembered.

After all this time, it could still come up twice in a row. On that strip of storefronts, many things changed the day of the murder, many of which never switched back. Women were no longer alone at work. Never. No one worked at night.

In the years since the murder, the travel agency Andersen worked for changed spaces and was closer than ever to the crime site.

The Provenance Gallery was now a beauty salon. She was friends with the new proprietors and considered them friends, but she still couldn't enter that building without thinking about what had happened there. Andersen went into the salon only a few days before and had talked with the owner. He asked Andersen if she was around at the time of the unpleasantness. Andersen said, "Oh yeah." He asked that she keep it quiet. He didn't want his clientele thinking his parlor was a haunted house.

Just as it had been before, that end of Palm Avenue was still the quieter part, although a new modern parking garage had increased pedestrian traffic, and additional streetlights meant it was no longer the darker end of the street. A lot of money had been pumped into sprucing that stretch, creating a modern, seemingly safer nocturnal vibe.

The turnover, life's turnover, was always under way, and several of the businesses from Joyce Wishart's day were gone, new businesses in their place. That was just a normal symptom of the tough times everyone had been going through for the past few years. Maybe, after enough time passed, the block could be completely renewed, and doors again could be left open.

The people who remember still do it in their own way, largely alone, and life goes on.

Sally A. Trout, whose interior design firm was only two doors away from the Provenance Gallery, said she had been changed forever by the murder. She still found the subject hard to think about, even though years had passed. She couldn't walk past "that space" without being overwhelmed by creepiness.

She shivered every time.

It wasn't the fault of the people who operated that space now, of course, but that kind of bad energy *stayed*. Then again, maybe she had it wrong. Maybe traumatized people carried the bad energy inside them, and it wasn't at the crime scene at all. The people who went there now, and didn't know what had occurred there, couldn't feel it. But Trout could feel it—because she remembered.

Her office still had a "panic button," in case she and her workers were ever accosted by an intruder— a security measure that would have seemed bizarre during the innocent days before the murder. She still supplied her largely female staff with Mace so they could feel safer going to and from their cars at the bookends of each day. She had a retail office in a different location now, but it remained policy that no one was allowed to work alone.

* * *

Marcia Corbino, the Sarasota art historian, completed a second fictionalized version of Wishart's murder and Murphy's trial. As of March 2011, she was having the work edited in hopes of getting it published.

Bob Ardren, the writer for *Sarasota Magazine* who volunteered a DNA sample during the days after Wishart's murder, died at age sixty-seven of cancer on January 1, 2008.

Reedy Photoprocess, which employed Murphy for six months back in the early 1980s, made a tough but efficient transition to digital photography. There came a time when all equipment had to be thrown away and replaced with new equipment, but the business survived. The location in Pasadena where Murphy worked was sold many years ago and is currently a Veterans of Foreign Wars (VFW) post.

Murphy's brother Dean and his wife Alane still operate the Boat in the Moat Restaurant near Solomon's Castle.

Elton Murphy bragged, "My brother also books all the tours of the thousands of people who visit Solomon's Castle yearly."

As it turns out, in the twenty-first century, Murphy's delusions regarding the SEALs police— squads of avengers seeking out those who falsely claimed to be SEALs—turned out to be not so far off the mark.

There was in reality a small band of veterans and civilian volunteers scattered across the country who *have* dedicated their existence to exposing phony ex-SEALs.

The problem, barely a blip until 2011, became an epidemic after a Navy SEAL killed Osama bin Laden. All of a sudden every con artist in the country was adding the SEALs to their résumés.

One guy, Steve Robinson, a former SEAL from Forsyth, Missouri, even wrote a book called *No Guts, No Glory: Unmasking Navy Seal Imposters*.

Bibliography

Corbino, Marcia. "A Fine Madness." *Sarasota Magazine,* November 2003. Available online at *www.sarasotamagazine.com/Articles/Past-Issues/2003/November-2003/A-Fine-Madness.aspx*

Kipling, Kay. "Death of an Art Dealer." *Sarasota Magazine,* November 1, 2005. Available online at *http://sarasotamagazine.com/Articles/Past-Issues/2005/November-2005/Death-of-an-Art-Dealer.aspx*

About the Author

Originally from Rochester, New York, Michael Benson is a graduate of Hofstra University. He is the author of *Betrayal in Blood*, *The Burn Farm*, *Killer Twins*, *Mommy Deadliest*, and *Watch Mommy Die*. He currently lives in Brooklyn, New York.

MORE SHOCKING TRUE CRIME
FROM PINNACLE